Walter Benjamin's Other History

Weimar and Now: German Cultural Criticism
Martin Jay and Anton Kaes, General Editors

Walter Benjamin's Other History

Of Stones, Animals, Human Beings, and Angels

Beatrice Hanssen

UNIVERSITY OF CALIFORNIA PRESS

Berkeley / Los Angeles / London

University of California Press
Berkeley and Los Angeles, California

University of California Press, Ltd.
London, England

©1998 by The Regents of the University of California

Library of Congress Cataloging-in-Publication Data

Hanssen, Beatrice
    Walter Benjamin's other history: of stones, animals, human
beings, and angels / by Beatrice Hanssen
        p. cm.—(Weimar and now ; 15)
    Includes bibliographical references and index.
    ISBN 0-520-20841-2 (alk. paper)
        1. Benjamin, Walter, 1892–1940—Philosophy. I. Title.
    II. Series.
    PT2603.E455H36 1998
    838'.91209—dc21   97-30170
                                                             CIP

Printed in the United States of America
9 8 7 6 5 4 3 2 1

The paper used in this publication meets the minimum requirements of American
National Standards for Information Sciences—Permanence of Paper for Printed Library
Materials, ANSI Z39.48–1984.

Contents

Acknowledgments

This study was conceived and written for the most part between 1987 and 1992, during a period of intense preoccupation with Continental theory and philosophy. I am especially indebted to the Humanities Center at Johns Hopkins University and its Program in Comparative Literature and Intellectual History for providing an academic environment in which many disciplinary boundaries could be crossed. I am particularly grateful to Jacques Derrida for his generosity and intellectual hospitality during a 1990 research period in Paris, above all for the conversations about Benjamin's "Critique of Violence" and "Force of Law." Memorable also during that period were the Talmudic readings by Emmanuel Levinas which I attended. In Berlin, I benefited greatly from the intellectual rigor with which Michael Theunissen analyzed *Being and Time*. The dialogue with my students at Harvard University and Stanford University, where I was a Mellon Faculty Fellow in 1995–96, allowed me further to refine my argument. Most of all, I am indebted to Hent de Vries for our many exchanges about the Frankfurt School. For their support or encouragement during various stages of my work in Baltimore or Cambridge, I would like to thank Martin Jay, Werner Hamacher, and Samuel Weber; Russell Berman, Cathy Caruth, Dorrit Cohn, Edward Dimendberg, Marjorie Garber, Andreas Huyssen, Barbara Johnson, Anton Kaes, Richard Macksey, Winfried Menninghaus, Werner Sollors, and Maria Tatar. Finally, I dedicate this book to Hildegard and Karin Rieder Hanssen.

Note on Translation

In some instances, slight adjustments to the diction of existing translations have been made to enhance their fidelity to the original. Such excerpts are identified parenthetically.

Abbreviations

B	Benjamin, *Briefe*
BüK	Benjamin, *Benjamin über Kafka*
C	Benjamin, *Correspondence of Walter Benjamin*
GS	Benjamin, *Gesammelte Schriften*
I	Benjamin, *Illuminations*
O	Benjamin, *Origin of German Tragic Drama*
R	Benjamin, *Reflections*
SW	Benjamin, *Selected Writings*

Introduction

In his 1921 essay, "The Task of the Translator," Walter Benjamin argued that translations should be defined neither with respect to their producer nor to their recipients. While "art . . . posits man's physical and spiritual existence," Benjamin maintained, "in none of its works is it concerned with his response. No poem is intended for the reader, no picture for the beholder, no symphony for the listener."[1] Benjamin's rather unusual claim can be read as a methodological demarcation against the psychologism of contemporary translation theories, as well as the discipline of historical linguistics, or, again, as a critique of reception theory, as some critics have noted. However, more than just methodological reflections, these remarks are indicative of the radically new philosophy of history and critique of the subject that emerged in Benjamin's writings of the 1920s and 1930s. For if, as the translation essay suggested, a "consideration of the receiver never proves fruitful" for aesthetic deliberations, it is because there exists a profound difference between the history of artworks, on the one hand, and human history, on the other.

Many of the critical and philosophical writings that belong to Benjamin's so-called metaphysical, pre-Marxist period, but also those following his turn to historical materialism, deserve to be reinterpreted in light of an aspect of his philosophy of history that, for the most part, has been left unexamined: the ethico-theological call for another kind of history, one no longer purely anthropocentric in nature or anchored only in the concerns of human subjects. Indeed, in his 1925 habilitation, *The Origin of German Tragic Drama,* Benjamin most fully spelled out this original conception of a natural, nonhuman history, coupling it with a critique of the philosophy of the subject, which would culminate in his redefinition of the theological concept *Kreatur*.

To trace these crossroads in Benjamin's thought, this study starts with a somewhat unusual constellation in that it links Benjamin to two philosophical contemporaries, Theodor W. Adorno and Martin Heidegger. As far as the constellation Benjamin-Adorno is concerned, the study revisits aspects of the intense long intellectual relationship that existed between both, a relationship that toward the end was fraught with disagreement and conflict. In recent years, quite some attention has been devoted to their disputes over aesthetic theory, sparked especially by Benjamin's preparatory work for the Arcades Project and documented in their correspondence from the 1930s.[2] Too much emphasis on the later disputes may serve, however, to obfuscate how Adorno—as one of Benjamin's earliest, enthusiastic readers—from the very start recognized the radical potential of his thought. For it was Adorno who early on deciphered the subversive significance of one of the most enigmatic terms in Benjamin's *Trauerspiel* book, namely the category of natural history.[3]

As for the constellation Benjamin-Heidegger, Heidegger's philosophy will serve in many ways as the negative foil that will bring the singularity of Benjamin's thought into better relief. Such a juxtaposition is warranted because of the often deceptive similarities that exist between their work. Thus, in her introduction to *Illuminations* Hannah Arendt held that Benjamin's "whimsical figure of the collector who gathers his fragments and scraps from the debris of the past" showed "close affinity" to Heidegger's reconceptualization of tradition.[4] Throughout his writerly career, however, Benjamin made great efforts to differentiate his thought from the German philosopher's, being quite vexed when a review in a German-language Soviet journal called him "a follower of Heidegger," a judgment based on the essay Benjamin wrote about Goethe's *Elective Affinities*.[5] Earlier, in Berlin in 1930, Benjamin had hoped to set up with Bertolt Brecht a critical reading group that was meant to demolish Heideggerian philosophy,[6] much as Adorno would make it his lifelong business to rid Continental philosophy of the jargon of authenticity. It is then precisely because of the uncanny points of convergence between Benjamin's and Heidegger's thought—evident, for example, in their common project of overcoming the shortfalls of humanism—that it becomes all the more urgent to mark off their deep-seated differences.

Part I of this book, titled "Toward a New Theory of Natural History," reconsiders Benjamin's philosophy of history by pursuing the genealogy of the materialistic category "natural history" from his *Origin of German Tragic Drama* to Adorno's lecture "The Idea of Natural History" and *Negative Dialectics*. Historians such as Michel Foucault and Wolf Lepenies have isolated the rise of "natural history" that occurred in the eighteenth century—exemplified by the work of Linnaeus—as a significant epistemological break in Western conceptions of historiography. But Benjamin's appropriation of the category proved to be highly unorthodox. With this term, he first of all referred to a process of transience and to a logic of decay that radically undermined Enlightenment and post-Enlightenment conceptions of human history, anchored in categories of human freedom and historical teleology. Following Adorno's suggestion that the *Trauerspiel* book implicitly contested Heidegger's theory of "historicity," I argue that Benjamin's positive validation of natural history was meant to overcome the limitations of historical hermeneutics, whose category of "meaning" (*Sinn*) remained grounded in the understanding of a human subject. In showing how Benjamin's new model of history fundamentally questioned the idealistic legacy that underwrites historical hermeneutics, I propose an alternative reading of the concept "origin" (*Ursprung*), on which the epistemo-critical prologue to the *Trauerspiel* book is structured. Thus, at least initially, my analysis suggests that Benjamin's profound reformulation of the term sought to merge the premises of transcendental philosophy with what traditionally is said to fall outside its boundaries: the contingency, singularity, transience, or alterity of history.

The chapters in part I show how for Benjamin the operations of natural history appeared refracted through the mourning play (*Trauerspiel*), whose vicissitudes he regarded to be exemplary of modernity. "The Turn to Natural History," for example, examines Benjamin's conviction that the predominance of natural history entailed a falling away from pure "historical" time into inauthentic "spatialization" and a temporality of transience that came to typify modernity. Similarly, the aesthetic theory that emerges from the *Trauerspiel* book—located mainly in the section "The Ruin"—established the status of the work of art as that of a remnant, relic, or ruin left in the wake of the demise of transcendent meaning.

In these and other passages it is clear that Benjamin read the *Trauerspiel* filtered through the secularization thesis, which—especially through Max Weber's sociological writings—had come to exemplify the predicament of modernity. Other parts of Benjamin's study, however, chart a return to the theological. In light of the theological residue that unmistakably weighs down the *Trauerspiel* book, the claims to antifoundationalism that Adorno discovered in Benjamin's philosophy of natural history need to be modified to a certain extent. To be sure, Adorno was interested mainly in Benjamin's search for another origin, *Ursprung,* or "primal leap,"[7] one that was no longer of the order of the Greek *arche,* the foundation of Western epistemology and ontology; at the same time, he failed to pursue the theological ramifications that followed from Benjamin's philosophical quest. The chapter "Natural and Sacred History" therefore takes up a question that Adorno left unanswered: how to understand the dialectic between sacred and natural history that shapes Benjamin's work. Through a comparative reading of the 1922 Goethe essay and the final, theological chapter of the *Trauerspiel* study, I argue that these two seemingly disparate strands interlock in his theory of allegory. Challenging some established interpretations in Benjamin scholarship, my analysis suggests not only that allegory counts as a radically new antisystematic figure signifying the disruptive force of history but also that it was meant to dismantle the figures of self and interiority, symptomatic of the philosophy of consciousness.

While part I chiefly engages with Benjamin's philosophy of history, part II shifts the perspective to his critique of the subject, showing to what degree his project for a new historiography was bound up with a profound reappraisal of the subject of idealism. Here I examine what could be called Benjamin's *de-limitation* of the human subject through a reading of the figures of stones, animals, and angels that one finds scattered throughout his writings.[8] His concern with these images was often shaped by questions concerning ethics, the law, and justice, subjects that form a sometimes tacit yet persistent subtext in his writings. Above all in his redefinition of the theological term *Kreatur* Benjamin most thoroughly probed the limits, even limitations, of a Kantian ethics and humanism.

In addressing the legacy of classical humanism, Benjamin chiefly proposed two different kinds of critique, one ethical in nature, the other political and related to the debates about humanism that preoccupied German intellectuals during the Weimar period and under national socialism. Against the background of humanistic Marxism, the chapters "Limits of Humanity" and "Benjamin's *Unmensch*" examine his explicit treatment of classical humanism in several essays written in exile. How divided Benjamin was as regards the merits and limits of the humanistic tradition emerges particularly clearly if one juxtaposes his epistolary collection, *Deutsche Menschen* (German People), to the long essay on Karl Kraus that he finished in 1931. While the collection of letters hoped to wield classical humanism against the dehumanizing horrors of national socialism, the Kraus essay renounced the ideals of the Enlightenment in order to advance a humanism that, paradoxically, advocated the figure of a destructive "in-human" (*Unmensch*), whose force was symbolized by Paul Klee's vengeful angel, *Angelus Novus.*

Before Benjamin's ethical critique of humanism can be taken up, it is first necessary to revisit the category of nature. As "The Mythical Origins of the Law" suggests, Benjamin's analysis of mythical nature rests on Judaic figures of thought, attesting to the incontrovertible legacy of Judaic law and justice in his thought. Throughout his intellectual career, Benjamin took to task mythical nature and fate, concepts that not only pervaded the Greco-Christian philosophical and religious tradition but also shored up its ethico-juridical discourse. Rejecting contemporary forms of vitalism, animism, biologism, and Darwinism, all of which validated natural or pure life, Benjamin favored a Judaic conception of justice, which, ultimately, was anchored in the realm of language.

Such essays of Benjamin's as "Critique of Violence" or the later Kafka study articulate a call for more primordial forms of responsibility and justice that antedate the hegemony of the Greek ontophilosophical tradition. In this respect, Benjamin's work needs to be placed in the context of a distinct ethico-theological tradition, one to be found also in the work of Levinas and Derrida, no less than in Adorno's critical philosophy. This summoning of an altogether different responsibility is most obvious in Benjamin's rethinking of the theological term *Kreatur* and most vividly expressed in the essay on the storyteller, also known as the Leskov essay. For in his reappraisal of Leskov's exemplary short story on the precious stone, "The Alexandrite," Benjamin proposed a form of ethical contemplation that ultimately was meant to transcend the self-absorption of melancholia and, with it, the restrictive confines of a subjectivity turned inward.

In charting these multiple patterns through Benjamin's work, this inquiry in many ways follows an inverse course. Starting off with high philosophical, epistemological questions regarding Benjamin's attempt to rethink the status of history, the study progressively follows him into the deepest recesses of his thought, to that very point where the philosophical threatens to turn into the mystical. To be sure, Benjamin's mysticism articulated itself first and foremost through his interest in cabalism, evident early on in his 1916 language essay, "On Language as Such and the Language of Man." But his mysticism has not always been interpreted in a purely theological sense; often, it has also met with suspicion, only to be read as a sign of the obfuscation, latent irrationalism, or, worse still, anti-Enlightenment program that is said to inhabit some of his work. If Gershom Scholem was one of Benjamin's early companions in his study of the cabala, he also often turned into one of his harshest critics, chiding his friend for engaging in a dialogue with conservative or protofascist authors whose politics defied redemption. Jürgen Habermas's influential 1972 essay "Walter Benjamin: Consciousness-Raising or Rescuing Critique" set the tone for such a critical reception, charging that Benjamin's interpretation of the past in terms of *Jetztzeiten* favored a "conservative-revolutionary hermeneutics," which had a "highly mediated position relative to political praxis."[9] One of the most politically engaging essays to have been dedicated to Benjamin, Habermas's piece disputed the viability of his thought for a revolutionary program, stressing instead his affinities to the fated aesthetics of surrealism.[10] My study does not mean to contest the possible irrationalism that limits the political potential of Benjamin's thought. There is no doubt that several essays from the 1930s, for example, celebrate the anarchistic, destructive practice of a disturbing new class of in-humans (*Unmenschen*). Even if this category may have been inspired by an avant-garde program of the kind the French poet Apollinaire championed,[11] Benjamin's call for the radical destruction of the human and humanism still came dangerously close to the rhetoric of the subhuman (*Untermensch*) propagated by fascist ideologues.

Mindful of these cautionary remarks, this study nonetheless attempts to read Benjamin against the grain, aiming to recover an ethico-theological potential from under the mystical and even mythic images that traverse his work. The Kafka and Leskov essays prove particularly revealing in this respect, since they bear witness to an ethical responsibility that—sentient and prereflective—falls outside the dominant philosophical narrative plotted around the quest for the *arche* (origin) of being. With Malebranche, Benjamin called this new ethical modality the "natural prayer of the heart," or an extreme attentiveness (*Aufmerksamkeit*), characterized by a radical openness to the creaturely—that is, an alterity that surpassed the confines of the merely human. In this sense, I would suggest, his thought is *an-archic*—to use the innovative meaning of the word coined by Levinas—that is, on the other side of the Greek-Hellenic tradition. Thus, Levinas advocated a radically new "humanism of the other man," one that attended to a prehistorical, an-archical responsibility anterior to the philosophical hegemony of being and no longer to be contained in ontological categories. To be sure, he thereby refused to give up the project of humanism, replacing metaphysical humanism by an ethical "humanism of the other," while Benjamin on several occasions advocated leaving all humanisms altogether behind. Yet Benjamin too held a discourse of justice against the priority of the Greek *logos,* even if he used the term "attentiveness" rather than Levinas's "responsibility."

It is important to add that by addressing the question of humanism in Benjamin's thought, one does not simply impose an extraneous framework onto his work. Certainly, in recent years, the question of antihumanism has garnered much attention, especially through political controversies surrounding French theory and philosophy. Often associated with the worst of postmodernism, the critique of humanism has been taken to task for eliminating the normative foundations upon which ethico-political action is said to rest. As this book hopes to show, an analysis of Benjamin's position allows one not only to shed new light on these discussions but also to expand the stakes of the debate and, crucially, to uncover the ethico-theological side of his thought. Finally, it should be emphasized that such a turn to the ethico-theological is not meant to transform Benjamin into an antimodernist or to diminish his position as an archeologist of the modern, most obvious in the *Paris Arcades.* Yet it cannot be doubted that even in the 1930s Benjamin's thought failed to offer a blueprint for the Marxist revolution but instead incessantly returned to that which effectively precedes the political realm—the ethico-theological. Far from drawing upon an Aristotelian or Kantian rule-governed ethics, Benjamin time and again invoked a divine justness imaged by the just man (*der Gerechte*). In so doing, he failed to explain how the ethical and the political were to be negotiated, or how an attentiveness for the creaturely was to be negotiated with a political model anchored in human agency, just as he failed to prove the political viability of a program that would join Marxism to Jewish mysticism. For these lasting incongruencies in his thought there is perhaps one figure in particular that can stand as an allegory. For, next to the images of stones, animals, and angels that traverse his work, there is one figure that ultimately emerges in all its uncanny characteristics and that heads off the theses on history: it is that of the seemingly semiautonomous chess-playing machine of historical materialism, in which sits crouched the dwarflike figure of theology.

PART I

Toward a New Theory of Natural History

At the end of the chapter "World Spirit and Natural History" in *Negative Dialectics* (1966), Adorno invoked the *Trauerspiel* study, arguing that Benjamin's materialist theory of natural history fundamentally challenged Hegel's philosophy of history. Through its emphasis on the transitory, or the process of decay that marked history, the *Trauerspiel* study, Adorno maintained, initiated the turn to another form of history, one no longer idealistic in nature. By suggesting that history and nature were "commensurable" in the moment of transience that befell both, Benjamin's study in fact contested the idealistic dichotomy between history and necessity, human freedom and nature, which it replaced with "natural history." Welding together nature and history, this term not only pointed to the originary unity and dialectical interaction between nature and history but also took note of historical contingency and of what Adorno, in his 1933 habilitation on Kierkegaard, had called real history, or "the irreversible and irreducible singularity of the historical fact."[1]

Adorno's enthusiastic validation of the *Trauerspiel* study in fact returned him to a thesis already developed in his early Frankfurt writings, which took leave of the phenomenological framework that still defined his dissertation, *The Transcendence of the Material and the Noematic in Husserl's Phenomenology* (1924).[2] Showing the first traces of an emerging materialistic critique of phenomenology, Adorno's dissertation was written under the direction of Hans Cornelius, the academic philosopher who mainly was responsible for Benjamin's failed attempt to be habilitated in Frankfurt. It was no small feat then that Adorno's programmatic lecture "The Idea of Natural History" (1932), in the context of a scathing critique of both phenomenology and Heidegger's new ontology, chose to introduce the *Trauerspiel* study as a noteworthy new text that managed to break with the idealistic tradition in German philosophy. Considering that Adorno defined the task of the new Frankfurt philosophy *against* the foil of the prominent school Heidegger already had established, the gist of his argument—despite his inordinately layered, often allusive style—will deserve closer attention. In the process, a number of questions will need to be raised. What does it mean, first of all, for Adorno to hold the *Trauerspiel* study against Heidegger's *Being and Time*? What are the theoretical and political implications of emphasizing the centrality of natural history rather than sacred history (*Heilsgeschichte*) in Benjamin's writings? And, a crucial question, how does this notion succeed in surmounting the idealistic legacy Adorno discerned in Heidegger's hermeneutical concept of historicity (*Geschichtlichkeit*)? Chapter 1, "Adorno and Benjamin— Against Historicity," pits Adorno's work against Heidegger's theory of historicity, developed in paragraphs 72–77 of *Being and Time*. To the degree that Heidegger traced natural history back to "world history" and renounced a temporality of transience, his theory of historicity must be set off from the "logic of decay" that Adorno first recognized in the *Trauerspiel* book and fully developed in *Negative Dialectics*.

This contrastive reading will set the stage for an examination of Benjamin's particular understanding of the concept of "natural history." Apart from deploying the term in its technical sense, whose history Wolf Lepenies documented in *Das Ende der Naturgeschichte* (The End of Natural History), the *Trauerspiel* study confers at least two additional meanings upon the term, as indicated by a slight difference in orthography.[3] For one, in the epistemo-critical prologue Benjamin uses the term "natural history" in the sense of *natürliche Geschichte* to delineate the specific historic mode that typifies the work of art. With respect to this first terminological usage, it becomes apparent that Benjamin advocated a nonhuman, and even nonhumanistic, history, which often found its privileged *topos* in the work of art.

But if the prologue dwelt on the natural history (*natürliche Geschichte*) of the artwork, the remainder of the study developed the term "natural history"—now spelled *Naturgeschichte* and sometimes *Natur-Geschichte*—in yet another sense. Figuring as a central historico-philosophical category, the term was meant to unlock the historic disposition of the baroque. Insofar as the mourning play was the product of secularization, it initiated a transition from historical time to a preoccupation with space and spatialization, resulting in what Benjamin called the dehistoricization of history. But if the baroque announced the onset of modernity, then the turn to natural history through secularization, exemplified in the mourning play, also asked about the status of the modern work of art as such. Is it no more than a fragment, a remnant, or relic, left in the wake of the excision of the transcendent? If so, does such a conception of art itself retain what one could call metaphysical remainders? In probing these issues, the analysis will circle back to the interrelations between sacred and natural history, thematized in the *Trauerspiel* book's final, theological chapter.

CHAPTER 1

Adorno and Benjamin

Against Historicity

Presented to the Kant Society at Frankfurt in 1932,[1] Adorno's lecture "The Idea of Natural History" traced the development of the concept of natural history in recent philosophy from Scheler's ahistorical, early phenomenology, which remained grafted onto a Platonic dualism between a static realm of Ideas and historical contingency, to Heidegger's theory of historicity (*Geschichtlichkeit*), which radically broke with phenomenology's blindness to history. Although Adorno never explicitly mentioned *Being and Time,* no doubt he had one particular section of Heidegger's study in mind, namely the chapter "Temporality and Historicity,"[2] which aimed to radicalize Dilthey and Yorck's concept of historicity by seeking to think the "ontic" and the "historical" in their originary unity.

As the social historian Herbert Schnädelbach has concisely argued, new ontology was the school in phenomenology that attempted to overcome the transcendental pitfalls that still adhered to Husserlian phenomenology.[3] Acknowledging this tradition, Adorno, in an initial moment, conceded that new ontology had been the first to point to "the irrevocable entwinement of the elements of nature and history,"[4] thus apparently superseding the nature–spirit opposition that marked subjective idealism. Similarly, he accepted that new ontology, in interpreting history as an ontological *Grundstruktur* (foundational structure), meant to account for history's most extreme dynamism (*äußerste Bewegtheit*). Yet Heidegger's philosophy relapsed into the fallacies of transcendental philosophy, or the philosophy of consciousness, when it presented historicity as an existential structure, turning it into a fundamental determination (*Grundbestimmung*) of *Dasein*.[5] Showing how new ontology's category of structural totality and its insistence on "possibility" rather than "reality" were idealistic remainders, and how its covert transcendental formalism could not adequately account for the historically contingent, the empirical, or facticity, Adorno located new ontology's main deficiencies in the logic of tautology and identity on which it proved to be founded. Its tautological tendency "results from the fact that a being that is historical is placed under the subjective category of historicity."[6] Thus, he rejected what he considered to be the flawed point of departure that informed *Being and Time,* namely, the question about the meaning (*Sinn*) of Being and its privileged point of access, or *Dasein,* through which this question was mediated. In essence, then, Adorno charged that the hermeneutical circle fundamentally amounted to a logical fallacy, for historical contingency and transience radically escaped its grasp, thus exposing the real limits of Heidegger's hermeneutics of meaning.

The program the new Frankfurt philosophy was to realize consisted in the overcoming of the idealistic legacy that burdened new ontology, thus wresting a genuine turn in the philosophy of history. Aiming to achieve what he called an "ontological reorientation of the philosophy of history,"[7] Adorno set out to show that nature and history constituted a concrete unity. This radical philosophical turn thus entailed that, first of all, an old, outmoded conception of nature needed to be discarded—that is, the belief that nature was "that which has always been there, that which as a fatefully organized, pre-given being bears human history, indeed appears in human history, and constitutes that which is substantial in human history."[8] This conceptual change was to go hand in hand with an equally profound transvaluation of human history, which he defined as the appearance of the qualitatively new in the same. As he maintained, "the point is not to find a being that shores up historical being or like a pure being inhabits history; instead, one must understand historic being itself as an ontological, that is, natural being. The retransformation of concrete history into dialectical nature forms the task of the ontological reorientation of the philosophy of history: the idea of natural history."[9] In his comprehensive study on Adorno and Heidegger, the philosopher Hermann Mörchen takes passages such as these to mean that Adorno still harbored an idealistic principle of identity and a substantialist conception of nature, amounting to nothing less than the phantom return of the traditional, metaphysical signification of Being.[10] A more attentive reading of Adorno's lecture, however, suggests the opposite. Not only does the lecture introduce the category of transience as a dialectical principle, but by positing transience as originary, Adorno inveighed against those theories that held nature to be an ahistorical "arche-principle" or primeval origin. Moreover, Adorno discerned the beginnings of such a critique of philosophical foundationalism in the work of Lukács and Benjamin.

Offering a comparative reading of Lukács's *Theory of the Novel* (1914–15) and the *Trauerspiel* book, Adorno established that both works shared a common purpose, namely the transvaluation of nature and the natural. As he noted, Lukács diagnosed the effects of modern capitalism in his theory of "second nature," a term that signaled the world of convention, reification, and petrification, as well as the ensuing alienation of the subject and his life-world, an alienation giving rise to a "charnel-house of long dead interiorities."[11] Initially, Lukács's *Theory of the Novel* thus seemed to foreground the problems posed to cognition, interpretation, and a hermeneutics of meaning, once things have lost their look of familiarity and are no longer ready at hand. In reality, however, Lukács relinquished the critical potential of his initial insight when he framed this loss of transcendent meaning by means of a salvational horizon within which such losses were to be recuperated. Benjamin's analysis, Adorno believed, managed to bring about a decisive change in perspective. For the *Trauerspiel* study, he argued, rejected such suprahistorical, transcendent meaning in favor of an analysis that lingered on transience and a logic of decay. Instead of resurrecting the skeleton of history, Benjamin's theory of allegory unearthed the debris of human history. "Whereas in the symbol destruction is idealized and the transfigured face of nature is fleetingly revealed in the light of redemption," Benjamin wrote, "in allegory the observer is confronted with the *facies hippocratica* of history as a petrified, primordial landscape. Everything about history that, from the very beginning, has been untimely, sorrowful, unsuccessful, is expressed in a face—or rather in a death's head."[12] Under Benjamin's critical gaze, allegory was transformed into the figure of natural history, which now exposed the ur-history of signification (*Urgeschichte des Bedeutens*)—that is, the incontrovertible historicity that defines all human acts of signification. Henceforth, Adorno emphasized, allegory was to be understood as a constellation that comprised the ideas of nature, history, signification, and transience—a constellation that, without fusing these terms, preserved their facticity and uniqueness.

Put differently, "natural history" referred to the mutual imbrication of nature and history, for both converged in the moment of transience that befell both. As such, Benjamin's novel conception of this old term put to shame all philosophical claims to foundationalism, including the traces of essentialism that seemingly still beleaguered his own conception of ur-history (*Urgeschichte*). For what surfaced in ur-history was nothing less than the process of destruction, decay, and transience; and what lay at the origin, Adorno implied, was not nature but originary decay: "It cannot just be a matter of showing that ur-historical motifs reappear in history time and again; instead, one must show that ur-history as transience carries the motive of history in itself."[13] In other words, Benjamin's study did not simply revert to a philosophy of origins.[14] Instead, the originary entwining of nature and history pointed to a duplicitous origin and to originary transience, which not only corroded the assumption of a primary substance or *arche* but also took leave of the metaphysical conception of nature as originary immediacy.[15]

As Adorno underlined in a notice he appended to the second German edition of *Negative Dialectics,* the thoughts first developed in this 1932 lecture were taken up again in the book's chapter "World Spirit and Natural History."[16] However, if the programs formulated in these texts seemingly converged, still the stakes of both were markedly different. True, the early lecture mounted a critique against phenomenology, yet Adorno never intended to leave philosophy's ontological framework. Instead, he sought to historicize ontology and to ontologize the philosophy of history—as he put it chiastically—through the introduction of a new dialectical category, that of transience. The latter, he contended, was "the deepest point, at which history and nature converge."[17] But by the time the term "transience" reemerged in 1966, the focus of Adorno's attention had shifted to Hegel's conception of world history, whose inflection by an insidious "natural growth" (*Naturwüchsigkeit*) he now sought to uncover.[18] In fact, when the term "transience" reappeared in *Negative Dialectics,* it seemed to have acquired even more of a programmatic status than was the case in the 1930s. Together with other, pariahlike terms that for centuries had been excluded from philosophical discourse, "transience" proved worthy of the philosopher's attention, as Adorno established in the study's introduction:

The matters of true philosophical interest at this point in history are those in which Hegel, agreeing with tradition, expressed his disinterest. They are

nonconceptuality, individuality, and particularity—things which ever since
Plato used to be dismissed as transitory (*vergänglich*) and insignificant, and
which Hegel labeled 'lazy Existenz.' Philosophy's theme would consist of
the qualities it downgrades as contingent, as a *quantité négligeable*. A matter
of urgency to the concept would be what it fails to cover, what its abstrac-
tionist mechanism eliminates, what is not already a case of the concept.[19]

Antisystematic philosophy, Adorno held, was to bring about the disenchantment of the concept, which required that philosophy equip itself
with a conceptual apparatus that could account for the nonidentical and
the transitory without obliterating them. Philosophical understanding
was, paradoxically, "to unseal the nonconceptual with concepts, without making it their equal," meaning that philosophy henceforth was
to be informed by a logic of disintegration and decay.[20] Spelling the
dissolution of Hegel's logic of identity, negative dialectics was to be
conceived of as a process that transpired through the contradictory
encounter between the real and methodical reflection.

To be sure, the term "transience" is only a component aspect of such
a logic of disintegration.[21] Yet the term, as it surfaces in *Negative Dialectics*, warrants special attention, particularly since it was inextricably
interwoven with Adorno's theory of temporality. For one thing, the
charge of "crypto-idealism" that Adorno leveled at new ontology in
his 1932 Frankfurt lecture reappeared in *Negative Dialectics*.[22] With it,
Adorno again contested Heidegger's ontologization of history because
of its detemporalization of time and neglect of transience, charging
that in *Being and Time* "time itself, and thus transiency, is both
absolutized and transfigured as eternal."[23] To gauge fully the critical
import of Adorno's analysis, it is crucial not to read his use of the
term "transience" as identical to the fallen, inauthentic conceptions of
time that traditionally have traversed the history of philosophy. On
numerous occasions, Adorno, to be sure, explicitly rejected inauthentic
modalities of time. Yet he located such an inadequate temporality in
chronological, quantitative, mechanical time, as well as in Bergson's
equally metaphysical attempt to recuperate another experience of time
in *durée*.[24] To claim, then, as Mörchen does, that Adorno's conception
of transience articulated the mere passing of time (*das Vergehen der
Zeit*), which—following Plato's *Timaeus*—was no more than the reverse "image of eternity,"[25] is to imply that his own critique of idealism
and of its legacy in phenomenology is merely the inversion of idealism's
ahistorical Platonism. As Mörchen implied, Adorno's critique did not
escape the metaphysics of presence and presencing. Indeed, we shall see

later that Adorno's philosophy did not fully rid itself of all metaphysical traits. However, Mörchen failed to credit negative dialectics for its attempt to subvert the ontologization or detemporalization of time. Furthermore, his analysis thus also remained blind to the new mode of reading offered by negative dialectics. Adorno's version of critical theory did not simply seek to read the philosophical texts of tradition anew but in addition hoped to render legible another history, one that lay "congealed in things."[26] At stake, then, was the history of things, or, as he phrased it, "that which exists as a text of its becoming."[27] In a passage striking for its Benjaminian flavor, Adorno called negative dialectics a responsiveness to the gaze of things: "The means employed in negative dialectics for the penetration of its hardened objects is possibility—the possibility of which their reality has cheated the objects and which is nonetheless visible in each one."[28] "World Spirit and Natural History" demonstrated such a new mode of reading when it distinguished between history's hidden possibilities and the ideological overlays it had received, particularly from German idealism. Hegel's attempt in his *Philosophy of Right* (Grundlinien der Philosophie des Rechts) and in *Reason in History* (Die Vernunft in der Geschichte) to construct a reality through which the reconciliation of the general and the particular could take place had to falter, for, in the concepts of the state, *Sittlichkeit,* duty, and *Volksgeist,* the violence of the general could be seen to prevail. In the section "Detemporalization of Time," Adorno presented Hegel's objective idealism as the executor of Kant's transcendental aesthetics for which time was an a priori condition of possibility, itself "exempted from time."[29] By equating "the absolute idea of totality with the passing of everything finite" and by sacrificing temporal existence to the presencing of eternity, Hegel hypostatized time as eternity.[30] As Adorno recapitulated in the study's final part, entitled "Meditations on Metaphysics," "temporal existence, by virtue of the destruction inherent in its concept, serves the eternal, which represents itself in the eternity of destruction."[31]

It was at this very point, however, that an insidious naturalness manifested itself in the Hegelian system. For in confounding the distinctions between *phusis* and *thesis* in the *Philosophy of Right* and in qualifying freedom—realized through the legal system—as spirit's "second nature," Hegel inadvertently exposed a "natural growth" that beset the spirit. When read dialectically, these passages in fact attested to the valence of Marx's category of natural history—a category, Adorno suggested, that no longer was mired in the determinism it seemingly inherited from its roots in social Darwinism. For, as a footnote from *The German Ideology* showed, already the early Marx had sought to set adrift the metaphysical antithesis between nature and history when he noted: "We know only a single science, the science of history. History can be considered from two sides, divided into the history of nature and the history of mankind. Yet there is no separating the two sides; as long as men exist, natural and human history will qualify each other."[32] In sum, the eruption of nature's violence and the mythical in Hegel's philosophy of history conclusively showed that his economy of equivalence and identity carried the seeds of its own destruction, located in the very transience and decay of the finite that his philosophical system hoped to control. At the same time, such an insidious force was the dialectical kernel that allowed Hegel to get the better of himself, pushing him beyond the limits of his own system. It is in this sense that one must understand Adorno's closing remarks: "Where Hegelian metaphysics transfigures the absolute by equating it with the total passing of all finite things, it simultaneously looks a little beyond the mythical spell it captures and reinforces."[33]

Postscript: Natural History and the Hermeneutical Circle

The critical ramifications of Adorno's—and, by implication, Benjamin's—theory of natural history become even more apparent if one turns to a contrastive and somewhat more detailed reading of the section "Temporality and Historicity" in *Being and Time,* and of paragraph 75 in particular. Indeed, it is no coincidence that in criticizing traditional, so-called inauthentic conceptions of history Heidegger made some seemingly innocuous yet crucial references to the notion of transience, seeking to devalue the discipline of natural history. In accordance with the existential analysis of the Hegelian term "world" set forth in the first part of *Being and Time,* which treated the relationship between history and time, the study's second part now made natural history subservient to "world history."

Of the inauthentic conceptions of history that needed to be repudiated, Heidegger noted, one in particular proved pernicious—namely, the erroneous reduction of history to the past. This conception of the past explained why, particularly in the nineteenth century, historiography (*Historie*) had been reduced to mere historicism—in other words, to the antiquarian collecting of rests, remainders, remnants, or so-called historical material commonly put on display (*vorhanden*) in museums. Playing with the homophony between *Vergangenheit* and *Vergängnis*—a word play irrevocably lost in English—Heidegger underscored the etymological and, indeed, conceptual relations between both: the view of history as that which is "past" (*Vergangenheit*) corresponded to a fallen conception of time, or *Jetztzeit*, defined precisely by transience (*Vergängnis*) or "the passing of time" (*Vergehen*).

In a passage that examined the historical character of antiquities, Heidegger questioned this privileging of the past and the historical object, commenting that it went hand in hand with the belief that the traces of decay in objects provided the very blueprint of history. That the transitory character of the museum artifact (*Zeug*) constituted its historicity was a position to which Heidegger strongly took exception: "The gear [*Gerät*] has become fragile or worm-eaten 'in the course of time'. But that specific character of the past which makes it something historical, does not lie in this transience [*Vergänglichkeit*], which continues even during the Being-present-at-hand of the equipment in the museum."[34] Rather, what had decayed, what was past, was the world of a former *Dasein*, in which these things once appeared as ready-at-hand (*Zuhandenheit*). *Dasein* itself could never be past, only *da-gewesen*, insofar as it was originally and primarily historical. By contrast, equipment (*zuhandenes Zeug*), including the cultural artifacts on display in museums, proved historical only in a secondary sense—that is, only insofar as it participated in the world of *Dasein*. As such, he added, these objects could be called world-historical (*Welt-geschichtlich*).

Crucial to this analysis was that nature too—in its modality of "environing nature" (*Umweltnatur*) and as "the very soil of history"[35]—was qualified as world-historical, illustrating that, ultimately, it could be traced back to the world of *Dasein*. For, as Heidegger underscored, the ready-to-hand and the present-at-hand—including nature—were grounded in the world of *Dasein*:

With the existence of historical Being-in-the-world, what is ready-to-hand and what is present-at-hand have already, in every case, been incorporated into the history of the world. Equipment and work—for instance, books—have their 'fates'; buildings and institutions have their history. And even Nature is historical. It is *not* historical, to be sure, in so far as we speak of 'natural history'; but Nature is historical as a countryside, as an area that has been colonized or exploited, as a battlefield, or as the site of a cult. These entities within-the-world *are* historical as such, and their history does not signify something 'external' which merely accompanies the 'inner' history of the 'soul.' We call such entities "the *world-historical*".[36]

Not only did Heidegger exemplify what he meant by nature as "historical soil" by means of a string of examples that were either exploitative or belligerent in nature. Ultimately, the term "natural history" was relegated to the domain of inauthentic history. At first sight, this should not come as a surprise. Heidegger thus rejected the positivistic conception of natural history, referring to F. Gottl's *Die Grenzen der Geschichte* (The Limits of History).[37] Thus, he mainly inveighed against the methodological division between the nomothetic natural sciences and the ideographic human disciplines, advocated by the neo-Kantians Wilhelm Windelband and Heinrich Rickert.[38] But in fact he also took to task his own earlier writings on the discipline of history, notably the 1915 lecture "Der Zeitbegriff in der Geschichtswissenschaft" (The Concept of Time in Historiography), a crucial early text to which we shall return in due course. By turning to Dilthey and Yorck's more original conception of historicity, he sought to overcome his earlier neo-Kantian links, since, after all, he had written the 1915 lecture in Freiburg under Heinrich Rickert.[39] In other words, on the one hand Heidegger returned to the work of Dilthey and Yorck to think the originary unity of the "ontic" and the "historical," which he recognized in their correspondence; on the other hand, he also hoped to move beyond historical hermeneutics so as to gain a fundamental-ontological vantage point.

However, it is fair to say that Heidegger's qualification of nature as secondary also testified to a deep-seated set of uncontested presuppositions, including an unreflective anthropomorphism. While seeking to surpass the methodological "division of labor" between the sciences, his analytic also reinscribed certain epistemological assumptions of the human sciences (*Geisteswissenschaften*). For one thing, a notion of cultural history surreptitiously guides the analysis of historicity and of the "world-historical." True, in paragraph 73 of *Being and Time* he implicitly discredited his own early conception of history as the progressive production of culture, or "the objectification of the human spirit."[40] However, as Michel Haar has argued in *Le Chant de la terre* (Song of the Earth), the reduction of nature to the present-at-hand and the ready-at-hand in paragraph 14 testified to a covert yet prevailing technological perspective in *Being and Time*.[41] Only in the later

Introduction to Metaphysics and the essay on the work of art would the derivative significance his earlier work ascribed to nature be replaced by a meditation on the relation between *phusis* and *aletheia,* indicative of how his interest shifted from historicity to the history of Being.[42]

This excursion into the intricacies of Heidegger's philosophy has made the following point more obvious: by redefining the term "natural history" as he did, Adorno clearly contested the hermeneutical and humanistic assumptions of "new ontology," specifically its reduction of historicity to a "Grundbestimmung von Dasein" (fundamental determination of *Dasein*). Put differently, despite Heidegger's aspiration to destroy the metaphysics of the subject, the privileged position that he accorded to the status of the question and to the exemplary *Dasein* remained expressive of a tacit but all the more profound humanism.[43] Indeed, in spite of pronounced theoretical and methodological differences with the Frankfurt School, recent French philosophical critiques have again taken up this Adornian perspective. Thus, counter to the wave of interpretations that primarily extolled the so-called radical or even nihilistic elements of Heideggerian hermeneutics—of which Vattimo's *The End of Modernity* could be seen to be representative[44]— more recent readings have increasingly directed their attention to the humanistic legacy of *Being and Time.*[45]

Benjamin shared this new philosophical project with Adorno, seeking to explode the hermeneutic circle and to revalidate a concept of nature that was neither mythical in character nor the reified object of instrumental reason. In fact, at around the same time that Adorno wrote his lecture on natural history, Benjamin formulated his notion of the dialectical image in the N-notes of the Arcades Project. Different from both phenomenology's ahistorical "essences" and Heidegger's historicity, the dialectical image—a key term in Benjamin's "dialectic at a standstill"—was said to carry a historical index that distinguished it from the phenomenological *eidos*: "What differentiates images from the 'essences' of phenomenology is their historic index. (Heidegger seeks in vain to rescue history for phenomenology abstractly, through 'historicity.')"[46] At this point it seems necessary, then, to take up again Adorno's observation, quoted earlier, that the seeds for a critique of historicity could already be found in *The Origin of German Tragic Drama.* At the same time, it will be important to correct Adorno's reading somewhat, along lines indicated earlier. To repeat, Adorno's lecture exclusively addressed the concept of natural history operative in the main part of Benjamin's study and failed to scrutinize the quite different use to which it is put in the prologue. In other words, Adorno's "Idea of Natural History" exclusively addressed Benjamin's notion of *Naturgeschichte* as used in the chapters dedicated to the *Trauerspiel*, omitting to examine its alternate use in the prologue. As we shall see, while the prologue set up the frame for the theory of natural history at the core of the *Trauerspiel* study, it did not yet do so by centering on the figure of allegory. Instead, the prologue led into an analysis of the historic modality that qualified the artwork and aesthetic forms and that Benjamin carefully demarcated from human and world history (*Weltgeschichte*) no less than from historicist ventures to map its course in art history (*Kunstgeschichte*).

CHAPTER 2

The Epistemo-Critical
Prologue Reconsidered

With his philosophical assessment of Benjamin's habilitation, Adorno was among the few who early on identified its radical
implications. However, while Benjamin's theory of allegory in its antisystematic, anti-idealistic force has since found general acceptance and
applications, the study's epistemo-critical prologue (*erkenntniskritische
Vorrede*) has, by contrast, often been regarded as hermetic or arcane.
Meant as a decisive contribution to the methodological debates that
dominated the nineteenth and early twentieth centuries, Benjamin's introduction advanced a "Platonic theory of science" (eine platonisch auf
Darstellung der Wesenheiten gerichtete Wissenschaftstheorie),[1] which
was to provide the foundation for philosophy, the philosophy of history, and philosophical aesthetics. But when seen from a contemporary
perspective, the prologue's return to Plato's doctrine of Ideas, which
it called "philosophy at its origin" (*GS* 1:209), must seem not so much
untimely as curiously out of time as the entry to a study that would
come to be regarded as one of the cornerstones of modernity. Nor
is it readily apparent how such a return to Platonism could be recon-
ciled with a radically new philosophy of history—a point already made
by an early critic who saw in what he considered to be Benjamin's
"Pseudoplatonism" "the most dangerous malady that can befall anyone
who deals with historical matters either *ex professo* or out of his own
inclination."[2]

In light of these apparently contradictory moments, which seem
to divide the prologue from the main study, the following analysis
returns to the *Trauerspiel* book's prologue to explore more closely
the conceptions of history it offers. In particular, I will examine to
what degree Benjamin intended to provide a fundamental critique of

contemporary theories of history and their roots in subject philosophy by means of the introduction of two new historical categories—namely, those of the "origin" and "natural history" (*natürliche Geschichte*). For although the prologue circled back to Plato, it cannot be read merely as an unqualified return to the origins of Western metaphysics. Instead, Benjamin hoped to surmount the ahistoricism of Plato's doctrine of Ideas by means of a radically new "philosophical history" centered on the category of the "origin." Indeed, the philosophical significance of Benjamin's theory of origin lies in the fact that it articulates an attempt to overcome the dualism between historical contingency and the ahistorical, transcendent Ideas, thus proposing an alternative reading of Plato's *ta phainomena sōzein*. At the same time, the prologue was also meant to intervene in contemporary philosophical discussions about history and historiography. Continuing a line of thought already presented in Benjamin's earlier writings, such as the translation essay, the theory of the origin targeted at least two intellectual currents: historicism and neo-Kantianism. Through the notion of origin, Benjamin attacked the inductivism of empiricist forms of historicism as he saw these manifested in the humanities, specifically in art history and literary studies. Conversely, by describing the origin as a dialectic between historical singularity and repetition, Benjamin also challenged the southwest German neo-Kantian differentiation between the historical and natural sciences.

Part of the complexity of the prologue, however, stems from the fact that it not only engaged with methodological concerns but combined such "profane" intentions with theological ones. Such a merger of intentions is apparent in Benjamin's reinterpretation of the doctrine of Ideas along cabalistic lines—which defined the Idea not as *eidos* but as the divine Word, suggesting that the profane origin must be thought in relation to a divine Origin. Within this theological framework, the terms "nature" and "history" likewise take on an added dimension—in a sense yet different from the one described in Adorno's Frankfurt lecture—insofar as they come to betoken Greek and Judaic conceptions of nature and history respectively.

It is in this double context, I would argue, that one also needs to situate the second historical category that Benjamin deploys in the study's introduction, that of "natural history" (in the sense of *natürliche Geschichte*). Insofar as the term was introduced to define the history *of* the artwork in its distinction from human history, it differed from the historical analysis of *Naturgeschichte* provided in the main body of the study while nonetheless remaining related to it in spirit. Like the notion of origin, it served to interrogate the relation between historical change and the "nature" of the Ideas, whereby "nature" is to be understood in the metaphysical sense of "essence." But by emphasizing that the history of the artwork was intrinsically different from human history, Benjamin also took up a theme that had already implicitly organized the translation essay, thus indicating the close affinities between natural history (*natürliche Geschichte*) and what he earlier had called the work's "natural life." Indeed, in many ways, the prologue can be seen as the culminating point in Benjamin's search for an *objective* grounding of history in the work of art, so typical of the writings he produced in his so-called German period. What motivates Benjamin's early reflections on history (and what links many of his early texts together) is the project to overcome the pitfalls of subjectivism and transcendentalism in historical thinking.[3] Thus, while his 1918 Kant text "On the Program of the Coming Philosophy" and the 1919 dissertation on the early romantics had already tried to shed the fallacies of subject philosophy through the introduction of terms such as "objective experience" (*GS* 2:163) and an objective "I-less reflection" (*Ichfreie Reflexion; GS* 1:40), in the *Trauerspiel* prologue Benjamin perhaps most explicitly rejected the model of reflective consciousness in favor of the linguistic nature of truth (*O* 38; *GS* 1:218). This new way of seeing history, Benjamin further suggested, was to be matched by a new model of historical analysis and understanding, one that was no longer determined by intuition (Croce) or *Einfühlung* (Dilthey, R. M. Meyer) but was receptive to what was now called the objective interpretation of phenomena. Finally, by thus questioning the limits of historical understanding, Benjamin's prologue, I would submit, at once proved to be informed by a distinct ethico-theological call for another form of history, one no longer purely ruled by the concerns or categories of human agency. In order better to explore the intricate texture of the historical model Benjamin advanced with the principles of origin and natural history, I shall first pursue its ties to some of his earlier writings—the Kant essay, the dissertation and translation essay, as well as an important letter Benjamin sent to Florens Christian Rang—and then return to the prologue.

I

    As one can learn from his correspondence with Scholem, Benjamin's early thoughts about philosophy and historiography took shape during a period in which he intensely studied Kant's system of thought. In the fall of 1917, he still hoped to dedicate his dissertation to the philosopher, oscillating between Kant's philosophy of history and his notion of the "infinite task."[4] But by December of the same year he experienced a complete disillusionment with respect to Kant's philosophy, sparked by his reading of "Idea for a Universal History from a Cosmopolitan Point of View" and "Perpetual Peace."[5] These texts, Benjamin confided to his friend, warranted a critical response for failing to reveal the "ethical side of history" and for adopting the perspective and methodology of the natural sciences. Targeting the limits of Kantian philosophy, Benjamin above all took aim at neo-Kantianism, especially the empiricist concept of experience (*Erfahrung*) that Hermann Cohen set forth in *Kant's Theory of Experience* (1871). While much of his correspondence with Scholem was critical of Kant's epistemology, his response nonetheless remained markedly complex, even divided. Perhaps Benjamin's position is best characterized in his own words, as an attempt to disregard the letter or minutiae of Kant's writings in order to be attentive to their essence or typology, as he explained to Scholem in a letter of October 22, 1917. Although he admitted that he could not yet formulate what "this 'essential' something consists of," he stressed that it would relate to Kant's "struggle to *conceive doctrine itself*."[6] Thus, it was ultimately through a revision and expansion of the Kantian system that he aimed to incorporate philosophy into religious doctrine—a near-utopian project, which he set out to accomplish in his 1918 Kant essay, "On the Program of the Coming Philosophy." At the same time, Benjamin's letter concentrated on the tensions among the dogmatism of religious doctrine, religious tradition, and historical change—tensions he likewise hoped to resolve. As he argued, the philosophy of history, which exposed the "historical development of knowledge," was to be brought to bear upon religious doctrine (*Lehre*). The letter thus looked ahead to the very dualities that would still occupy Benjamin in the epistemo-critical prologue to the *Trauerspielbuch*. Repeating that he planned to devote his dissertation to Kant and history, Benjamin again underlined the importance of historical thought for religious doctrine while at the same time voicing his first misgivings about Kant's theory of history:

I believe I recognize the ultimate reason that led me to this topic [Kant and history], as well as much that is apropos and interesting: the ultimate meta-physical dignity of a philosophical view that truly intends to be canonical will always manifest itself most clearly in its confrontation with history; in other words, the specific relationship of a philosophy with the true doctrine [*die wahre Lehre*] will appear most clearly in the philosophy of history; for this is where the subject of the historical development of knowledge for which doctrine is the catalyst will have to appear. Yet it would not be entirely out of the question for Kant's philosophy to be very underdeveloped in this respect. (*C* 98–99, slightly modified)[7]

Despite his interest in the position of religious doctrine, Benjamin's notable insistence on the historical genesis of knowledge seemed to show affinities to Dilthey's enterprise of replacing Kant's ahistorical a priori with a critique of historical consciousness. This is borne out by "On the Program of the Coming Philosophy," which took on Kant's epistemology, criticizing it for its blindness to the transient or historically defined character of the mechanistic, indeed empirical, notion of experience upon which it rested. Arguing from a position of historical relativism that—initially at least—indeed looked remarkably like Dilthey's, Benjamin defined Kant's epistemology as a *Weltanschauung* (worldview), one typical of the ahistorical and areligious philosophy of the Enlightenment. At the core of the essay, however, lay Benjamin's attempt to reclaim absolute experience and to establish firmly the foundations for metaphysics. For, with "On the Program of the Coming Philosophy," he meant to offer "prolegomena to a future metaphysics," which, while grounded in Kant's typology, would be able to account for "a deeper, more metaphysically fulfilled experience," thus providing "the logical place and logical possibility of metaphysics." Ultimately, he described the task of the coming philosophy as follows: "to create on the basis of the Kantian system a concept of knowledge to which a concept of experience corresponds, of which the knowledge is the doctrine."[8] The essay thus targeted what Adorno, in his "Meditations on Metaphysics," was to define as the Kantian block or "the bar erected against the absolute."[9] Like Benjamin before him, Adorno emphasized that there existed a contradiction in the historical nature of Kant's alleged ahistorical formalism; but Benjamin went further than Adorno when he criticized Kantian epistemology for being founded on a base and "singularly temporal" empirical experience that, counter to the philosopher's intentions, failed to ground cognition on certainty and timeless truth. Benjamin's programmatic Kant text intended to correct this by dislodging the concept of experience from a predominantly empirical consciousness and by introducing the singularly new notion of objective experience, founded exclusively on a pure transcendental consciousness.

Invoking phenomenological data about the perception of the in-sane and so-called primitive, preanimistic peoples, Benjamin boldly subverted philosophical tradition when he suggested that Kant's cogni-tive, empirical consciousness was itself no more than "a type of insane consciousness."[10] In so doing, he not only turned the Kantian tradition inside out but in fact meant to expand the notion of experience to in-clude religious experience and the phenomenon of madness. Radically questioning the rational stronghold of cognition, Benjamin sought to "de-limit" the rational subject, a project that would become even more pronounced in his later writings on psychoanalysis and surrealism.

Kant's epistemology, then, was labeled mythical for failing to discard the traditional subject–object divide and for retaining a "sublimated conception of a corporeal-spiritual I"[11]—a description meant to qualify the transcendental ego. Objective experience, by contrast, hinged on a pure transcendental consciousness. In fact, insofar as this consciousness was stripped of its subjective qualities, it could perhaps best be called—following Michel Haar's definition of the term—quasi-transcendental in nature.[12] As Benjamin wrote:

[An] objective relation between empirical consciousness and the objective concept of experience is impossible. All genuine experience rests upon the pure epistemological (transcendental) consciousness, if this term is still us-able under the condition that it be stripped of everything subjective. The pure transcendental consciousness is different in kind from any empirical consciousness, and the question therefore arises of whether the application of the term consciousness is allowable here.[13]

By thus drastically expanding the paradigm of experience, Benjamin did nothing less than shake the very foundations of epistemology. But the term "objective experience" also looked ahead to Benjamin's later theory of *Erfahrung,* particularly as presented in the Baudelaire essay, where he would set the concept against Dilthey's vitalistic and subjectivistic notion of *Erlebnis* (lived experience). Turning *Erfahrung* into the yardstick with which to measure the vicissitudes of modernity, Benjamin there would understand the waning of experience as the irrecoverable loss of tradition.

In the addendum to the Kant essay, finally, Benjamin further erased the Kantian demarcations among metaphysics, epistemology, and religion, as well as the boundaries between critical and dogmatic phi-losophy. Characteristically, the field of epistemology was turned inside out when Benjamin proposed to call all of philosophy epistemology: "All philosophy is thus theory of knowledge, but just that—a theory, critical and dogmatic, of knowledge."[14] Both critical and dogmatic theory were now said to fall within the domain of philosophy: the "reformulation of 'experience' as 'metaphysics' means that so-called experience is virtually included in the metaphysical or dogmatic part of philosophy, into which the highest epistemological, i.e., the critical [part] is transformed."[15] In calling for a concept of experience that was virtual in nature and encompassed all possible modes of experience, the Kant essay thus expressed the "unitarian approach" that shored up the 1916 language essay, "On Language as Such and on the Language of Man."[16] For in the final analysis the "mathematical-mechanical" model of experience was to be supplanted by a profoundly innovative theoretical position that outdid the Copernican revolution Kant aspired to have introduced in the field of philosophy. Insofar as it related "knowledge to language, such as was attempted by Hamann during Kant's lifetime,"[17] this daringly new paradigm looked ahead to Benjamin's large-scale plan— more fully developed in the *Trauerspielbuch*—to exchange the reflection model of the philosophy of consciousness for the insights of a full-fledged philosophy of language. But, before Benjamin could complete that step, he first needed to think through the reflection model, exhausting all its possibilities until he reached its limit. He would do so in his dissertation, which, instead of focusing on Kant, would be dedicated to the romantics' aesthetic theory, or as the title indicated, to "The Concept of Art Criticism in German Romanticism."

2

_____

In the Kant essay, Benjamin believed that philosophy, through its encounter with religious doctrine, or "knowledge of religion," could gain a mediated access to the absolute. Conversely, in his dissertation Benjamin demonstrated how the artwork was to partake of the absolute through the mediation of critical reflection. Turning away from Kant's transcendental philosophy, Benjamin now addressed the early romantics' theory of *Kritik* and their "undogmatic," "free," or "liberal" formalism[18]—a formalism that would prove foundational to his early thought, judging from the prologue to the *Trauerspielbuch*.[19] A letter to Scholem, dated June 1917, had already lauded the early romantics for their audacious attempt to lay bare the form of religion, just as Kant had uncovered the subjective conditions of form in theoretical philosophy. Central to the dissertation was the claim that Schlegel and Novalis had transposed an innovative conception of (transcendental) form into the realm of art and art criticism. Thus, individual, empirical form (*Darstellungsform*) was the organ through which the work of art partook in the absolute, which itself was to be seen as an immanent medium of reflection and a continuum of forms. Art criticism in turn was an act of reflection that not only potentiated (*steigern*) the reflective seed embedded in the work's form but in fact itself unfolded in the medium of absolute reflection. The early romantics' conception of form thus proved indebted to Fichte's theory of reflection—a "thinking of thinking"—in which thinking (form) became matter and thus was elevated to a thinking of the second degree. Yet if Fichte's early philosophy was centered on the *Ich,* with the romantics such a mode of thinking no longer was carried out by an I, whether an absolute or an empirical one. Instead, art criticism amounted to I-less reflection (*Ichfreie Reflexion*), while the absolute itself was an objective medium of reflection—that is, a system of multiple, multifarious connections that could encompass lower centers of reflection, including the individual work of art. Discrete form functioned as a liminal marker (*Grenzwert*), as the work's a priori or *Daseinsprinzip.* As the kernel or very possibility of reflection lodged in the work of art, individual form was the principle through which the work was to be transported into the medium of forms. Foundational to this transcendental theory of art was a "double concept of form"—that is, the relation between the individual form of a work of art and objective, absolute form, both of which were mediated through irony:

The particular form of the individual work, which we might call the presentational form [*Darstellungsform*], is sacrificed to ironic dissolution. Above it, however, irony flings open a heaven of eternal form, the idea of forms (which we might call the absolute form), and proves the survival [*Überleben*] of the work, which draws its indestructible subsistence from that sphere, after the empirical form, the expression of its isolated reflection, has been consumed by the absolute form. The ironization of the presentational form is, as it were, the storm blast that raises the curtain on the transcendental order of art, dislodging this order and in it the immediate existence of the work as a mystery.[20]

The violent force of objective irony or "irony of form" was to dissolve individual, empirical form so that the individual work could be unveiled as a mystery. Form was the condition of possibility ingrained in the individual work, allowing it to endure beyond its dead, profane form as it was activated through objective, reflective irony. Devising a figure of thought that in various guises would resurface in his early as well as mature work, Benjamin understood the relation between artwork and criticism in terms of survival (*Überleben*). Not surprisingly, the term gained center stage in "The Task of the Translator," where—linked to the act of *Über-setzen*—it became anchored in a new theory of history, notably, history conceived as the progressive movement of translations.

3

In the opening paragraphs to "The Task of the Translator," Benjamin introduced translation as a form and a law that was lodged in the original as its very "translatability." The essay thus from the start situated the praxis of translation with respect to a law that, while immanent to the original, at once transcended it. Insofar as translatability provided the conditions of possibility of every translation, it could perhaps be called an objective quasi-transcendental structure.[21] However, rather than representing an ahistorical, atemporal a priori, translatability in reality was to be thought of as a temporal kernel located in the original—to use a figure much cherished by Benjamin—that ensured the original's endurance or survival (*Überleben*). The temporality of translatability was the condition of possibility of the work's history, for it enabled its survival and its mnemonic inscription in tradition, even if this tradition, Benjamin wrote, should pass unnoticed by humans. Thus, the transcendental structure of translatability, as a mode of temporality, was to be carefully distinguished from individual translations. Inasmuch as individual translations were dependent on the original's fame, they were its latest manifestation, for the "life of the originals attains in them to its ever-renewed latest and most abundant flowering."[22] While the translation unfolded, unfurled, perpetually renewed, and transformed the original, it at once sprang forth from it, finding its condition of possibility in the original's afterlife. This reciprocal, mutual interdependence between translation and original is what Benjamin qualified as a natural or "vital connection" (*ein Zusammenhang des Lebens*) flowing forth from the work's "natural life" (*I* 71; *GS* 4:10–11).

But the terms "life" and "afterlife" (*Überleben, Fortleben*), Benjamin cautioned, should not be read as metaphors. Nor could they be defined in terms of the conception of an amorphous soul or the monism and hylozoism that characterized the theory of psychophysics proposed by Gustav Theodor Fechner, with which Benjamin at one point, if only for a brief moment, had been fascinated.[23] Further, the term "life" could not be restricted to the life of the living organism, to organic corporeality, or to animalism. Instead, Benjamin grounded the natural and natural life in the historical finally to identify life itself as *history:*

The concept of life is given its due only if everything that has a history of its own, and is not merely the setting for history, is credited with life. In the final analysis, the range of life must be determined by history rather than by nature, least of all by such tenuous factors as sensation and soul. The philosopher's task consists in comprehending all of natural life through the more encompassing life of history. (*I* 71; *GS* 4:11)

Benjamin's statement that history was more primordial than nature would seem to form part of the philosophical critique of vitalism and its monistic principle, laid out also in the "Critique of Violence" (*GS* 2:201).[24] Yet his willingness to entertain the organic term "life" remained very much informed by the discourse of romanticism and by what he then still regarded to be the early romantics' profound insight in "the life of literary works" (*I* 76; *GS* 4:15). For Benjamin, as we saw, the artwork's participation in the absolute was ensured through critical reflection and objective irony. Clearly, then, the structure of survival and potentiation that lay at the foundation of the translation essay was a legacy from the dissertation, except that translation now had come to take the slot of romantic critique and objective irony. If translation transposed the work of art into a higher realm, this realm was now no longer a continuum of forms but, quite explicitly, a linguistic one. By transporting the original into a "more definitive linguistic realm" (*I* 75; *GS* 4:15), the medium of translation now proved to be a more prominent moment than critique or objective irony in the artwork's afterlife. Indeed, translation was the "highest testimony" of the work's life (*I* 76; *GS* 4:15). Not until *The Origin of German Tragic Drama* would Benjamin design a thanatological model of interpretation, when he redefined critique as mortification in an attempt definitively to dismantle its organic, romantic legacy. Nonetheless, it is telling that "Task of the Translator" no longer deployed the structure of "objective reflection" or of an "objective" transcendental consciousness still present in the Kant text.

As the essay advanced, a remarkable shift took place from the history of the work per se to the history of language and to history as language. Insofar as the transformations that the work underwent through translation signaled the growth of language, translation was the very organon (*Werk*) or medium of language. But while history was "at work" in translation, its operations could not be mapped by means of the derivative, philological categories of historical linguistics. This discipline, Benjamin wrote, purported to trace the genealogy of languages by means of the questionable theory of their descent or parentage (*I* 74; *GS* 4:74). In a manner reminiscent of Nietzsche's critique of historicism and his ascription of antiquarian philology to the German *Bildungstrieb,* Benjamin leveled his invectives at the philological and historiographic presuppositions that informed so-called dead theories of translation.[25] To the derivative categories of empiricist historiography Benjamin opposed the suprahistorical, intensive kinship or innermost relation among languages. By this he meant that, "a priori and apart from all historical relationships" (*I* 72; *GS* 4:12), languages were related to one another by their intentionality to pure language. Although translations could not themselves produce or bring about this hidden relation among languages, they nonetheless could represent it, "realizing it in embryonic or intensive form" (*I* 72; *GS* 4:12). But while individual translations remained singularly temporal and secondary in nature, they were granted a vital spark by the original, "catch[ing] fire on the eternal life [*Fortleben*] of the works and the perpetual renewal [*Aufleben*] of language" (*I* 74; *GS* 4:14). Poised somewhere between poetry and religious doctrine, profane translations thus became the testing ground for the "hallowed growth of languages" (*I* 74; *GS* 4:14)—a growth, Benjamin contended, that would last until their messianic end, until revelation. Until then, translations measured the distance from this end, exposing "how far removed is their hidden meaning from revelation, how close can it be brought by the knowledge of this remoteness" (*I* 74–75; *GS* 4:14).

What was peculiar about the eschatological model Benjamin laid out in these passages was that individual, singular translations were said to point proleptically to and anticipate revelation; they were its "intensive—that is, anticipative, intimating—realization" (*I* 72; *GS* 4:12). While the translation aspired to pure language, which was its end or *eschaton,* by the same token it was indebted to an economy of restitution in that it was to restore the original logos or divine *arche.*[26] Only through literal translation (*Wörtlichkeit*)—that is, through the word-by-word rendition of the primary text, whose model Benjamin admired in Hölderlin's Sophocles translations—could the translation remain faithful to the divine Word. From the movement of languages, the translation was to wrest pure language, "which no longer means or expresses anything but is, as expressionless and creative Word, that which is meant in all languages" (*I* 80; *GS* 4:19). The operation of translation was to turn the agent or power that symbolized—pure language—into the symbolized by hitting on the stratum in language that at once erased meaning, intention, communication.

While the divine Logos was the absolute principle that enabled every potential future translation, again it could not be interpreted as an ahistorical, atemporal, eternal, transcendent ground, even though it was called suprahistorical (*I* 74; *GS* 4:13). Benjamin's translation essay here took up moments from the 1916 language essay, "On Language as Such and on the Language of Man," which explained the originary fall and the episode of Babel as a fall into the empirical realm and as the separation from the divine Name, signaled by the sundering of language's nominative functions from its cognitive ones. If according to the 1916 essay this historic division eventually could be redressed through language's magic force, the translation essay, even more emphatically, thought the relation between pure language and the empirical languages as one of immanence. Pure language was the becoming of language or the movement of languages, for "that which seeks to represent, to produce itself in the evolving [*Werden*] of languages, is that very nucleus of pure language" (*I* 79; *GS* 4:19). As such, this interrelation was structurally similar to what the prologue would call the esoteric "hidden symbolical side" of language, which lay covered under its overt profane signification, and to what Benjamin later in his "Doctrine of the Similar" would term the "non-sensuous similarity" between languages.[27] Pure language, then, as the movement of language, was immanent to the diversity of empirical languages, yet it transcended them. At the risk of pressuring the limits of the German language, one could perhaps say that in Benjamin's essay the German term for translation (*Übersetzen*) no longer only denoted "transfer" or "transposition," as it does etymologically, but also pointed to transcendence, to a law (*Gesetz*) that transcends, that is *über*, above. Inasmuch as this transcendence manifested itself in translation, it was also at once immanent. As such, its ur-image (*Urbild*) was the interlinear version of the scriptures. Pure language as translation was that which inhabited and exceeded singular languages and idioms.

Rather than merely distinguishing the history of the work from human history, Benjamin's essay thus seemingly inverted their relation to allocate a certain precedence to the history of the work, showing how the tradition of translation, or history as translation, transcended human history. But its mode of transcendence was such that it announced itself as a task, as the law to translate, which was at once immanent to the history of humans. To push the implications of such an inversion to their limits: the history of the work and its translations was an objective, nonhuman, nonhumanistic history, for it was distinguished by relational concepts (*Relationsbegriffe*) and by relations, which, as Benjamin wrote, would guard their most central significance only "when they are not in advance exclusively related to humans" (*GS* 4:10). Precisely this form of history will be renamed natural history in the prologue to *The Origin of German Tragic Drama*.

4

The interconnections between the translation essay and the *Trauerspiel* book's prologue, which are underscored by a footnote in the prologue (*O* 47; *GS* 1:227), cannot be adequately explored unless one is attentive to a transitional text: a letter of Benjamin's to his friend and mentor Florens Christian Rang, from whom he had received the main impetus to reconsider Plato's doctrine of Ideas.[28] Dated December 9, 1923, the letter not only advanced some preliminary observations about "the specific historicity of works of art" (*C* 224; *B* 322) but, centrally, aimed to find common ground between the Platonic Ideas and the hermeneutical principle of interpretation. If in the *Timaeus* and the *Symposium*, Benjamin wrote to Rang, Plato had delineated the realm of Ideas in relation to art and nature, then what yet remained to be accomplished was the interpretation of historical and sacred texts by means of the doctrine of Ideas.

Written during a period when Benjamin was immersed in preparatory readings for *The Origin of German Tragic Drama,* the letter sketched the first contours of the methodological breakthrough the prologue was intended to accomplish. At the same time, there was an unmistakable proximity to the translation essay, for the letter re-addressed "the question of the relationship of works of art to historical life" (*C* 223; *B* 322) by means of an oppositional model that pitted an inauthentic, fallen form of temporality against a more authentic, intensive form of timelessness. Oddly enough, in an initial moment Benjamin seemed to suggest that the historicity of the work of art was ahistorical. But this description clearly carried polemical weight, for, like the translation essay, the letter entailed a scathing critique of historicist historiography and, particularly, of contemporary forms of art history. With its categories of causality, teleology, generations, and parentage, art history, Benjamin declared, projected a genealogical model of human history onto the work of art. While human history, seen from the perspective of the history of peoples, allowed for the study of the "extensive" connections or parental relations between generations, the relationships that existed between works of art were, by contrast, timeless and "intensive." Because of their intensive, atemporal character, works of art showed an elective affinity to philosophical systems. Empiricist art history and historicist accounts of philosophy, which chronicled the history of philosophers, dogmas, or ideas, were to make way for a genuine concern with philosophy and the work of art, whose historicity could be unlocked only by means of interpretation:

the specific historicity of works of art is the kind that can be revealed not in "art history" but only in interpretation. For in interpretation, relationships among works of art appear that are timeless yet not without historical relevance. That is to say, the same forces that become explosively and extensively temporal in the world of revelation (and that is what history is) appear intensively in the world of silence and closure (and this is the world of nature and of works of art). (*C* 224; *B* 323)[29]

Against revealed history, with its linear, extensive, quantitative temporality, was set another, intensive, qualitative history that no longer functioned as a theatrical stage (*Schauplatz*) or domicile for mankind. Drawing on a cosmogonic model, reminiscent, as we shall see, of the essay on Goethe's *Elective Affinities,* the letter recast the difference between these realms as that between the "day of history" and the "night of nature," between the "sun of revelation" and the Ideas, which were stars that shone in the night of nature: "Works of art are thus defined as models of a nature that does not await the day and thus does not await judgment day either; they are defined as models of a nature that is neither the staging ground of history nor a human domicile. The salvaged night" (*C* 224; *B* 323). Echoing Heraclitus's famous fragment *phusis kruptesthai philei,* this other realm was a withdrawn, intensive world of closure that comprised not merely the realm of nature but the work of art as well, whose secrets could be disclosed only by means of interpretation—a term to be taken both in a strict hermeneutical sense and in the sense of scriptural exegesis. Whether or not Benjamin intended this world of closure covertly to refer to a Heraclitean conception of *phusis*, the theme is a familiar one in his writings, for it testifies to the persistence with which he sought to integrate a Judaic history of revelation with a Greek notion of *phusis*. Further, the letter demonstrates a conceptual model similar to the one that underpinned the translation essay: the reference to the intensive, pure language of the translation essay has made way for a world of closure—that of the work of art and of nature—that was to be brought to revelation by means of interpretation. Especially in light of the focal position the letter allocated to interpretation, it can be said to be a nuclear conception of the principle of "objective interpretation" that was to emerge in the prologue to *The Origin of German Tragic Drama*.

5

_____

With the epistemo-critical prologue, Benjamin hoped to secure the methodological ground for his study of the German *Trauerspiel*.[30] Written at a time when he had already turned away from the neo-Kantian paradigm of his formative years, the prologue became an attempt to intervene in the methodological battles or so-called *Methodenstreit* that were being waged in the exact sciences and the humanities.[31] The result was a proposal for a new theory of science, which ideally was to serve as a methodological foundation not only for philosophy but also for the philosophy of art and literature. That Benjamin intended to provide methodological recommendations for these respective fields can be gleaned from the tripartite structure he gave to the prologue: a first part (*O* 27–38; *GS* 1:207–18), which renounced the priority of epistemological questions in philosophy and centered on a cabalistic reinterpretation of Plato's doctrine of Ideas; a middle section (*O* 38–48; *GS* 1:218–28), which shifted the focus to the philosophy of art and literary history to define "philosophical history" as the "science of the origin"; and a final part (*O* 48–56; *GS* 1:228–37), which reviewed the reception history of the baroque and the *Trauerspiel*, whose "pre- and post-history" would be defined by the medieval mystery play and expressionism.

If the prologue called for a return to the origin of metaphysics, it was because already at its origin, with Plato, philosophy considered its main concern to be truth rather than cognition, which would be privileged by the Kantian tradition (*O* 30; *GS* 1:209). Although the term *erkenntniskritisch* seems to suggest that the prologue proposed a transcendental critique of the conditions of possibility that underlie cognition, the title instead should be taken quite literally to mean a definitive and radical repudiation of epistemology and transcendental philosophy.[32] In Benjamin's well-known call for the "death of intentionality," the entire tradition of the philosophy of consciousness from Kant to Brentano and Husserl, marked as it was by the primacy of cognition, interiorizing consciousness, and reflection, was put to the test. Instead of giving priority to epistemological questions, the task of the philosopher consisted in the philosophical representation (*Darstellung*) of Ideas. Unlike mathematics, which sought to eliminate representation in its quest for knowledge, philosophy existed in the perpetual confrontation and engagement with the question of representation. Precisely because truth could not be grasped by means of cognition or the concept, philosophy was to find its propaedeutic in the philosophical and theological tractatus, whose methodology was representation as detour. Only the tractatus and related experimental forms, such as the essay, enabled the philosopher to be receptive to the pre-given, transcendent force of truth.

Benjamin's delineation of the task of philosophy in terms of representation, the use of the inconclusive tractatus, and the turn to the micrological, as critics have pointed out, first of all targeted the claims to totality of idealistic philosophical systems, no less than those of positivism. Equally important, however, was the emphasis Benjamin placed from the start on the linguistic form of truth, indicating the pronounced historico-philosophical agenda that underpinned the prologue. For in positing that the sign systems of the mathematical sciences neglected representation and the linguistic nature of truth, Benjamin implied that these disciplines of necessity also denied its historical order: "Philosophical doctrine is based on historical codification. It cannot therefore be evoked *more geometrico*" (*O* 27; *GS* 1:207). The prologue thus resumed the critique of Kant's predilection for mathematical formalization, whose shortcomings Benjamin had already taken up, along distinctly Hamannian lines, toward the end of his "Program of the Coming Philosophy."[33]

Despite its overt allegiance to Plato—whose definition of truth as beautiful in the *Symposium* Benjamin invoked to underscore further that truth eludes cognition—the prologue cannot be read merely as an unconditional surrender to Platonism. Instead, Benjamin fused Hellenistic and Judaic figures of thought, when in a revision of the 1916 language essay he established truth as the precinct of the divine Name and defined the task of the philosopher as an *anamnesis* not of intuitable but of linguistic Ideas.[34] Insofar as the philosopher was "to release" the Idea "from the heart of reality as the word, reclaiming its namegiving rights," it was not Plato but rather Adam, Benjamin maintained, who was "the father of philosophy" (*O* 37; *GS* 1:217). Crucially, if philosophy was to realize itself through the recollection and recovery of its forgotten origins, it ultimately was to revert to the divine Origin. The overlay of such a Greek model on a Judaic one is further borne out by a passage in an earlier draft of the introduction, in which the realm of Ideas was quite explicitly redefined with respect to revelation. To explain the *chorismos* or salvation of the phenomena in the Ideas, Benjamin invoked a legend recounted by Salomon Maimon. The mode in which the Ideas both constituted the sphere of truth and participated in it was that of the "mise-en-abyme" markings or tracings on the stones covering the Sinai. These "have impressed upon them the pattern of a leaf (tree), whose peculiar nature consists in the fact that it reproduces itself immediately on every single piece of stone that has broken off from a stone block, and this in infinity" (*GS* 1:934).

Proposing a thorough reassessment of the philosophical tradition, Benjamin thus sought to think through the very foundations of philosophy while also aiming to dismantle the conceptual apparatus that upheld some of the more prevalent misconceptions in the discipline of history. How tightly these different levels of analysis were interconnected, indicating that for Benjamin there could be no contradiction between the theological and scientific intentions of the prologue, is clearly evident if one subjects the category of origin to closer scrutiny.

6

The methodological precautions that determined the analysis of philosophy in the opening section of the introduction also appeared in the second part, which dealt more narrowly with the philosophy of art and literature. Defining the discipline of philosophical aesthetics as "a theory of Ideas of the art forms" (*GS* 1:226), Benjamin took issue with the legacy of the philosophy of consciousness and psychologism to be found in aesthetics and literary studies. To account for the historical dimension of the work of art, he argued, the philosopher should renounce not only inductive, empiricist literary history but also the deductive and classificatory principle of genre studies, as well as the alternative notion of "a genetic, concrete classification," described in Benedetto Croce's *Grundriß der Ästhetik*. The study of the artwork's origin alone adequately could take stock of its historical dimension:

Origin [*Ursprung*], although an entirely historical category, has, nevertheless, nothing to do with genesis [*Entstehung*]. The term origin is not intended to describe the process by which the existent came into being, but rather to describe that which emerges from the process of becoming and disappearance. Origin is an eddy [*Strudel*] in the stream of becoming [*der Fluß des Werdens*], and in its current it swallows the material involved in the process of genesis. That which is original [*das Ursprüngliche*] is never revealed in the naked and manifest existence of the factual; its rhythm is apparent only to a dual insight. On the one hand it needs to be recognized as a process of restoration and reestablishment, but, on the other hand, and precisely because of this, as something [unfinished and] incomplete [*Unvollendetes, Unabgeschlossenes*]. There takes place in every original phenomenon a determination of the form in which an idea will constantly confront the historical world, until it is revealed fulfilled, in the totality of its history. Origin is not, therefore, discovered by the examination of actual findings, but it is related to their [pre- and post-history] [*Vor- und Nachgeschichte*]. The principles of philosophical contemplation are recorded in the dialectic which is inherent in origin. This dialectic shows singularity and repetition to be conditioned by one another in all essentials. The category of origin is not therefore, as Cohen holds, a purely logical one, but a historical one. (*O* 45–46; *GS* 1:226; modified translation)

By qualifying the origin as a historical rather than a logical category, Benjamin envisaged the neo-Kantian attempt to ground philosophy in a logic of the origin, advanced by Hermann Cohen in his *Logik der reinen Erkenntnis* (Logic of Pure Knowledge; 1902). Cohen's theory of the origin was thus stripped of the positive validation it received in Franz Rosenzweig's *Star of Redemption,* which had considered Cohen's definition of the origin as "determined nothingness" to be a decisive break with Hegel's foundation of logic in being.[35] But the term must also be distinguished from the historicist, causal concept of genesis (*Entstehung*). Instead, Benjamin presented the origin as an eddy in the stream of becoming and defined the task of philosophical concept formation as "to establish the becoming of phenomena in their being" (das Werden der Phänomene festzustellen in ihrem Sein; *O* 47; *GS* 1:228). By thus bringing together being (*Sein*) and becoming (*Werden*), Benjamin's language at first might seem to resemble Nietzsche's rhetoric and the latter's return to the origin (*Anfang*) of Greek philosophy as it was interpreted by Heidegger in "Nietzsche's Fundamental Philosophical Position."[36] Heidegger argued that Nietzsche had sought to bring together as a whole Parmenides' being and Heraclitus' becoming, or, on the one hand, being as "fixated" and "permanent" and, on the other, being as "perpetual creation and destruction."[37] But Nietzsche's conception of the will to power, which in aphorism 617 of the *Will to Power* he defined as "to stamp [*aufprägen*] Becoming with the character of Being,"[38] was entirely at odds with Benjamin's thought. Indeed, if in his early writings Benjamin seemingly adopted a "plastic principle," it was none other than that of the divine Name, which, insofar as it transcended phenomenality, existed as the power that "determines [*prägen*] the essence of this empirical reality" (*O* 36; *GS* 1:216). Free of Nietzschean implications, Benjamin's notion of the origin instead was precisely an attempt to move *beyond* the theory of eternal return, which he regarded to be the manifestation of a mythical power in history.

That the new term "origin" was meant to revoke the fallacies not only of neo-Kantianism and historicism but also of Nietzsche's eternal return is clear if one reads the prologue in conjunction with the earlier draft. Benjamin considered Nietzsche's principle of repetition to be an inconclusive and insufficient explanation for one of the central antinomies of history, namely that a principle of repetition manifested itself in the form of historical periods or epochs while history itself was a singular and unrepeatable process. In fact, what Benjamin aspired to accomplish with his new notion of origin was nothing less than to think together, and to bring together in one term, historical singularity and repetition. The passage from the draft that discussed this specific aspect of the origin is worth quoting at greater length. Having distinguished the term from Cohen's logic of the origin, Benjamin wrote:

But the phenomenon of the origin is not conceivable to a conception of history that considers only flat, causal forms of history. Instead, it belongs to a conception of history whose center is formed by the analysis of historical time and that sees the latter's epochs not as the constructions of a subjective mode of seeing [*Anschauungsweise*] but as part of an objective and teleological rhythm, in which the connections of causality appear under moral concepts. Such a conception of history, for which the border between natural and world history should become seriously problematic, would regard

repetition as an essential moment in every form of periodization that oc-
curs in natural and world history and would turn the question in what sense
repetition can appear in history—itself an unrepeatable course—into the
experimentum crucis of its philosophy of history. This is an experiment that
the doctrine of eternal return may have sought to conduct but failed to solve.
(*GS* 1:935)

Although the category of origin was a historical one, history could
not be conceived of on the basis of the natural law of causality.
A historiography that truly accounted for the origin was to analyze
historical time, whose epochs or periods were not purely given to a
subjective form of intuition. Instead they were marked by an objective
and teleological rhythm that exceeded the finite bounds of subjective
historical cognition and philosophical concept formation. When seen
from such an innovative historical perspective, Benjamin implied, the
usual antinomies between causality and morality and between natural
history and world history, part and parcel of the idealistic tradition, no
longer held.

There can be no doubt that Benjamin's comments on historical
singularity and repetition also addressed contemporary discussions
about historiography and, more specifically, the southwest German
neo-Kantian taxonomy, which had differentiated the nomothetic natural sciences from the ideographic science of history. This taxonomy
was originally introduced by Wilhelm Windelband in his 1894 lecture
"History and Natural Science" and further developed by Heinrich
Rickert in *The Limits of Concept Formation in Natural Science*.[39]
By establishing methodological distinctions between the disciplines
that addressed anomic, historical singularity and those that mapped
repeatable, general, or universal natural laws, this school hoped to
prove and found the possibility of a *science* of history.[40] Benjamin, by
contrast, thought the relationship between singularity and repetition
in an entirely different way, seeing the two as no longer mutually
exclusive. Thus he suggested that the conventional borders between
natural history and world history vanished because the so-called diacritical principle of repetition in fact could be seen to transpire in
both realms. Such an obfuscation of difference, however, did not
signal the emergence of an eternal return or the manifestation of a
mythical power. Instead, the crossing of the boundaries between the
two realms indicated what perhaps is best described as the redemption of ahistoric, mythic nature by a Jewish history of revelation.
With regard to this Greek–Jewish encounter, Thorleif Boman's study

Hebrew Thought Compared with Greek could be said to be particularly revealing. While the theoretical framework of this study is indisputably dated in that it links Bergson's notion of *durée* to the Hebrew conception of time, which it holds against a Greek-Hellenistic neo-Kantianism, by the same token it provides a helpful insight into the very intellectual climate within which Benjamin was working during the 1920s. Boman contrasts the Greek theory of eternal return and the principles of repetition and causality, foundational to the natural sciences, with the Judaic doctrine of eschatology and teleology, which traditionally guided not only its philosophy of religion but also its ethical teachings. The Greek-Hellenistic science of history, which originated with Herodotus and Thucydides, views in historical transience merely the workings of the principle of eternal repetition that also rules nature. Transient nature is therefore sharply distinguished from the divine realm of intransient, invariant Ideas. To this Greek constellation, Boman holds the Judaic account of God's revelation in history: "God revealed himself to the Israelites in history and not in Ideas; he revealed himself when he acted and created. His being was not learned through propositions but known in actions."[41] That with his theory of the origin Benjamin intended precisely such a salvation of nature can be gleaned from an addendum to the *Trauerspiel* study. Inspired by Georg Simmel's study of Goethe,[42] Benjamin, in a moment of belated revelation, recognized in the origin a transposition of Goethe's ur-phenomenon from the realm of nature to that of history. It is, one speculates, as if the leaf, which figured as the ur-phenomenon in Goethe's morphology of plants, suddenly had unfolded itself to become the cabalistic leaf stamped on the stones of the Sinai that had been at the center of Salomon Maimon's legend. "'Origin,'" Benjamin wrote in his addendum, "is the concept of ur-phenomenon—the theologically and historically differentiated, theologically and historically vital, concept of ur-phenomenon transposed from the pagan realm of nature into the Jewish realm of history. 'Origin,'" he continued, "is the ur-phenomenon in a theological sense. This is the only reason it can bring the concept of authenticity to completion" (*GS* 1:954).[43] Not unless one left behind the parameters of the historical sciences, Benjamin's prologue suggested, could one think together singularity and repetition and discern history's objective teleological rhythm, with its double rhythm of restoration and inconclusiveness. For what returned in the singular, transient historical process was not mythic nature but revelation; and what was repeated as the seal of the origin (*Ursprungssiegel*) or authenticity in every singular artwork was not representative of a deductive genre principle but nothing less than the imprint of the divine Origin.[44] Thus, the singular, original phenomenon (*das Ursprüngliche*) was granted its historical dimension and originality by dint of the mode and degree to which it participated in the Origin or the foundational moment of revelation. Offering a critique of idealism's anchoring of the real in the faculties of the subject (*O* 46; *GS* 1:226), Benjamin located the imprint of authenticity (*Echtheit*) *in* the phenomenon. The methodological principle of a philosophy of origins thus called for a recognition or anamnesis of the seal of origin (*GS* 1:227) in the phenomenal. Anything but a Platonic anamnesis of the *eidos,* this was a recognition of the divine imprint of revelation, or what in the original draft was qualified as the recognition of the phenomenon as a representative of long-forgotten connections to revelation (*GS* 1:936). Again, Benjamin's methodological enterprise appeared refracted through a concern with the eschatological model we already encountered in the translation essay. Just as the individual translation at once restored and proleptically announced revelation, so the singular, originary phenomenon was held to be the anticipatory and necessarily inconclusive restoration of revelation.

7

In the second and third parts of the published prologue, Benjamin seemed to engage in a more "profane" methodological debate. Thus he sought to rethink Plato's *sōzein ta phainomena* by dialectically joining, in the category of origin, the realm of the static Ideas to dynamic contingence—that is, to the transience or dynamism (*Bewegtheit*) of historical change (*GS* 1:947). As an endeavor to set into motion the Platonic sphere of Ideas and to uncover the historical dimension of truth in its full facticity, the project of the epistemo-critical prologue could well be defined as the "historicization of ontology." In this very specific sense, one must also understand Benjamin's cautionary remarks that the concept of being particular to the science of philosophy needed to reflect the history of the phenomena. Its task was "to establish [*feststellen*] the becoming of phenomena in their being. For in the science of philosophy the concept of being does not satisfy itself by means of the phenomenon, but only in the exhaustion of its history" (das Werden der Phänomene festzustellen in ihrem Sein. Denn der Seinsbegriff der philosophischen Wissenschaft ersättigt sich nicht am Phänomen, sondern erst an der Aufzehrung seiner Geschichte; *GS* 1:228).[45] The term *feststellen* no longer simply carried the more common significations of "to observe" or "to pinpoint," but, insofar as the passage sought to come to terms with historical flux in its relation to historiography, it also bore the connotation of "to set at a standstill." Applied to the philosophy of art this meant that out of all the possible empirical manifestations of the mourning play or its "extremes," the science of the origin was to dislodge and represent what amounted to the very Idea of the mourning play. Its historical dimension, which lay encrypted in the Idea, consisted in its "pre- and post-history"—that is, in a history that was no longer present as event or occurrence but only virtually present, as a content of the Idea. Crucially, Benjamin here distinguished a pure and "pragmatically real" human history from what he called the work's "natural history." As a transcendent yet *historical* realm, it was no longer real but instead virtual in nature:

The representation of an idea can under no circumstances be considered successful unless the whole range of possible extremes it contains has been virtually explored. Virtually, because that which is comprehended in the idea of origin still has history, in the sense of content [*Gehalt*], but not in the sense of a set of occurrences [*Geschehen*] that have befallen it. Its history is inward in character and is not to be understood as something boundless but as something related to essential being, and it can therefore be described as its [pre- and post-history]. This [pre- and post-history] of such essences is—as a token of their having been redeemed or gathered into the world of ideas—not pure history but natural history [*natürliche Geschichte*]. The life of the works and forms that need such protection in order to unfold clearly and [unperturbed] by human life is a natural life [*natürliches Leben*]. [Here follows a footnote reference to "The Task of the Translator."] Once this redeemed state of being in the idea is established, then the presence of the inauthentic—that is to say natural-historical—[pre- and post-history] is virtual. It is no longer pragmatically real but, as natural history [*die natürliche Historie*], is to be inferred from the state of completion and rest [that the essence has achieved]. (*O* 47; *GS* 1:227)

The natural life or natural history of the artwork lay salvaged and apparently stabilized, set at a standstill (*festgestellt*) in the Idea or essence of the phenomenon.[46] If Benjamin qualified this form of history as "inauthentic" (*uneigentlich*), this label nonetheless did not carry the strong overtones it had received either in so-called philosophies of decay or in Heidegger's fundamental-ontological reinscription of the term in *Being and Time*. As can be inferred from the passage, the inauthenticity of the work's natural history was said to distinguish it from pragmatic history, from a human history of *pragmata* or deeds.[47] Indeed, the unorthodox, paradoxical meaning Benjamin granted to the term "natural history" (*natürliche Geschichte*) becomes clear if one takes into account the reference to "The Task of the Translator." The prologue here invokes anew Benjamin's earlier theory of the natural life and survival (*Überleben*) of the work of art, as well as the theorem that the historical had to gain precedence over the natural. As mentioned before, within the context of the Platonic doctrine of Ideas, the term "natural history" took on an added dimension. For inasmuch as the historical lay encased in the essence or "nature" of the Ideas, natural history simultaneously signified the historical "dynamization" of the intransient Ideas or essences. Much as in the earlier translation essay, the phrase "to unfold clearly and unperturbed by human life" indicated that the life or history of the work of art gained a certain independence from human, pragmatic history.

The turn to such an objective history to which these lines testified was mirrored by the passage on objective interpretation and Leibniz's monadology with which Benjamin closed his methodological discussion of the philosophy of origins. Said to be structured like a Leibnizian monad, the Idea contained a representation of all possible phenomena, which, taken collectively, constituted the world. In its capacity as monad, the Idea thus projected an image of the world, as which it was its objective interpretation. Already the letter to Rang had set up a correlation between Leibniz's monadology, the Ideas, and the hermeneutical principle of interpretation. Invoking the concept of monad, Benjamin suggested to Rang that "the task of interpreting works of art is to gather creatural life into the idea. To establish it [*festzustellen*]" (*C* 225; *B* 323). Writing about how the principle of interpretation as "mortification" was to supplant all current practices in the discipline of aesthetics, Benjamin presented the Ideas as "the means of an establishing [*feststellend*] interpretation" (*C* 225; *B* 323). The transition from the plan sketched in the letter, which still qualified the Ideas more or less as tools or devices of interpretation, to a full-fledged theory of objective interpretation thus marked a significant turning point. While in the letter the praxis of "establishing," used in the sense of "to define" or "to pinpoint," primarily seemed to be under the control of an interpreting subject, in the prologue this moment was superseded by objective interpretation, or the "*pre-stabilized* representation of phenomena" (*O* 47; *GS* 1:228) in the Idea. As such, this change in emphasis only served to give more force to the central insight that had already organized the earlier parts of the prologue—namely, that if truth was essentially linguistic in nature, its very texture transcended the limits of human cognition.

To sum up, the critical potential of an objective hermeneutics resides in Benjamin's attempt to surpass the confines of subject philosophy and its relics in historiography, evident when he reformulated the task of the philosopher as the injunction to immerse himself in the real in order to dislodge its objective interpretation. In the history of Benjamin criticism, this principle of objective interpretation, together with the monadology, have been read as early formulations of the later materialistic conception of "objective construction," which was to become central to the theses on history and the Arcades Project.[48] Further, in the call for the historian's openness to the objective text of phenomena, Benjamin likewise anticipated what in the Arcades Project would be called a receptiveness to the legibility of the historic index that marked the dialectical image. To be sure, these connections to the later work do not clear the epistemo-critical prologue from the charges of metaphysics or even mysticism to which it has been subjected. Thus its reader may rightly question whether Benjamin's monadology and the encapsulation of the historical in the Idea, while ostensibly overcoming the received notion of Ideas as intransient or invariant, does not conversely entail a reification of history and a submission of the singular to the reign of the general. Notwithstanding these precautions, however, it cannot be overlooked that Benjamin's project of dislodging historical understanding from the entrapments of the reflective subject stands in stark contrast to what Adorno in his "Idea of Natural History" described as the tautological structure of understanding projected by the hermeneutical circle. Similarly, while Benjamin's conception of the work's natural history, at a remove from human history, may not be entirely free of the idealism that characterized the tradition of philosophical aesthetics, one can nonetheless discern in it what could perhaps best be called the ethico-theological call for a different kind of history, one no longer purely anthropocentric in nature or anchored solely in the concerns of a human subject. Benjamin would explore this topos further in his analysis of the figures of nature and natural history that lie at the core of *The Origin of German Tragic Drama*. Thus, the prologue may not so much bar the entry to the *Trauerspiel* book as perhaps provide the very key to it.

CHAPTER 3

The Turn to Natural History

Directed against the methodological shortcomings of nineteenth-century historicism, which classified the mourning play as "a necessary but inessential transitional manifestation" (*O* 100; *GS* 1:278), Benjamin's study on the baroque aimed at "a critical examination of the form of the *Trauerspiel*" (*O* 53; *GS* 1:234). Opposing idealistic and formalistic aesthetic theories no less than their positivistic counterparts, the study set out to define the historic specificity of the German baroque play by demarcating it from other historical periods and theatrical forms such as Attic tragedy or the contemporary expressionistic play. In the study's first part, "*Trauerspiel* and Tragedy," Benjamin sought to salvage the *Trauerspiel* from the anachronistic Aristotelian categories that had been applied to it in the past, particularly during the periods of German classicism and idealism. Placing the *Trauerspiel* against the backdrop of the Counter-Reformation, seventeenth-century theories of natural law, and the inception of an absolutist theory of the state, he argued for a new historical typology that would allow for a rigid demarcation between mourning play and tragedy. Thus, while tragedy remained firmly embedded in the world of Greek antiquity, ruled as it was by a temporality and ethics of decision (*Entscheidung*), the mourning play was to be seen as a secularization of the medieval mystery play (*O* 78; *GS* 1:257).

The first part of the *Trauerspiel* study examined the mourning play mainly from the perspective of political anthropology and genre studies, while its second half, titled "Allegory and *Trauerspiel*," mostly relied on the discipline of semiotics, offering a historico-philosophical analysis of allegory, from classicism through German idealism and beyond. Seeking to wrest allegory from the aesthetic tradition, Benjamin criticized what he called—using a turn of phrase that alluded to Machiavelli—the unlawful usurper on the scene of aesthetics: the romantic theory of the symbol. But if he set his analysis off against the predominance of the romantic symbol, he also paid homage to the theories of Friedrich Creuzer and Joseph von Görres, whose principal accomplishment, he emphasized, consisted in the introduction of the element of time into the field of semiotics.

In spite of Benjamin's endeavor to provide a new historico-philosophical contribution to the study of the baroque, however, the *Trauerspiel* book has been received primarily as his earliest document on the origin of modernity, not in the least because of the foundational status allegory was to acquire in his unfinished, monumental study of modernity, the Arcades Project. That Benjamin established methodological and thematic parallels between both texts has been well documented.[1] To a certain extent, the present analysis situates itself within this tradition in that it reads the *Trauerspiel* book predominantly as a study on the literary, aesthetic, and philosophical foundations of the modern era. Yet it does so by concentrating on particular observations of Benjamin's that seem to have gone all but unnoticed in the scholarship. Indeed, in presenting the German mourning play as an exemplary text that revealed modernity's condition, Benjamin's position toward the onset of modernity remained as conflicted as it would be in the later essay "The Work of Art in the Age of Mechanical Reproduction," which likewise hailed modernity while simultaneously lamenting tradition's untimely loss. That this ambiguous attitude already characterized his analysis of the *Trauerspiel* comes to the fore in the complex category of natural history, whose meaning, as used in the main body of the study, tended to shift. In the course of the investigation, natural history could either signal the temporality of transience or, quite to the contrary, refer to the dehistoricizing tendency that marked baroque drama. Inflected by the dialectical operations of allegory, the mourning play nonetheless essentially remained a flawed literary form or genre. If—unlike Greek tragedy—it addressed the vicissitudes of contemporary history, still it failed to embrace a genuine philosophy of history, which would not be realized until the arrival of classicistic theater. For in turning to natural history the mourning play brought about a spatialization (and hence de-historicization) of history—a dynamic Benjamin captured by what he called the "setting-to-stage" of history.[2] To gauge fully the implications of Benjamin's analysis, it will be necessary to review the complexity, even ambiguity, of the term

Naturgeschichte (sometimes spelled *Natur-Geschichte*) as it migrates through the *Trauerspiel* study. A brief elucidation of its usage therefore seems appropriate.

According to the history of the concept provided in Wolf Lepenies's important study *The End of Natural History* (Das Ende der Naturgeschichte), natural history usually refers to the atemporal, ahistorical conception of nature typical of the natural sciences and common before the advent of evolution theory or the historicization of nature that took place in the eighteenth century. Crucially, the discipline of natural history, of the type practiced by the Swedish botanist Linnaeus, for example, did not yet conceive of nature as temporal—a revolutionary insight that eventually would profoundly change the sciences. Instead, Linnaeus championed a classificatory, taxonomical, topological, and therefore essentially *spatial* conception of nature. This static view of nature did not challenge, but co-existed with, the older theological idea that nature was an infinite chain of being and thus ultimately the product of divine creation.[3]

Whenever Benjamin invoked the term "natural history" in this technical sense—specifically in the *Trauerspiel* study's first part—it essentially expressed the dehistoricization of history that baroque drama put on display. As if further to compound the intricacies of the term, however, natural history for Benjamin not only defined an inauthentic concept of nature common to the natural sciences (outer nature) but also referred to the renaissance of natural law that occurred in the sixteenth and seventeenth centuries and, finally, to the emerging discipline of anthropology (inner nature). To document the baroque's obsession with the workings of natural history, Benjamin relied extensively on Wilhelm Dilthey's influential study of the Renaissance and Reformation, *Die Funktion der Anthropologie in der Kultur des 16. und 17. Jahrhunderts* (The Function of Anthropology in the Culture of the Sixteenth and Seventeenth Centuries; 1904).[4] Part of Dilthey's monumental study on the human sciences (*Geisteswissenschaften*), this work argued that the nineteenth-century philosophy of life (*Lebensphilosophie*) had its roots in the discipline of anthropology, which originated in the sixteenth and seventeenth centuries. As Dilthey demonstrated, the dawning of the modern age witnessed the rise of the analysis of affects, temperaments, characters, types, and physiognomy; the study of the physiological determination of the psyche; and the examination of human nature in its various developmental stages and responses to the environment. These new disciplinary developments gave rise, Dilthey maintained, to "a doctrine of how to conduct life [*Lebensführung*], an evaluation of life values, in short, a philosophy of life."[5] Among the decisive factors that helped develop the nascent anthropologies was, first, the need to found law, state, and religion rationally on universal and invariable laws; second, the rediscovery of the Roman stoa; and, third, the application of the methods and principles of the mechanical natural sciences to the psyche, constituting what came to be known as the psychophysical system.[6] In the connections Benjamin drew between the stoic theory of affects, on the one hand, and natural law, on the other, he clearly proved indebted to Dilthey's study. As he noted: "The function of the tyrant is the restoration of order in the state of emergency: a dictatorship whose utopian goal will always be to replace the unpredictability of historical accident with the iron constitution of the laws of nature. But the stoic technique also aims to establish a corresponding fortification against a state of emergency [*Ausnahmezustand*] in the soul, the rule of emotions" (*O* 74; *GS* 1:253). Linking Carl Schmitt's theory of the sovereign and the state of exception to Dilthey's insights, Benjamin thus established that judicial theory sought to ground the legitimacy of the sovereign's supremacy in the state of creation or nature.[7] Like Adam, he suggested, the monarch or prince was considered to be "lord [*Herr*] of all creation" (*O* 85; *GS* 1:265).

It must at first come as somewhat of a surprise that Benjamin appeared to be indebted to Dilthey's study, not in the least in view of the implicit critique of vitalism that runs through the *Trauerspiel* book. This connection is less startling, however, once one takes into account the pronounced theoretical distinctions that exist between Benjamin's and Dilthey's projects. Dilthey's focus on the new anthropology and its philosophy of (human) nature must be understood in the context of his attempt to lay the foundations of the human sciences.[8] In stark contrast, Benjamin's analysis seemed to do nothing less than cast doubt on the alleged foundational status of anthropology. For not only did the baroque's excessive interest in nature lead to the destruction of historic ethos, as he claimed, but its emerging anthropological frame at bottom remained incompatible with a genuine philosophy of history. Insofar as the baroque historically preceded the rationalism of the Enlightenment, which conceived of history as the progressive completion of human freedom and morality, its theatrical productions lacked the ethos that would come to characterize Schiller's historical drama (*O* 89; *GS* 1:268). Pushing this line of argument still further, Benjamin contended that baroque drama reduced world history to the narrow scale of medieval chronicle. The calamities that befell the sovereign or state never proved to be the result of an offense in the realm of moral action but resembled natural catastrophes, thus attesting to "the natural aspect of the course of history" (*O* 88; *GS* 1:267). The only action the *Trauerspiel* depicted, Benjamin added, mostly took the form of "the painstaking analysis of the calculations of political intrigue" (ibid.). Here Benjamin's interpretation took up a point he had made in his 1919 essay, "Fate and Character." In accordance with the views of the neo-Kantian philosopher Hermann Cohen, this essay had criticized all ethical systems that, rather than anchoring morality in action, based it on an invariable, immutable character, thus submitting to stoicism's doctrine of eternal return. Pursuing this line of thought still further in the *Trauerspiel* study, Benjamin now seemed to suggest that the mourning play staged the return of a stoic, ahistorical cosmic conception of the world when it presented historical events as if they belonged to a "pre-history conceived in natural-historical terms" (*O* 89; *GS* 1:268). Lohenstein's dramatic work especially demonstrated how ethical reflection was blocked by the excessive use of a metaphorical language that set up analogies between the historical and the natural, thus "resolving historical and ethical conflicts into the demonstrations of natural history" (*O* 90; *GS* 1:269). Clearly, then, Benjamin's invocation of Dilthey can hardly be read as an acceptance of the latter's ideological position. For, as the German philosopher Odo Marquard has suggested in another context, Dilthey's philosophy of life subordinated the philosophy of history to anthropology: history merely bore witness to the workings of an unchangeable human nature, while historical change and contingency for their part were recuperated under the term "worldview" (*Weltanschauung*). Benjamin's position thus corroborates Marquard's thesis that, since the end of the eighteenth century, philosophical anthropology—or "the philosophical theory of man that became possible through the turn to the human life-world and fundamental through the turn to nature"[9]—has not only stood opposed to but in fact been incompatible with a true philosophy of history.

How, then, did Benjamin avoid the pitfalls of the conservative anthropology Dilthey embraced? Instead of accepting the latter's anthropological premises, he charged that the "dehistoricization of history," characteristic of baroque drama, in reality testified to modernity's secularization process. Further, as was the case with his theory of natural history, Benjamin's conception of secularization turned out to be profoundly idiosyncratic, even out of step with philosophical tradition. To be sure, the precise connotations of the term "secularization" are as varied as the history of its usage in theology, philosophy, and historiography, so that, as Hans Blumenberg has maintained, the term cannot purely be reduced to a common denominator—for example, the excision of transcendence. Blumenberg's fame in the German philosophical and historiographical debates of the 1960s derived from his attempt to topple the received notion that modernity was the product of a secularization process, a view firmly established by Max Weber and further elaborated by Karl Löwith. The critic Michael Makropoulos, however, has noted that Carl Schmitt's work, no less than Benjamin's, attested to a Weberian climate of relativism and analysis of values that foregrounded the dangerous absence of "premises of action in a contingent world."[10] Makropoulos primarily found proof for this view in Benjamin's later Baudelaire studies, but the signs of the stronghold that the secularization thesis had over Benjamin's thought are equally visible in the *Trauerspiel* study. In other words, unlike Blumenberg, Benjamin never contested the validity of defining modernity as the effect of secularization. Rather, what proved noteworthy was the very unorthodox way in which he conceived of the symptoms of such secularization, namely, in topological and temporal terms. Put succinctly, for Benjamin secularization announced the fall away from religious, historical time into an inauthentic, excessive preoccupation with space and spatialization—a predicament for which, once again, the natural sciences were to be held partly responsible. Much as Adorno's early and mature work proved to be fascinated with the philosophy of time, so Benjamin seemed to have been significantly influenced by contemporary debates about (historical) time. To no small degree, the *Trauerspiel* study responded to far-reaching changes in the conceptions of time and space that defined the nineteenth and early twentieth centuries and found expression in Bergson's and Husserl's influential philosophies of time. To be sure, the impact of these new conceptions of time on Benjamin's thought truly emerged in the later Baudelaire studies, the technology essay, and the Arcades Project—studies that challenged Bergson's *durée* or even the astral time that marked Auguste Blanqui's model of revolutionary change. By and large, however, the importance of time in the *Trauerspiel* study seems to have gone unnoticed in the critical responses to the study,[11] even though Benjamin cast the formal characteristics of baroque drama in terms of temporal and spatial coordinates. In the secularization or spatialization of historical time, in the "setting to stage" (*Schauplatz*) of history, he located one of the profound innovations that marked the mourning play and, by implication, modernity. Or, as he phrased it economically, "history merges into the setting" (*O* 93; *GS* 1:271). Seen from this perspective, the study's first part can be read as an extended, methodical reflection on the projection of time into space, or what Benjamin called "the transposition of the originally temporal data into spatial inauthenticity [*Uneigentlichkeit*] and simultaneity" (*O* 81; *GS* 1:260). Granted, then, that the *Trauerspiel* book established that the instauration of modernity implied a fall from historical time into an inauthentic form of spatialization, how is one to conceive of historical time? And, further, in what respect does such a spatialization of time also amount to secularization?

That the *Trauerspiel* study should define secularization as the "spatialization of time" appears significant in light of Benjamin's later writings, particularly an entry in the N-convolute to the Arcades Project. Having offered a series of often aphoristic reflections about the epistemological foundations of historiography, Benjamin suddenly raises a question that seems to reflect back on the *Trauerspiel* book:

Pursue the question of whether a link exists between the secularization of time into space and the allegorical perspective. The former, in any case, is hidden in the "world view of the natural sciences" of the second half of the century, as becomes apparent in Blanqui's last composition. (Secularization of history in Heidegger.)[12]

Short as this entry may be, it telescopes a cluster of issues that were at the crux of the theory of modernity Benjamin laid out in the Arcades Project. Thus, the entry linked the spatialization of time, symptomatic of the natural sciences, to the tract *l'Éternité par les astres,* which the revolutionary Auguste Blanqui wrote while in prison. From other convolutes to the Arcades Project, it is evident that Blanqui's astral time for Benjamin expressed the same fated course of time that also imbued Nietzsche's *Will to Power.* Influenced by Karl Löwith's *Nietzsche's Philosophy of the Eternal Return of the Same,* Benjamin contested the essentially ahistorical, even mythical, premises that upheld Nietzsche's mature work. While Benjamin plainly voiced his suspicion of Nietzschean vitalism in the D-convulute of the *Passagen-Werk* and elsewhere, it is less obvious how one is to understand the entry's rather cryptic parenthetical remark that Heidegger secularized and, presumably, "spatialized" history. Read, however, in conjunction with Benjamin's famous note on the dialectical image,[13] the theoretical implications of the entry readily issue forth. At stake this time too was Heidegger's theory of historicity. For in note N3, 1 Benjamin opposed his notion of the dialectical image, "that in which the Then and the Now come together into a constellation like a flash of lightening" (GS 5:578),[14] to Heidegger's historicity and the "essences" (*Wesenheiten*) of phenomenology, which do not carry a historical index but fall outside genuine historical time (*historische Zeit*; GS 5:178). Further, in another convolute of the Arcades Project, Benjamin defined historical time as eminently dialectical, arguing that it had to be distinguished, first, from the irresolvable antinomies that imbued the liberal notion of progress; second, from Kant's idea of infinite perfectibility; and, finally, from Nietzsche's eternal return (ibid.). Given, then, that the process of secularization corroded historical time, how exactly did Benjamin understand the latter term?

The concept of historical time recurs with a certain persistence in Benjamin's writings but takes on different conceptual shades according to the respective methodological and theoretical shifts his thought underwent.[15] Central to the Arcades Project and the theses on history, as several critics have observed, the category already emerged in his earliest work, notably in the short 1916 essay "*Trauerspiel* and Tragedy."[16] These early instances reflect Benjamin's engagement with methodological and epistemological questions that were at the heart of contemporary debates about the discipline of history and historiography. Most influential for Benjamin's thought were Simmel's "The Problem of Historical Time" ("Das Problem der historischen Zeit" [1915]) and Heidegger's Freiburg inauguration lecture, "The Concept of Time in Historiography" ("Der Zeitbegriff in der Geschichtswissenschaft" [1916]), which originally appeared in *Zeitschrift für Philosophie und philosophische Kritik*.[17] In a letter to Scholem of November 11, 1916, Benjamin mentioned Heidegger's lecture only to label it as an "awful piece of work, which you might, however, want to glance at, if only to confirm my suspicion, i.e. that not only what the author says about historical time (and which I am able to judge) is nonsense, but that his statements on mechanical time are, as I suspect, askew" (C 82; B 129–30). In a somewhat later letter, Benjamin mercilessly dismissed Simmel's "The Problem of Historical Time," calling it "an extremely wretched concoction" (C 106; B 162). Written in Simmel's last theoretical phase, the lecture discussed the issue in the context of what he regarded to be the most vexing "antinomy" of historiography—namely, the irresolvable conflict between the discipline of history and events

(*Geschehen*), a term to be understood in a vitalistic sense as the continuity of "experienced life" (*erlebtes Leben*).[18] Because historiography was a theoretical construct, it threatened to mortify (*Entlebendigung*)[19] this vitalistic continuity, turning it into atomistic, discrete (temporal) units.

Heidegger's Freiburg lecture did not share Simmel's vitalistic suppositions but took as its starting point the neo-Kantian opposition between the nomothetic and the ideographic sciences in order to elucidate the concept of time operative in historiography. Heidegger's goal was ultimately to contribute to the foundation of a logic or theory of science (*Wissenschaftslehre*) for the cultural sciences by means of the analysis of one of its foundational logical elements—namely, time.[20] Thus, Heidegger sought to deduce the logical structure of the concept of time from its function in historiography and, eventually, from the ends of historiography.[21] Whereas the concept of time in the natural sciences was homogeneous, to be determined quantitatively[22] and, consequently, spatially (a factor especially evident in non-Euclidean geometry), the concept of time in the cultural sciences was fundamentally qualitative in nature. In seeking to determine the relations that existed between singular past events, which were marked by a "qualitative otherness," the science of history remained value oriented, a point established by Heidegger's teacher Heinrich Rickert.[23]

Understandably, Heidegger's rigorous lecture with its neo-Kantian starting point had to leave Benjamin dissatisfied. Nevertheless, his disenchantment with Heidegger's perspective, expressed in the 1916 letter to Scholem, didn't simply reflect his rejection of a neo-Kantian perspective in determining historical time. During this early phase, he also seemed to be uninterested in defining historical time for the purposes of the science of history. How then, one might justifiably ask, did Benjamin conceive of the concept "historical time" if he sought to disengage it from the established epistemological concerns of contemporary historiography? The answer is to be found in his 1916 essay "*Trauerspiel* and Tragedy."

Much like Heidegger's lecture, Benjamin's essay started by setting historical time off from the physical, astronomical clock time of the natural sciences. Although historical time, which Benjamin described as "infinite in every direction and unfulfilled in every instant" (*GS* 2:134), might at first seem similar to physical time, there existed a seminal difference. Unlike the concept of time in the natural sciences, which for Benjamin remained an empty form, the continuum of historical time could be brought to completion.[24] Benjamin defined physical time as "the possibility of spatial changes of a certain magnitude and regularity—namely that of the clock hand—taking place simultaneously with spatial changes of a complex structure" (GS 2:134). This definition of physical time as the (spatial) measurement of movement derived from the Greek philosophical tradition, more precisely from Aristotle's definition of time as *arithmos kinēseos* in *Physics*, book 4.[25]

Although Benjamin called time a form, he did not subscribe to Kant's conception of time as a subjective transcendental form of intuition. Conceived instead as an *objective* transcendental form, historical time could not be related back to a transcendental subject, nor could it be brought to completion by mere events—in other words, by empirical history. Refusing the philosophical conceptions of objective no less than subjective time, Benjamin qualified historical time as religious time.[26] "This idea of completed time, which forms the dominating historical idea of the Bible, is called: messianic time" (GS 2:134). Seen against biblical, divinely completed time, physical time appeared as no more than an endless succession of discrete moments—in other words, as an inauthentic, empty infinitude.

Having established the specificity of historical time, Benjamin now argued that it was only on the basis of their distinctive positions relative to this authentic time that tragedy and the mourning play could be demarcated from one another. If historical time was defined by the historical idea of a messianically completed time, tragedy remained ruled by an individually completed time while the mourning play displayed the historical idea of repetition. Using language reminiscent of Hölderlin's annotations to *Oedipus* and *Antigone*, "*Trauerspiel and Tragedy*" suggested that the death of the tragic hero resulted from his inability to survive completed time and from the subsequent guilt he brought upon himself as he sought individuation in defiance of the Greek gods. Historically more recent, the mourning play no longer pointed to a "higher life" or realm of transcendence. Instead, it was caught in an infernal game of reflections destined to display the empty mirror image of transcendence, which it infinitely reflected and deflected. It is not hard to notice how the essay thus pointed to the romantic trope of reflection that was to take up a prominent role in the dissertation on romantic *Kritik* and return in the *Trauerspiel* study. Moreover, the mourning play proved to be determined by a temporality of repetition that was remarkably similar to what Benjamin in "Fate and Character" (1919) and the *Trauerspiel* study would call an inauthentic, "parasitical" time (GS 2:176; 1:115).

Through the distinctions it drew between empty and completed time, "*Trauerspiel* and Tragedy" placed itself within the long-standing tradition in Western philosophy of discriminating authentic from inauthentic modes of temporality. The temporal spheres to be discerned in this essay—to use a Kierkegaardian term—already announced the typology of authentic and inauthentic time that would become constitutive of Benjamin's work as a whole. As an endless, tedious succession of moments or a linear continuum, chronological time, for example, equaled the temporal modality of antiquarian historicism—a discipline that, as the later theses on history insisted, reduced history to a mere chronicle. In addition, such a chronological concept of time upheld the ideology of progress against which Benjamin later would hold the radical temporality and discontinuity of the shock and the dialectical image. Finally, the 1916 essay advanced an early critique of the eternal return, whose spectral temporality would form the target of the Baudelaire texts and the later analysis of modernity in terms of the eternal recurrence of the New.[27]

The typological distinctions that Benjamin introduced in the 1916 sketch partly reappeared in the *Trauerspiel* book, whose first part—not by accident—was titled after the essay. If the mourning play transformed time into space, it was because a more authentic temporality, that of a messianically completed time, served as the implicit background of Benjamin's analysis. The fall from authentic, historical time into space, typical for baroque drama, emerged in the predominance of three inauthentic temporal modalities: chronological time, its inversion, *acme,* and, finally, the cyclical, eternal return of the same. It is to a brief review of these three inauthentic modalities that I would like to turn in the remainder of this chapter.

If in the first part of the *Trauerspiel* book Benjamin assessed the mourning play as the secularization of the medieval mystery play, it was because it displayed a realm of "pure immanence" resulting from the loss of all eschatology (*O* 81; *GS* 1:259). The fact that the worldly pains of the tyrannical sovereign often approximated those of the Christian martyr or even the passion of Christ served as an indication that the mourning play retained a formal, structural similarity with the mystery play. At the same time, Benjamin contended, the secularization thesis needed to be modified, for the worldly stage of the mourning play still remained placed under the arch of sacred history (*O* 78–79; *GS* 1:257). Whereas the Renaissance poet projected the possibility of an imminent apocalyptic finality (*Endzeit*), the ideal of the baroque playwright, by contrast, was the "acme," that is, "a golden age of peace and culture, free of any apocalyptic features, constituted and guaranteed *in aeternum* by the authority of the Church" (*O* 80; *GS* 1:259). In the profane baroque play, the image of transcendence appeared only by proxy, through the spectral double of ghosts and spirits who, in Benjamin's reading, became the defense mechanisms the baroque playwright devised as he sought to counteract the loss of eschatology in the wake of the theological upheavals that shook the period. In the more sophisticated Catholic Spanish plays, and above all Calderon's dramas, Benjamin added, an attempt was made to regain the illusion of transcendence through the game of reflection—that is, through the simulated entry of transcendence by means of mirrors, crystals, or puppets (*O* 81; *GS* 1:260), a device later adopted by the German romantics. The less sophisticated German baroque play, however, relapsed into an adulation of the state of creation, a phenomenon that helped to explain the sudden popularity of the pastoral play. Yet despite these national differences, both theater forms demonstrated what Benjamin termed "the transposition of originally temporal data in a spatial inauthenticity and simultaneity" (ibid.).

Nowhere was the transformation of historical temporality into prehistorical nature more evident than in the pastoral play, which transposed historical events into the prehistorical days of creation, depicting a prelapsarian state of nature or pure timelessness. At the same time, Benjamin took issue with a contemporary critic who went so far as to suggest that this enchantment with nature indicated a flight from time:

> The decisive factor in the escapism of the baroque is not the antithesis of history and nature but the comprehensive secularization of the historical in the state of creation. It is not eternity that is opposed to the disconsolate chronicle of world-history, but the restoration of the timelessness of paradise. History merges into the setting. And in the pastoral plays above all, history is scattered like seeds over the ground. "In a place where a memorable event is said to have taken place, the shepherd will leave commemorative verses in a rock, a stone, or a tree. The columns dedicated to the memory of heroes, which can be admired in the halls of fame erected everywhere by these shepherds, are all resplendent with panegyric inscriptions." The term "panoramatic" has been coined to give an excellent description of the conception of history prevalent in the seventeenth century. (*O* 92; *GS* 1:270–71)

The critic Benjamin took to task was Herbert Cysarz, who in his innovative study *Deutsche Barockdichtung: Renaissance-Barock-Rokoko* (1924) had described the "unstratified nonform" of baroque drama as

"panoramatic," noting how baroque playwrights popularized the medieval technique of the "speculum."[28] Also called *Weltspiegel* in German,
this theatrical device resulted in the stringing together of often disparate
scenes and eventually would be replaced by the more clearly delimited
modern stage (*Schauplatz*).[29] Possibly inspired by Cysarz's comments,
Benjamin observed that this tendency toward spatialization also was
apparent in the graphic adornments that embellished the published
plays. But where Cysarz's interests were, strictly speaking, philological,
Benjamin really aimed to uncover the historico-philosophical nature
of these formalistic features in an attempt, ultimately, to disclose the
baroque frame of mind. This ambitious intention may help explain
the sometimes inventive connections Benjamin detected between the
artistic and philosophical productions of the time. Thus, as he speculated, the poet's preference for spatial and panoramic structures found
its corollary in the philosopher's system, particularly in Leibniz's new
conception of calculus:

If history is secularized in the setting, this is an expression of the same metaphysical tendency which simultaneously led, in the exact sciences, to the
infinitesimal method. In both cases chronological movement is grasped and
analyzed in a spatial image. The image of the setting or, more precisely, of
the court, becomes the key to historical understanding. For the court is the
setting *par excellence* [*der innerste Schauplatz*]. (*O* 92; *GS* 1:271)

More revealing still, this tendency toward spatialization, expressed
in the exact sciences or Leibniz's infinitesimal method, surfaced in
yet another field, that of politics. For, if the epoch appeared to be
dominated by calculation, then yet another sense of the term was at
play: political calculation. Arguing that the schemer, popular in baroque
drama, should be seen as the precursor of the ballet master, whose
dance steps measured the periphery of space, Benjamin proposed the
following gloss of Lope de Vega's play *El palacio confuso*: "In contrast
to the spasmodic [*sprunghaft*] chronological progression of tragedy,
the *Trauerspiel* takes place in a spatial continuum, which one might
describe as choreographic. The organizer of its plot, the precursor of
the choreographer, is the intriguer" (*O* 95; *GS* 1:274). In setting up
an analogy between the schemer and the choreographer, Benjamin
evidently played on the double meaning of "to calculate"—that is,
both its mathematical sense of "computation" and the calculations
(*Berechnungen*) of political intrigue. For the calculations of the schemer
were the expression not only of "a mastery of the workings of politics"

but also of an "anthropological, even a physiological knowledge which fascinated him" (*O* 95; *GS* 1:274). In line again with Dilthey's study, then, Benjamin held that these calculations attested to the same mindset that led Machiavelli to found his politics on anthropology. At the same time, as suggested earlier, this passage also voiced Benjamin's covert critique of anthropology or, more precisely, of the colored interpretation this field had received within Dilthey's vitalistic framework. For insofar as this emerging discipline conceived of man as a pure natural force (*Naturkraft*),[30] it confined him to his animality and the afflictions of calculable affects—that is, "the calculable driving mechanics of the creature [*Kreatur*]."[31] As the manipulator and calculator of human nature, the Machiavellian intriguer exemplified how the faculties of reason and will had gone awry. Ultimately, his actions represented the dubious ascendance of spirit (*Geist*), as Benjamin contended, in a reading that—were it not for its ideological incompatibilities with Heidegger—for a moment at least seemed to approximate Heidegger's condemnation of the history of metaphysics as a metaphysics of the will.

Metaphorical language, Benjamin added, was the tool of the poetic schemer. In the preference baroque poets displayed for metaphors that established analogies between the psyche and the mechanisms of the clock, the metaphysics of calculation again proved to be operative. Dilthey's analysis of the baroque concept of psychophysics may have influenced Benjamin when he observed: "In Geulincx's celebrated clock-metaphor, in which the parallelism of the psychological and physical worlds is presented schematically in terms of two accurate and synchronized clocks, the second hand, so to speak, determines the rhythm of events in both.[. . .] The image of the moving hand is, as Bergson has shown, essential to the representation of the non-qualitative, repeatable time of the mathematical sciences" (*O* 96–97; *GS* 1:275). The passage is significant, for it invoked Bergson's *Essai sur les données immédiates de la conscience* (Time and Free Will; 1888), which not only contested the stronghold of psychophysics but also rebuked inauthentic, so-called spatialized notions of time, or *temps espace*. Indeed, Bergson's psychological theory criticized the concept of physical, measurable clock time used in the natural sciences for presenting an "endosmosis"—that is, for confounding temporal succession and spatial simultaneity, which resulted from the projection of time (*durée*) into space.[32] If Benjamin likewise questioned the "projection of temporal progress into space" (*O* 94; die Projektion des zeitlichen Verlaufes in den Raum; *GS* 1:273), he did not, however, promulgate the vitalistic vantage point that Bergson championed. As Adorno was to note in *Negative Dialectics,* Bergson's philosophy was premised on "the irreconcilability of *temps durée* and *temps espace*," showing the scars of a divided consciousness or "the wound of that split consciousness whose only unity lies in being split."[33] To be sure, Benjamin's rejection of the Bergsonian model would be more pronounced in the later essay "On Some Motifs in Baudelaire," which rigorously criticized Bergson's vitalistic concept of *durée,* as well as the definition *Matiére et mémoire* (Matter and Memory) had offered of memory as "the contemplative actualization of the stream of life."[34] However slight the reference to Bergson in the *Trauerspiel* study may seem, there can be no doubt that Benjamin did not intend to celebrate an inner, organic, vitalistic self[35] but merely sought to underscore the all-pervasive presence of a politics of calculation.

That the third inauthentic form of temporality—the kind of spectral temporality that manifested itself in Nietzsche's eternal return—appeared prominently in the last pages of the study's second chapter is no accident. For it is here that Benjamin discussed the ethico-political consequences of the fall into natural history. As the mourning play relinquished the realm of moral action and historical responsibility, so the reign of fate and creaturely guilt made itself felt:

> Fate is not a purely natural occurrence—any more than it is purely historical. Fate, whatever guise it may wear in a pagan or mythological context, is meaningful only as a category of natural history in the spirit of the restoration-theology of the Counter-Reformation. It is the elemental force of nature in historical events, which are not themselves entirely nature, because the light of grace is still reflected from the state of creation. But it is mirrored in the swamp of Adam's guilt. (*O* 129; *GS* 1:308)

Quoting from his earlier essays, "Critique of Violence" and "Fate and Character," Benjamin reiterated that the characters presented in the mourning play, and more particularly in the tragedy of fate, did not constitute real tragic subjects: "The subject of fate cannot be determined" (*O* 132; *GS* 1:310). Instead, individuation had made a place for the operations of an ill-defined fate, while the agents of dramatic action proved to be the contingent, creaturely passions. These passions in turn set into motion the theatrical props or requisites, which acquired an uncanny second life, proving that the rule of fate incurred "the breaking down of action into fragmented, thing-like elements" (*O* 133; *GS* 1:312). The force of the uncanny similarly manifested itself in the dreams and spectral appearances the mourning play paraded. Dreams, ghostly apparitions, the terror of the end, "all of these are more or less closely orientated around the theme of death, and in the baroque they are fully developed, being transcendental phenomena whose dimension is temporal, in contrast to the immanent, predominantly spatial phenomena of the world of things" (*O* 134; *GS* 1:313). Although the revenant seemingly pointed toward the distant presence of a transcendental beyond and therefore to another temporality, Benjamin instead once again foregrounded the tendency toward spatialization to which the phenomenon attested. Noting that the plays' action was often set at around midnight, as in Shakespeare's *Hamlet,* he explained:

There is a good reason for associating the dramatic action with night, especially midnight. It lies in the widespread notion that at this hour time stands still like the tongue of a scale. Now since fate, itself the true order of eternal recurrence, can only be called temporal in an unauthentic, that is parasitical sense, its manifestations seek out time-space [*den Zeit-Raum*]. They stand in the narrow frame of midnight, an opening in the passage of time, in which the same ghostly image constantly reappears. (*O* 135; *GS* 1:313–14; modified translation)

In the appearance of ghosts Benjamin sensed the manifestation of fallen time, the rule of a "parasitical," eternal recurrence he had addressed in "Fate and Character." Insofar as these ghastly apparitions were the messengers of fate, they made their entry through "the narrow frame of midnight" in an endless, repeated procession. As such, they were the manifestations of a world beyond history, for, as he noted, the "spirit world is ahistorical" (*O* 135; *GS* 1:314). Once again, then, the baroque play depicted a realm of pure immanence and spatialization, or what Benjamin now called *Zeit-Raum*.[36] Ruled by spectral time, the time of phantoms, the mourning play did not display the temporality of discrete, singular decisions (*Entscheidungen*) typical of tragedy. Instead, it fell privy to a temporality of repetition, whose operations announced themselves in the play's seemingly ornamental repetition of scenes.

For all its apparent uncanniness, however, the insidious temporality Benjamin saw at work in the mourning play also had larger theoretical repercussions for his emerging aesthetics. How exactly Benjamin's analysis of the entrapments of natural history reconfigured his aesthetic theory forms the subject of the following chapter. Only after we have fully explored the various manifestations of natural history can we return to the dialectical constellation

Natur-Geschichte that figured so prominently in Adorno's Benjamin interpretation. If the preceding analysis focused mainly on the dehistoricizing tendency of the baroque's fascination with natural history, the next chapter returns to the temporality of transience to unravel the implications that can be drawn from it for the discipline of aesthetics. To do so, it is necessary to read Benjamin's historical interpretation of the mourning play together with the later technology essay, "The Work of Art in the Age of Mechanical Reproduction." One question that as yet has remained unresolved is the following: to what degree did Benjamin define the modern artwork as in essence belated (*nachträglich*), thus uncovering its structure as that of the remnant? And, related to that question, how did he establish the temporality of transience as a dynamic, dialectical principle typical of modernity?

CHAPTER 4

The Aesthetics of Transience

In the fields of contemporary aesthetics, literary criticism, and the philosophy of history, the iconoclastic potential of Benjamin's notions of allegory and the fragment has been well established. In the realm of historiography, the fragment is the figure that explodes the continuity of universalizing conceptions of history; in the realm of aesthetics, fragment and allegory destroy the totalizing gestures of metaphysical theories of art. Benjamin's reinterpretation of these figures has left an indelible stamp on current critical debates about modernity and the status of the modern artwork. But less attention has been devoted to the way in which the categories of decay and transience, at the center of the *Trauerspiel* study, anticipate the later materialistic theory of the work of art in an age of mechanical reproduction. Thus it could be argued that especially the section "The Ruin," which addressed baroque *ars inveniendi,* simultaneously raised some provocative, indeed fundamental, questions about the nature of the modern artwork. Put differently, Benjamin's preoccupation with transience was not simply motivated by the baroque's obsession with things in decay but equally concerned the temporal, historical, and processlike nature of the modern artwork.

In focusing on the work's temporality, Benjamin seemed to subscribe to those aesthetic theories that regard the temporalization of art to be one of modernity's main revolutionizing achievements, whether expressed in dadaism's celebration of the ephemeral or futurism's ill-fated "aesthetics of speed." By emphasizing such a temporality of transience, Benjamin shed doubt on one of the more persistent assumptions about art—its alleged endurance and permanence—thus rebuffing those time-honored metaphysical theories that continue, as Vattimo has put it, "to think in terms of the work as a necessarily eternal form, and, at a deeper level, in terms of Being as permanence, grandeur, and force."[1]

The point of this chapter, then, will be to reexamine whether Benjamin's theory of transience truly managed to break completely out of this older classical frame. For even though his new aesthetic model privileged the fragmentary and the transient, it still left some challenging questions unanswered. Can the work of art be conceived as a fragment, remnant, or relic, and, if so, of what is it a remnant? Is it conceivable that an aesthetic theory of the fragment still retains metaphysical remainders? And, given that Benjamin maintained that "allegory established itself most permanently where transitoriness and eternity confronted each other most closely" (*O* 224; *GS* 1:397), doesn't this observation still beg the question of how we must think this "encounter" between transience and the metaphysical category of eternity? If Benjamin at one point saw allegory as a salvific figure that imbued the dead objects of history with meaning, must not this salvation falter in the face of an eternity that has been forever lost? In seeking to answer these questions, Adorno's *Aesthetic Theory* will form an indispensable point of reference, for it could be argued that his aesthetics, with hindsight, further developed and drew out the implications of the theory of the artwork that lies encapsulated in the *Trauerspiel* book.

I

Temporal and topological modalities inform Benjamin's interpretation of symbol and allegory in the semiotic section of the *Trauerspiel* study. Following Görres and Creuzer, who introduced the category of time into the field of semiotics, Benjamin drew up a list of features that rigidly differentiated symbol from allegory. Arguing that the symbol expressed a mystical desire for timelessness—that is, for the mystical instant or standstill of time as eternity—he underscored that it consequently also lacked the dialectical potential of allegory. Quoting Creuzer's thesis that symbol and allegory "stand in relation to each other as does the silent, great and mighty natural world of mountains and plants to the living progression of human history" (*O* 165; *GS* 1:342),

Benjamin added that the symbol expressed an "organic, mountain and plant-like quality" that was counterchecked by the epic, narrative, and historic dimensions of allegory. Benjamin thus unquestionably relied on Creuzer's and Görres's scholarly insights, but he also changed their romantic model considerably, for, if Görres understood allegory to be the trope that best captured organic, vital human history, then Benjamin regarded it instead as figuring natural history or what he now called the "ur-history of signification and intention" (*O* 166; *GS* 1:343 mod. tr.). Stripped of "all 'symbolic' freedom of expression, all classical proportions, all humanity" (ibid.), allegory in reality opened up onto a landscape of death and devastation. In fact, the vista of destruction Benjamin conjured up at first seemed to have more in common with the havoc wreaked by the human passions and nature that Hegel evoked in his *Vorlesungen über die Philosophie der Geschichte* (Lectures on the Philosophy of History). If the philosopher-historian bemoaned worldly transience, Hegel speculated, this wrenching experience proved bearable only because of the hope that, in the final analysis, such historical ruin would be overcome once the absolute goal of world history was attained. Despite appearances, no such sublating intentions can be imputed to Benjamin's analysis at this point. For in allegory, death appeared as "the jagged line of demarcation between physical nature and significance." In allegory, the "*facies hippocratica* of history as a petrified, primordial landscape" (*O* 166; *GS* 1:343) were put on stage.[2]

Benjamin's theory of allegory usually has been taken to spell an end to all systematic and universalistic conceptions of history, but there are still other philosophical consequences that follow from it. First, insofar as allegory exposed a fissure between nature and signification, between *phusei* and *thesei,* it pointed to a postlapsarian, fallen, or conventional form of language, which was responsible for what Benjamin would term the mourning of nature.[3] As the production and positing of meaning, allegory thus exemplified nothing less than the foundational act of hermeneutics. Second, the baroque's obsession with allegory sprang from its profound interest in natural philosophy. Counter to the Enlightenment, which regarded human happiness to be the end or entelechy of nature, baroque allegory was the heir to renaissance humanism and its rediscovery of Horapollon's *Hieroglyphica.* Allegory eminently proved to be the product of a mystical natural philosophy, which was devoted to the arcane, the hieroglyphical, the iconological, and mysterious instruction: "From the point of view of the baroque, nature serves the purpose of expressing its meaning, it is the emblematic representation of its sense, and as an allegorical representation it remains irremediably different from its historical realization" (*O* 170; *GS* 1:347). So as better to render this distinctly new view of nature, Benjamin resorted to the language of numismatics, which captured the impress history left on nature: "For where nature bears the imprint of history, that is to say where it is a setting [*Schauplatz*], it has a numismatic quality" (*O* 173; *GS* 1:349). In other words, the process of history was to be likened to the impress of a stamp, leaving the "seal of the all-too-earthly" on fallen nature (*O* 180; *GS* 1:356). Using the language of impressing, stamping, or tracing, Benjamin concluded that the transformation of nature into the scene of history transpired much like the inscription of writing: "When, as is the case in the *Trauerspiel*, history becomes part of the setting, it does so as script. The word 'history' stands written on the countenance of nature in the characters of transience. The allegorical physiognomy of the nature-history, which is put on stage in the *Trauerspiel*, is present in reality in the form of the ruin" (*O* 177; *GS* 1:353). Like nature, so history lost its organicity, for it entwined with nature to become "nature-history." History no longer assumed "the form of the process of an eternal life so much as that of irresistible decay" (*O* 178; *GS* 1:353). In the end, then, the figure of spatialization returned in Benjamin's analysis, insofar as in allegory nature was granted a "countenance" (*Antlitz, Physiognomie*), impressed as it was with meaning.

In his rendition of things in decay, decomposition, and dissolution, the baroque playwright, Benjamin contended, retained a mimetic relation to nature. But the word *phusis* now no longer carried the meaning of "growth," as its roots in the Greek verb *phuō* would lead one to believe. "Nature was not seen by them in bud and bloom, but in the over-ripeness and decay of her creations. In nature they saw eternal transience, and here alone did the saturnine vision of this generation recognize history. . . . In the process of decay, and in it alone, the events of history shrivel up and become absorbed in the setting [*Schauplatz*]" (*O* 179; *GS* 1:355). Even if nature was still rendered mimetically, it could now only take the form of a *nature morte,* to borrow Adorno's reinterpretation of this painterly term.[4]

Having questioned the existence of organic nature, Benjamin turned to the status of the fragment—"the finest material in baroque creation" (*O* 178; *GS* 1:354)—only to probe further the false appearance of totality adulated by classicism. The baroque fragment was innately different from its romantic counterpart insofar as it resisted the uplifting movement of a reflective consciousness upon which the romantic theory of art was based.[5] Like the fragment, the ruin represented the "exuberant subjection of antique elements in a structure which, without uniting them in a single whole, would, in destruction, still be superior to the harmonies of antiquity" (*O* 178–79; *GS* 1:354). In this capacity, the ruin was structurally related to allegory, as well as to the baroque theory of *ars inveniendi*. Allegory, fragment, and ruin exposed (the word Benjamin used was *Ostentation*) the fabricated nature of the artwork— in other words, its character as an artifact. Out of the remnants and allegorical remainders left by classical antiquity the baroque poet or playwright constructed his textual ruins, thus destroying classical and neoclassical notions of harmony.

But more is at stake in these passages than simply an analysis of the *vanitas* motif, popular throughout the European baroque. Benjamin aimed not only to underscore the baroque's preference for transience and decay but also to foreground the paradigmatic switch that the baroque artwork brought about in the realm of aesthetics. The poet's mourning over transience revealed a profound insight in the precarious relation between the category of truth (*Wahrheitsgehalt*) and historical becoming. Although the artwork expressed a longing for endurance, it was inevitably and irrevocably subjected to decay. Paradoxically, as Benjamin seemed to suggest, the baroque work of art was characterized partly by a desire to endure, and partly by an insidious temporality that eroded its very claim to eternity. Interestingly, Benjamin captured this desire for permanence in a phrase that bordered on anthropomorphism: "The baroque work of art wants only to endure, and clings with all its senses to the eternal" (*O* 178; *GS* 1:353).[6] ·

To define further the confrontation between temporality and endurance that marked the baroque work, Benjamin resorted to the terminology of survival, which he had introduced in his 1921 translation essay.[7] The baroque artwork, he wrote, could not survive through critical reception, for over the course of time its influence and popularity had steadily waned. Ironically, through the violent force of critique and the works' subsequent "erosion" (*Zersetzung*) they achieved lasting endurance (*O* 181; *GS* 1:357). As such, Benjamin's interpretation attested to a remarkable dialectic: the baroque work of art survived in the very act of decomposition, brought on through the mortifying force of critique:

What has survived is the extraordinary detail of the allegorical references: an object of knowledge which has settled in the consciously constructed ruins. Criticism means the mortification of the works. By their very essence these works confirm this more readily than any others. Mortification of the works: not then—as the romantics have it—awakening of the consciousness in living works, but the settlement of knowledge in dead ones. Beauty, which endures, is an object of knowledge. And if it is questionable whether the beauty which endures does still deserve the name, it is nevertheless certain that there is nothing of beauty which does not contain something that is worthy of knowledge. (*O* 182; *GS* 1:357)

Underlying this analysis is the philosophical notion of *Schein* (appearance, semblance), which in the history of Western metaphysics has customarily signaled the site of beauty. What Benjamin seemed to propose, then, was that the artwork was to be relinquished to the dissecting activity of knowledge, through the mortification of *Schein* or aesthetic semblance. In this way, he fundamentally redefined the task of the art critic or, better yet, of the philosopher of art. From the material content of the artwork (*Sachgehalt*), the passage suggested, the critic was to release the philosophical truth content (*Wahrheitsgehalt*), for only the latter could in the final analysis ensure the work's endurance, located on the other side of ephemeral beauty.[8] Not until the veil of *Schein* had been rent and the work had been decomposed to the point where it revealed its allegorical, ruinous form could it actualize the salvific potential that lay embedded at its core: "In the allegorical construction of the baroque *Trauerspiel* such ruins have always stood out clearly as formal elements of the salvaged work of art" (*O* 182; *GS* 1:358). Following a figure of thought that he deployed earlier in his dissertation and the translation essay, Benjamin now established that the baroque work carried the seeds of its own critical dissolution. Insofar as criticism was mortification, it brought on the decomposition of the work's static, spatial form, thereby realizing its temporalization and processualization.

To what extent the excerpt transposed the notion of survival from the realm of translation into that of critique (*Kritik*) becomes apparent when it is situated within the context of Benjamin's development.[9] Not only does such a temporality of transience question classical aesthetics, founded on endurance and the artwork's participation in transcendence, epitomized by the *Schein* of the idealist symbol. But also the theory of transience articulated Benjamin's attempt to reconfigure the modern artwork, which he saw prefigured by the baroque mourning play. As such, this passage, as well as the earlier analytic of the temporality of repetition typical of the mourning play, look ahead to Benjamin's later comments on the artwork and in fact take on a distinctly dialectical significance when read from the standpoint of the later technology essay.

2

In his celebrated essay on the work of art in an age of mechanical reproduction (1935–38), Benjamin hoped to devise a set of revolutionary, materialistic theses that could not be appropriated by fascism. With that purpose in mind, the theses introduced a set of "fighting concepts" (*Kampfbegriffe*) that took on idealist conceptions of art such as "creativity and genius, eternal value and mystery" (*I* 218; *GS* 1:473).[10] Showing how mechanical reproduction, repetition, and reproducibility assaulted the work of art's "here and now," the essay set out to demolish the idealist concept of eternity.

Drawing on the insights of the Viennese school of art history, whose main representatives included Alois Riegl and Franz Wickhoff, Benjamin posited that the changed status of the artwork was a function of profound changes in the perception of time and space. But if Riegl and Wickhoff had studied the formalistic signature of perceptual changes that occurred over successive centuries, they had failed to take note of how societal transformations affected human perception. Thus the advent of technology in capitalism, together with the rise of mass media, Benjamin charged, had thoroughly transformed the perceptual apparatus. Further, under the impact of technological reproduction and reproducibility the work's *aura* had come under assault. With the word "aura," Benjamin invoked a term that would acquire a prominent status in his aesthetic theory. In the technology essay, this term first of all referred to the work's spatial and temporal coordinates—that is, to its topology, uniqueness (*Einmaligkeit*), and authenticity (*Echtheit*)—in short, to what Benjamin termed the work's "here and now." "Even the most perfect reproduction of a work of art," Benjamin observed at the beginning of the second thesis, "is lacking in one element: its presence in time and space, its unique existence at the place where it happens to be" (*I* 220; *GS* 1:475). Contesting the ontological claims to primacy of the original, Benjamin simultaneously queried to what extent these revolutionary transformations had radically changed the work's long-standing relation to history and tradition. How, the essay seemed to ask, did technology alter the artwork's position as a witness to human history? Going beyond the empiricist assumptions of art history, Benjamin maintained that the historic nature of the original could not simply be gleaned from its status as a palimpsest—a slate of matter (*hule*) in which the passing of history recorded its traces. Instead, the work's bearing witness to human history was a function of the position it occupied, first, through "various changes in its ownership," second, in the course of tradition or cultural transmission. He continued:

This unique existence of the work of art determined the history to which it was subject throughout the time of its existence. This includes the changes which it may have suffered in physical condition over the years as well as the various changes in its ownership. The traces of the first can be revealed only by chemical or physical analyses which it is impossible to perform on a reproduction; changes of ownership are subject to a tradition which must be traced from the situation of the original. (Ibid.)

At issue was the loss of the work's material endurance, as well as its ability to be a witness to human history:

The authenticity of a thing is the essence of all that is transmissible from its beginning, ranging from its substantive duration to its testimony to history which it has experienced. Since the historical testimony rests on the authenticity, the former, too, is jeopardized by reproduction when substantive duration ceases to matter. And what is really jeopardized when the historical testimony is affected is the authority of the object. (*I* 221; *GS* 1:477)

What was lost was the work's authenticity, its authority, its place in tradition—in short, its aura.[11] Mechanical reproduction brought about both a temporal and spatial displacement; if the original still occupied a unique position, then the reproduction now was made available to the masses; and, if formerly the original was fixed to a particular locus, such as, for example, the private collection, through the massification of art it now could become part of everyone's experience.

To demonstrate the decline of aura that afflicted historical and cultural objects, Benjamin turned to natural objects, defining their aura as the "unique phenomenon of a distance, however close it may be" (*I* 222; *GS* 1:479). It was this hallowed distance that had been blighted and in fact replaced by a new proximity, facilitated by an accelerated technologization and mass production of art.[12] Insofar as the reproduction satiated the "desire of contemporary masses to bring things 'closer,'" it was profoundly different from the original, a difference Benjamin again mapped by means of spatiotemporal terms: "Uniqueness and permanence are as closely linked in the latter as are transitoriness and reproducibility in the former" (*I* 223; *GS* 1:479). Both these displacements in time and space substantially altered, and virtually liquidated, the handing down of tradition through cultural heritage and patrimony (*Kulturerbe*). At once a destructive, even cathartic force, mechanical reproduction violently wrenched the artwork from the realm of tradition.

This dramatic structural change in the original, presented here as the effect of progressive technologization, is, to a degree, already announced in the *Trauerspiel* study, albeit not in materialistic terms. There the structural transformations that beset the baroque artwork, Benjamin implied, emerged in the period's noted preference for artifice. Indeed, the new structure of the mourning play could best be captured by means of the Latinate word *Ostentation,* in German "zur Schau stellen, zeigen." For not only did these plays indulge in hyperbolic displays of mourning, but they were also often staged on funereal occasions, indicating that they could become "plays for the mournful" (*O* 119; *GS* 1:298). In this respect, they proved to be influenced by and continued the theatrical tradition of the Italian Renaissance theater, which originated in the *trionfi* of Lorenzo de Medici.

What merits considerable attention in Benjamin's discussion of baroque ostentation, however, is the fact that the mourning play no longer obeyed the theatrical conventions of classical antiquity. As the paradigm of a secular modernity, the mourning play fundamentally differed from Greek tragedy, a difference that could best be rendered by means of topological and temporal coordinates:

> In the European *Trauerspiel* as a whole the stage is not strictly fixable, not an actual place, but it too is dialectically split. Bound to the court, it yet remains a travelling theater; metaphorically its boards represent the earth as the setting created for the enactment of history; it follows its court from town to town. In Greek eyes, however, the stage is a cosmic *topos*. (*O* 119; *GS* 1:298).

Inasmuch as the mobile stage of the traveling theater represented creation only by proxy, the topos or scene it displayed essentially remained inauthentic. Relying on the technology of the theatrical apparatus, the stage of the mourning play was mobile, mechanical, substitutable. In Greek open air theater, by contrast, the stage *was* identical with the cosmic topos, as Benjamin commented, citing Nietzsche's *Birth of Tragedy*: "the form of the Greek theater recalls a lonely valley in the mountains: the architecture of the scene appears like a luminous cloud formation that the Bacchants swarming over the mountains behold from a height—like the splendid frame in which the image of Dionysus is revealed to them" (ibid.). While classical tragedy transpired as a unique cosmic event (*Entscheidung*), the mourning play was ruled by repetition and repeatability, as well as by the psychological constraints of "an inner world of feeling [that] bears no relationship to the cosmos": "The Greek trilogy is, in any case, not a repeatable act of ostentation, but a once-and-for-all resumption of the tragic trial before a higher court. As is suggested by the open air and the fact that the performance is never repeated identically, what takes place is a decisive cosmic achievement" (ibid.). Dependent on an insidious law of repetition, the mourning play no longer was bound to a fixed topos or *cosmos* or to the authentic temporality or locatability of the singular "here and now." When these passages are held against Benjamin's later writings, it is hard not to read in them an early, if still hesitant, sketch of the repetition principle that would find full elaboration in the essay on mechanical reproduction—an essay to which we must now return.

3

In the fourth thesis of the artwork essay, Benjamin observed that the work's aura and uniqueness was "inseparable from its being imbedded in the fabric of tradition" (*I* 223; *GS* 1:479). To the degree that the *Trauerspiel* study not only claimed the mourning play as a decisive break with theatrical tradition but vigorously examined the very notion of tradition from within a historico-philosophical framework, another powerful parallel between these texts can be discerned. Using terms that recalled the translation essay, as well as Scholem's conception of religious tradition, the artwork essay defined tradition in quasi-vitalistic terms, as "thoroughly alive and extremely changeable" (*I* 223; *GS* 1:479)—a living tradition, however, that threatened to be liquidated by the destructive force of mechanical reproduction. The example Benjamin chose to illustrate the decline of tradition—the fate of an antique Venus statue in the Christian Middle Ages—is perhaps not as gratuitous as might at first appear. That such classical statues at the time were regarded to be mere idols drives home the point that these changes in the work's reception history expressed a profound transformation in its relation to tradition (*Traditionszusammenhang*). Also significant is the fact that the reference to Venus resonates with a passage from the last chapter of the *Trauerspiel* book. Drawing on Aby Warburg's groundbreaking study *Heidnisch-antike Weissagung in Wort und Bild zu Luthers Zeiten* (Pagan-Antique Prophecy in Word and Image during Luther's Time; 1920), Benjamin maintained that baroque allegory often staged a cultural confrontation between Christian medieval practices and Hellenistic tradition, which survived in the form of cultural artifacts, legends, and emblems. While the artwork essay sought to appraise the loss of tradition that occurred in the wake of mechanical reproduction, the *Trauerspiel* study argued that allegory came about at the cost of the loss of former life-worlds (*Lebenszusammenhänge*). Rather than stamping out classical tradition, Christian allegory, first in the Middle Ages, then during the baroque era, in fact inherited and assured the survival (*Fortleben*) of the disfavored antique Greek and Roman gods. Adopting Warburg's language, Benjamin read Christian allegory as a Janus-faced figure in which an Olympian world cohabited with a mythical, demonic one. Although the ancient gods ostensibly had fled, allegory preserved them in a creaturely form. Following the Greco-Christian tradition, which located abject sensuality in the body—the shroud to the soul—Benjamin now qualified allegory as the "attire of the Olympians, and in the course of time the emblems collect around it" (*O* 225; *GS* 1:399).

While the allegories common to Christian medieval tradition displayed a deep-seated awareness of earthly transience—a fate befitting human sin—the baroque, Benjamin held, went further when it sought to release the redemptive potential implanted in allegory. As Benjamin observed, "an appreciation of the transience of things, and the concern to rescue them from eternity, is one of the strongest impulses in allegory" (*O* 223; *GS* 1:397). Or, allegory "established itself most permanently where transitoriness and eternity confronted each other most closely" (*O* 224; *GS* 1:397). These passages implied that the true status of allegory could be gauged only on condition that it was no longer merely interpreted as a historically specific trope but rather as a form of memory or historical commemoration. In exhibiting the dead relics and remnants of tradition, depleted of their former life-worlds, allegory at once rekindled these same remainders with meaning, transfiguring them into objects of allegorical interpretation:

Alongside the emblems and the attire, the words and the names remain behind, and, as the living contexts [*Lebenszusammenhänge*] of their birth disappear, so they become the origins of concepts, in which these words acquire a new content, which is predisposed to allegorical representation; such is the case with Fortuna, Venus (as Dame World) and so on. The deadness of the figures and the abstraction of the concepts are therefore the precondition for the allegorical metamorphosis of the pantheon into a world of magical, conceptual creatures. (*O* 225–26; *GS* 1:399)

Furthermore, as a historico-philosophical category, allegory also testified to humanity's profoundly altered relationship with nature.[13] Insofar
as allegory stood for semantic overdetermination and oversignification,
it was responsible for what Benjamin, alluding to the mystical tradition,
described as nature's mourning. Allegory sardonically paid tribute to a
pantheon of antique gods, which, despite their apparent departure, still
lingered in cultural remainders, sculptures, temples, cloaks, shrouds,
and sanctuaries. Allegory, in short, was a *mementum* that retained
the former presence of the antique gods in a petrified, reified form.
"Allegory," as Benjamin phrased it in gnomic fashion, "corresponds
to the ancient gods in the deadness of its concrete tangibility" (*O* 226;
GS 1:400).

Apart from the commonalities noted so far, there exists yet another
point of correspondence between the technology essay and the *Trauerspiel* study—namely, the fact that both paid tribute to the secularization
thesis. At the same time, these structural similarities will now need to be
qualified somewhat more. For while the Venus statue mentioned in the
artwork essay served to demonstrate the loss of tradition as it changed
hands from classical antiquity to the Middle Ages, it still retained its aura
and uniqueness. In this regard, Benjamin went on to argue, it differed
intrinsically from the mechanically reproducible work of art, which
alone had precipitated an incisive break in the history of aesthetics.
Indeed, three radically distinct phases could be discerned in the history
of the artwork and the relation that it bore to tradition. In a first stage,
the work remained embedded in magical and religious rituals, which
bestowed a cult value (*Kultwert*) on it. Once again Benjamin made
reference to the aura of natural objects, comparing the work's cult value
to the "unique phenomenon of a distance, however close it may be."
In a second, secular phase, the work of art was divorced from its divine
origins, although it still retained, in weakened form, its ritual function
or original use value. Now, the authenticity (*Echtheit*) of the original,
which still entertained what Benjamin called a "parasitical" relation to
primeval rites, had to be understood as a secularization of cult value
(*I* 224; *GS* 1:481). In the third and final phase, that of the reproducible
artwork, this latent link to the ritual had been relinquished, insofar
as art now proved to be founded in politics rather than theology.
Going further than Adorno, who in his aesthetic theory held on to the
category of secularization as he defined the artwork, Benjamin claimed
that the age of mechanical reproduction canceled out the sacred cult
object *and* the secularized work of art: "for the first time in world

history, mechanical reproduction emancipates the work of art from its parasitical dependence on ritual. To an ever greater degree the work of art reproduced becomes the work of art designed for reproducibility" (ibid.). No longer did the word "parasitical" refer to the temporality of repetition and eternal return, as was still the case in the *Trauerspiel* study. Rather, it now stood for the dangers of fascism and ritualistic mysticism, from which art had to emancipate itself. Spelling an end to fascism's exploitation of art's cult aspects, mechanical reproduction announced a new era, for it provided the means—or so Benjamin believed—for a new, political foundation of art: "Instead of being based on ritual, [art] begins to be based on another practice—politics" (*I* 224; *GS* 1:482). Reproduction was no longer contingent to the reproducible work of art but defined its very essence. In particular, film proved to be grafted onto reproducibility—a term that, seen within the frame of Benjamin's writings, now structurally occupied the position of translatability. Reproduction and reproducibility not only accelerated the production process of the artwork but increased what Benjamin— further expanding Marx's value system—termed its "exposition value" (*Ausstellungswert*). Not only did mechanical reproduction destroy the work's cult value, as well as the shrine to the arcane secret it was believed to hold, but also it sundered art's links to the divine place (topos) on which the temple or shrine were formerly built. In modernity, Benjamin seemed to suggest—in marked contrast to Heidegger, whose essay on the work of art heralded the sacredness of the Greek temple[14]—the ancient temple no longer had any place. From now on, it could exist only as a ruin.

4

Much as the early Adorno had espoused Benjamin's emerging theory of natural history, the later Adorno—author of *Aesthetic Theory*—drew out the consequences of the theory of art that lay dormant in Benjamin's habilitation. Thus Adorno returned to Benjamin's thoughts on art's transience in the context of Hegel's conception of the death of art, interpreting the latter's diagnosis of this decline as follows:

The Hegelian perspective that the death of art might possibly be imminent is appropriate to its genesis. That he considered art transient and still attributed it to absolute spirit on the one hand matched the double character of his system, yet on the other hand gave rise to a consequence that he himself would never have drawn: the content [*Gehalt*] of art—according to his conception its absolute—did not dissolve in the dimension of its life and death. The content of art could well consist in its own transience.[15]

As a consequence, art realized itself only to the degree that it confronted its own inevitable transience and decay. In an age of mechanical reproduction, which was ruled by what Adorno considered to be the progressive de-artification of art (*Entkunstung der Kunst*), art was pushed to its limits. That Adorno here engaged in a covert dialogue not only with Benjamin's technology essay but also with the section "The Ruin" is evident in the following excerpt, which almost literally recapitulated the anthropomorphic image Benjamin had used to capture how the artwork clung to endurance. Building on Benjamin's insights, Adorno posited, "it is likely that the thought of duration only becomes acute, as soon as duration [*Dauer*] becomes problematic and as soon as the works of art, sensing their latent powerlessness, cling to duration."[16] Mechanical reproduction, which seemingly fulfilled the dream of "the rising omnipotence of durability," was also responsible, ironically, for the rapid decline of art's endurance. In fact, just as Benjamin had pointed to the entwining of history and truth in art, so Adorno's *Aesthetic Theory* argued that this false belief in art's endurance needed to be shattered. Only once this illusion was dispelled would art reveal its profoundly historical nature, showing how all along it had been implanted with a temporal kernel:

If art were ever to rid itself of the illusion of endurance it had unmasked; if it were to take its own transience out of its sympathy for the ephemeral into itself, then this would be in conformity with a conception of truth that does not posit truth as that which abstractly persists, but instead becomes conscious of its temporal kernel. If all art is the secularization of transcendence, then every form of art participates in the dialectic of enlightenment. Art presented itself with this dialectic in the aesthetic conception of anti-art. Art can no longer be thought without this moment. This doesn't mean anything less than that art must go beyond its own concept, in order to remain faithful to it.[17]

Inasmuch as the work of art carried a temporal kernel, it had to be thought of as a process, a (Joycean) work in progress; and, inasmuch as the artwork was becoming (*Werden*), it participated in and bore the stamp of history. The truth component of art was its transience, for "truth only exists as becoming [*Gewordenes*]."[18]

Adorno possibly pushed Benjamin's conception of art even further when he defined the artwork as essentially mournful in nature. Thus the modern work of art, he suggested, clung to endurance, in which it recognized its only chance of survival. Having secularized itself from magical cults and rites, art ended up being no more than "those pitiful allegories in church yards, the broken pillars of life."[19] Art, in other words, amounted to no more than remnants, remainders, leftovers: "Art remains after the loss of that element in it which once was to fulfill a magic, then a cult function."[20] Qualifying modern art as constituted in and by the loss of transcendence, Adorno implicitly raised the question of whether the artwork essentially was belated (*nachträglich*) in nature.

But a residual ambiguity, indeed a remainder of metaphysical presence, seemed to mark Adorno's analysis. Inadvertently, these reflections appeared to rely on a conception of time as eternity—in other words, on the same detemporalization of time (*Entzeitlichung der Zeit*) that, as we had seen earlier, typified idealistic systems. The same can be said about the discussion of natural history that Adorno advanced in his *Negative Dialectics* when he introduced the category of secularization. Citing the passage from the *Trauerspiel* book according to which history transpired as the writing of transience on the face of nature, Adorno qualified the operations of history by means of the categories of secularization and decline:

"When history, in tragedy, makes its entrance on the stage, it does so as writing." . . . This is the transmutation of metaphysics into history. It secularizes metaphysics in the secular category pure and simple, the category of decay. Philosophy interprets that pictography [*Zeichenschrift*], the ever new Mene Tekel, in microcosm—in the fragments which decay has chipped, and which bear the objective meanings. No recollection of transcendence is possible any more, save by way of [transience] [*Vergängnis*]; eternity appears, not as such, but diffracted through the most [transient].[21]

Going against the thesis presented in "Idea of Natural History," Adorno held that the refuse or remnants produced by historic decay now no longer spelled "transience" as their meaning. Instead, these relics were presented as ghostly objects, letters, traces—that is, as a spectral scripture of a forever mediated, inaccessible eternity. Inasmuch as these traces remained part of a metaphysical text or writing—the texts offered by tradition—these traces, it would seem, still operated as negative indexes of a lost presence, or as what Derrida, in another setting, has called "a negative mode of presence."[22] As such, they failed to become the indexes to another text, one that exceeded or de-limited the metaphysical text, the text of tradition. As a method and interpretive praxis, negative dialectics—as Adorno in fact had posited early on in his study—was to be thought of as the secularization of the holy scriptures. Entrenched in the interpretation of the texts of tradition, negative dialectics remained mindful of biblical exegesis, presenting a reading praxis that exalted "neither the interpretation nor the symbol into an absolute but [sought] the truth where thinking secularizes the irretrievable ur-image [*Urbild*] of sacred texts."[23] Anticipating the argument set forth in its final chapter, "Meditations on Metaphysics," Adorno's analysis of the *Trauerspiel* study emphasized how the traces of history were to be read as the secularization of metaphysical transcendence. In the final analysis, *Negative Dialectics* seemed to imply, the post-Hegelian era ought to be defined by means of a Marxian phrase—namely, as the *caput mortuum* of the absolute spirit.[24] Marked by the secularization of metaphysical categories, the modern era eventually exposed the deficit of Heidegger's category of meaning (*Sinn*), which, following the horrors of Auschwitz, was forever replaced by the forces of "absolute negativity."[25]

While these observations seemingly may have taken us far afield, Adorno's reflections are nonetheless equally pertinent for Benjamin's appraisal of the baroque and modernity. For inasmuch as Benjamin defined allegory as a salvific gesture by which the poet sought to forge an encounter between the transient and eternity, his analysis still begged the question of whether the prospect of eternity remained forever inaccessible. It is precisely this question, as will become apparent, that lies at the core of Benjamin's theory of allegory.

CHAPTER 5

Natural and Sacred History

In "The Idea of Natural History," Adorno established that Benjamin's theory of allegory exposed an originary contingence at the center of the history of meaning on whose frail grounds the discipline of hermeneutics had been erected. In emphasizing transience at the expense of permanence, Benjamin's conception of natural history proved to be directed against the Platonic metaphysical tradition, as well as its covert legacy in contemporary philosophical thought. From this radical change in the philosophy of history, Adorno argued, it followed that the philosopher was to exchange the plenitude of the symbol for the antinomies of allegory (*O* 174; *GS* 1:350) in order to embrace a radically new negative hermeneutic.[1]

But however compelling Adorno's insistence on such a depletion of originary meaning may be, one must wonder whether he did not too easily brush aside a certain equivocation that adhered to Benjamin's figure of allegory. To follow Adorno's reading too closely may mean not paying heed to the ambiguities that beset Benjamin's discussion of the figure, some of which we have already encountered. Indeed, despite its obvious materialistic overtones, allegory, as Benjamin deployed the figure in the *Trauerspiel* study, often seemed to take on conflicting connotations. To what extent the dialectics of allegory proved to be more elusive than Adorno was perhaps willing to acknowledge can be gauged, for example, from the diverse scholarly responses to the *Trauerspiel* book. Its various readers have privileged either the messianic, chiliastic implications of allegory or its antimessianic, disjunctive force, depending on whether its restitutive, resurrectional moments or its materiality have been underscored.[2] A similar equivocation, it should be added, befalls the status of the fragment or ruin, which can be read either as a subversion of the unifying grasp of systematic philosophy or as a remnant waiting to be redeemed. Given this remarkable interpretive divergence, it may not be altogether inappropriate to use Warburg's image of the Janus face (*Doppelherme*; *O* 225; *GS* 1:399) as a way of describing Benjaminian allegory. If the neo-Kantian philosopher Hermann Cohen, as Benjamin noted, deplored allegory's excess of signification, which stood opposed to "clarity and unity of meaning" (*O* 177; *GS* 1:353), it was this very same ambiguity that Benjamin chose to celebrate when he revalidated the depreciated rhetorical figure.

The question as to why Benjamin invested allegory with these conflicting operations can be answered, I believe, if one pits his 1922 Goethe essay against the final chapter of the *Trauerspiel* study, which promised to resolve the paradoxes of aesthetics by means of a theology of history. To be sure, the essay on Goethe's *Elective Affinities* deserves to be read on its own terms, as a significant contribution to Goethe scholarship. But it also presents a notable attempt to think through the categories of salvation and redemption. At first, it is hard to believe that the Goethe essay was written in the 1920s, not in Benjamin's earlier period of the Youth Movement, for—on the surface at least—it deals obsessively with mythical figures and seemingly ends up proposing a metaphysics of death. Upon closer study, it becomes clear that Benjamin hoped to replace the mythical realm with a Kierkegaardian ethics of decision (*Entscheidung*) as he moved from the realm of mythical sacrifice to an existential embrace of death. Nonetheless, in the course of defining this ethical model, Benjamin lapsed into a stereotypical representation of femininity as the site of aesthetic *Schein* and into an acceptance of the dubious insights that marked Bachofen's *Mutterrecht*.

Elective Affinities

In *The Origin of German Tragic Drama*, Benjamin posited that genuine literary critique was to consist in the "mortification" of texts, in contrast to the early romantics' infinite potentiation (*Steigerung*) of the artwork. While this interpretive model seemed informed by an economy of finality or finitude, the essay on Goethe's

Elective Affinities—completed just a few years before—proved to be defined by a distinct eschatological perspective. Structured according to a triadic model, the essay first described how a subterranean, telluric, mythical nature operated in Goethe's novel only to end with the image of an illuminated, starry sky and the hope of immortality. In a letter to Scholem, Benjamin stressed that the essay was first of all meant to lay the "groundwork to certain purely philosophical considerations" more than to offer a classical interpretation of a Goethe text. This may well explain why this extraordinarily complex essay can be untangled only by means of a reading that comes to grips with its underlying structure. For in keeping with the "cosmological" model that upheld some of Benjamin's other early writings, the essay exemplified his belief that the world was stratified according to conceptual and existential spheres whose connections were to be revealed through theology.[3] Through his reading of the Goethe novel, Benjamin ultimately aimed to uncover the ontotheological ground of its aesthetic and ethical strata. Using the metaphorical discourse of light and darkness—typical of Western metaphysics but also of cosmogonic myths—Benjamin's essay went beyond the level of textual analysis to show how artistic creation remained dependent on divine creation and, further, how the phenomenal realm of appearances (*Schein*) was constituted by and dependent on the violence of a nonphenomenal, expressionless (*ausdruckslos*) theophany.

In the first section of the essay, Benjamin posited that the novel's main characters had been reduced to mere toys in the grip of a destructive, demonic nature whose force became ever more prevalent as the moral, transcendent ground of Charlotte and Eduard's marriage progressively eroded. Set under the sign of astrological constellations— the incalculable game of *tuchē* and *anankē*, as well as the *daimon* and *eros*, all of which appeared in Goethe's poem Urworte, Orphisch— the novel, Benjamin wrote, in essence displayed a guilt-laden, archaic world of sacrifice, animism, and fetishism. Not only did it conjure up the empirical realm of necessity and creatural nature (the senses, corporeality, sexuality), but also it depicted formless, primordial chaos, or Manichaeistic matter (*hulē*)—"the magnetic force of the interior of the earth" and the material of Faustian alchemists:

Goethe said of it in his *Theory of Color* (Die Farbenlehre)—possibly around the same time—that to the attentive spectator nature is "never dead or mute. It has even provided a confidant for the rigid body of earth, a metal whose least fragment tells us about what is taking place in the entire mass." Goethe's characters are in league with this power, and they are as pleased with themselves in playing [*im Spiel*] with what lies below ground as in playing with what lies above. Yet what else, finally, are their inexhaustible provisions for its embellishment except a changing of backdrops of a tragic scene [*der Wandel von Kulissen einer tragischen Szene*]? Thus, a hidden power manifests itself ironically in the existence of the landed gentry. (*GS* 1:132–33)[4]

In referring to nature's play (*Spiel*), Benjamin may have had in mind the Greek notion of the game of chance, Heraclitus's *aiōn*, or even Schiller's *Spieltrieb*. More important, however, this image must be traced to the mythological figure of Eros, whose more benign version—that of an infant that throws away its toys—appeared in the work of Apollo of Rhodes, while his less benevolent guise was that of Eros Thanatos, the personification of death.[5] Customarily depicted with an extinguished torch in his hand, Eros Thanatos was the counterpart of the cosmogonic Eros of Hesiod's *Theogony* and of Orphism, which celebrated Eros as the *phanēs*—as the god who manifested himself as light. Eros Thanatos's force, the Goethe essay speculated, not only enacted itself in the realm of the senses and mythical nature that ruled the novel but also informed Ottilie's death drive or her "yearning for an absolute, final peace [*Ruhe*]" (*GS* 1:176). Figuring the eternal return of the same—of the kind described also in Freud's *Beyond the Pleasure Principle*—this death drive installed a "parasitical" or inauthentic time, at a far remove from an authentic, historical temporality. The result was a mantic, thaumaturgical universe in which random signs and their permutations were granted oracular significance evident, Benjamin argued, in the thanatological symbolism that dominated the novel.

In the dissolution of Eduard and Charlotte's marriage, Benjamin perceived the erosion of its ethico-theological foundations, giving rise to an inverted world in which mere appearance (*Erscheinung*) had taken the place of essence (*GS* 1:131).[6] In the play staged by nature, Goethe's characters—robbed of their individuality and last name—had been turned into mere representations or appearances of this mythical power, to the point where their actions amounted to nothing more than the "changing of backdrops of a tragic scene" (ibid.). It is not hard to read in these lines an allusion to Nietzsche's *Birth of Tragedy* or, more specifically, a pronounced critique of the latter's "artistic metaphysics."[7] Like the later *Trauerspiel* study, the Goethe essay criticized Nietzsche's conception of a primeval world genius, the *Ur-Eine*, whose plastic force hid behind mere appearances. Tellingly, Benjamin decidedly rejected Nietzsche's demotion of the realm of ethics to "the realm of 'appearances,'" to the region of "semblance, delusion, error, interpretation, contrivance, art."[8] Nor could he accept Nietzsche's principle of inversion, his reinscription of *Schein* in a physiology of art—in other words, his well-known reversal of Platonism, whose history he sketched in *The Twilight of the Gods*, "How the 'True World' Finally Became a Fable."[9] One can see this quite clearly in one of the preparatory fragments to the Goethe essay, where this Nietzschean principle is put on a par with melancholia, "the spirit of gravity [*Schwere*]" or the satanic inversion of the sacrament of marriage. The antics of this demonic force, Benjamin there suggested, manifested themselves in the attractions between the four characters at the heart of Goethe's novel as they were drawn to one another through a mysterious, fatal specular magic (*Spiegelzauber*):

Love here is nothing more than the appearance [*Schein*] of life; to the blind deadly passion of alchemical research this *Schein* even lends itself for the discovered, uncovered sacrament of marriage. The spirit of the black mass returns here; the sacrament takes up the position of love, love the position of the sacrament. The spirit of satanic success rules and marriage appears in an inverted way. For Satan is dialectical, and a sort of deceptive, happy success—the kind of semblance [*Schein*] to which Nietzsche deeply was enslaved—betrays him as does the spirit of gravity [*Schwere*]. (*GS* 1:838)

It is interesting to note, then, that in the final version of the Goethe essay Benjamin further pursued this logic when he presented the novel as the precinct of deceptive *Schein*. For the novel, he maintained, portrayed the very reversal of the novella,[10] which formed its redemptive core. Offering what amounted to an anagogical reading of the novella, Benjamin suggested that the near-fatal leap of the "marvelous children" in the novella represented final judgment (*GS* 1:169)—that is, the redemptive catastrophe that formed a counterpart to the dark interior of the "Hades-like" novel. If the scenes of the novel represented a fallen, Manichaeistic world, the novella instead managed to transcend the level of base matter:

With regard to the freedom and necessity that it reveals vis-à-vis the novel, the novella is comparable to an image in the darkness of a cathedral—an image which portrays the cathedral itself and so in the midst of the interior communicates a view of the place that is not otherwise available. In this way it brings inside at the same time a reflection of the bright, indeed sober day. And if this sobriety seems sacred, shines sacredly, the most peculiar thing is that it is not so, perhaps, only for Goethe. (*SW* 1:352; *GS* 1:196–97)

The fallen world of the novel became the site of phantasmal, aesthetic semblance, the realm of the senses and perception (*aisthesis*), or of what Western philosophy traditionally has qualified as "the inauthentic being common to all forms of metaphysics, the phenomenality of the sensuous."[11] Traditionally, this realm has counted as the inauthentic antipode to the intelligible, as well as to nonsensuous intuition (*Anschauung*). In line with this metaphysical legacy, Benjamin's theory of the artwork, as it took shape in the Goethe essay and its drafts, similarly allocated a subordinate position to the aesthetic, suggesting that it remained framed by an ontotheological horizon.

That for Benjamin the aesthetic realm fundamentally proved to be grounded in a theological sphere is confirmed by yet another early draft of the Goethe essay, which, crucially, invoked Mörike's well-known poem "Auf eine Lampe" (On a Lamp).[12] Called "Categories of Aesthetic Theory," this draft established that the sphere of semblance (*Schein*) and, with it, the aesthetic categories of perception and perceptibility belonged to the realm of the artwork or artifact. The latter sphere, Benjamin cautioned, should not be confounded with the nonphenomenal beauty (*scheinlose Schönheit*) of divine creation. The sharp distinction the fragment drew between creature (*Geschöpf*) and artifact (*Gebilde*) attests again to the fervor with which Benjamin contested romantic and neoromantic cosmogonic aesthetics. Hence his sharp critique, for example, of the figure of the autoproductive artist at the core of Stefan George's poetry, as well as the scholarly writings of the influential critic Friedrich Gundolf. Rather than seeing art as founded in the acts of a singular subject—as Kantian aesthetics had held—Benjamin believed the aesthetic realm to be determined by a theological *arche* or the thetic act of Genesis:

Creature [*Geschöpf*] and form [*Gestalt*]—object [*Gebild*] and form [*Form*]—must be distinguished from one another in that the former has been created while the latter has sprung forth. There is without the creator eidetically no creation and no creature; objects and forms, by contrast, can exist eidetically without an artist. Decisive, however, is that the act of creation leads to the existence of creation, the existence of the world. The origin of the work, by contrast, leads to its perceptibility from the very beginning. This lies in the original tendency [*Urtendenz*] of appearance [*Schein*]. The life of creation remains in the dark, in the shadow of the creator, until he separates himself from it. This removal of the creator is a moral act. He constitutes the sphere of perception in an unbroken, straight intention that originates in creation, which is good in itself and which, only because it is seen as "good," constitutes seeing. (*GS* 1:830)

Following this morphological conception of art, then, indeterminate matter or chaos was constrained through artistic form. Divine creation (*creatio ex nihilo*), by contrast, conformed to the rational theology of late rabbinical doctrine, according to which, as Scholem established, God separated himself from his creation in an act of love and not by conquering chaos, as mythical cabalism would have it. For its part, the realm of inauthentic *Schein,* which created the false illusion of totality and perfection, was to be shattered through the intervention of what Benjamin, following Hölderlin, termed the *caesura* of the expressionless (*das Ausdruckslose*). Insofar as the realm of the sacred denoted sublime beauty of the sort that exceeded mere appearance, Benjamin alluded to the Jewish *Bilderverbot* of the Decalogue—in other words, to the antimimetic injunction of the Bible. Centrally, however, the caesura reenacted the moment of divine separation—that is, the diacritical moment in which light was divided from darkness, giving rise to the faculty of human perception, which sprang forth from the ethico-theological *arche* laid down in Genesis: "And God said, 'Let there be light': and there was Light. / And God saw the light, that it was good: and God divided the light from the darkness" (Gen. 1: 3–4). Thus, the morality of divine creation impressed the seal of the expressionless onto the work of art.

The concerns expressed in this draft reappeared in the interpretation of *Elective Affinities,* notably in the image of the seal with which Benjamin sought to capture the relationship in the artwork between form and matter, *Sach-* and *Wahrheitsgehalt* (material content and truth content). The divine, cryptic, receding seal is a recurring topos in Benjamin's early writings, serving as a figure in which the Neoplatonic conception of form as "imprint" merged with the biblical tradition of the seals of creation.[13] This very same image had sealed off the 1921 essay "Critique of Violence," for example, which ended up establishing the interruptive power of divine violence in all its finality. "Divine violence, which is the sign and seal but never the means of sacred execution, may be called sovereign violence" (*R* 300). Much as in the *Trauerspiel* book, the figure of the seal thus expressed the plastic force (*prägende Gewalt*) of the nonphenomenal divine Name and divine Being—or, as the epistemo-critical prologue put it, "the state of being, beyond all phenomenality, to which alone this power belongs, is that of the name" (*O* 36; *GS* 1:216).

In comparing the fragment on *Geschöpf* and *Gebild* to the final Goethe essay, however, it is noteworthy that Benjamin originally distinguished three different forms of *Schein*—distinctions lost in the finished version. Still, these distinctions shed additional light on the complexities of the Goethe essay. For, as the early draft established, next to the beauty of art and sacred beauty—located beyond mere appearances—there existed yet another kind of beauty, this one demonic in nature:

> Beauty devoid of appearance [*scheinlose Schönheit*] is no longer essentially beauty but something greater. Correspondingly, a beauty whose appearance [*Schein*] no longer seeks to bind itself to totality and completion but remains free insofar as it intensively reinforces this beauty at the same time is no longer the beauty of art but a demonic beauty. The seductiveness of beauty rests on its shamelessness, the nakedness of appearance [*Schein*] by which it is armed. (Seduction of Saint Anthony). (*GS* i:829–30)

Defined as the realm of corporeal sensuality and seduction, this beauty, Benjamin contended, was no longer committed to totality and perfection but had been disengaged from all aesthetic ideals. Exposing the shameless nakedness of *Schein*, this fallen beauty therefore stood for creatural imperfection. Unmistakably, Benjamin placed his discussion of beauty in the Judeo-Christian tradition that equated nontruth or "nonbeing" (*to me on*) with original sin, creatural sexuality, and sensuality and, further, with an inauthentic form of temporality that eventually was to be overcome on the Day of Atonement.[14] Its traditional, privileged site was that of female sensuality and corporeality, as becomes clear from the reference to Saint Anthony's seduction. By associating this form of beauty with shamelessness, with the repealing of the cover of *Scham*—a word that is to be understood here in all its different meanings, as prudery, biblical nakedness, and the male/female reproductive organs—Benjamin invoked the age-old dualism of body and spirit together with the metaphysical discourse of veiling and unveiling. One of the more interesting texts that followed this tradition—and one with which Benjamin very likely was familiar—was Kierkegaard's *The Concept of Anxiety*. In this work's dialectical conception of the human subject, the individual was to be thought of as the frail synthesis of body and soul in concrete spirit. Rather than being merely an affect, shame essentially expressed the spirit's fear of sexual and corporeal determination: "The sexual is the expression for the prodigious *Widerspruch* ['contradiction'], that the immortal spirit is determined as man or woman (*genus*). This contradiction expresses itself in profound 'shame,' which pulls a veil over it and does not dare to understand it."[15]

It is thus significant that the Goethe essay put so much emphasis on Ottilie's status as a veiled beauty who forever was to remain at a distance. Inaccessible because of her self-absorbed rapture, for Benjamin she became the figure of aesthetic equivocation. She was the disappearing one (*die Schwindende*) who in languid death ultimately was subjected to a movement of withdrawal and distancing.[16] At the same time, her equivocal nature (*Zweideutigkeit*) appeared to be fundamentally different from the figures of femininity evoked, for example, in Nietzsche's work. For, insofar as Ottilie figured the deceptive appearance of innocence and virginity, or the "semblance of an innocence of natural life" (*SW* 1:352; *GS* 1:174), she symbolized the inversion of creatural culpability and naturality. As such, her equivocation resulted from her alleged sexual or erotic impurity. In fact, the manner in which she is described recalls the fervor with which Benjamin, in an early metaphysical text of 1916, had decried Socrates's maieutics for being "an erection of knowledge" (*GS* 2:131). Socrates's philosophy, this Nietzschean piece suggested, contaminated the spiritual purity of the male *Genius* and male creativity, which was to be thought of as conception without gestation. In this youthful essay, which showed the nefarious influence of the Youth Movement, Benjamin further used crass language to denounce the encroachment of the sexual on the spiritual and, related to this, of the literal on the figurative. For as the boundaries between the sexual and the spiritual were erased, a demonic undecidability, he argued, made its appearance.

In line with this early essay, the Goethe interpretation opposed the demonic equivocation and exteriority of Ottilie's *Schein* to the interiority of her character,[17] as well as to the unequivocal certainty (*Entscheidung*) of the spirit:

To be sure, like natural guilt, there is also a natural innocence of life. The latter, however, is tied not to sexuality—not even in the mode of denial—but rather solely to its antipode, the spirit (which is equally natural). Just as the sexual life of man can become the expression of natural guilt, his spiritual life, based on the variously constituted unity of his individuality, can become the expression of natural innocence. This unity of individual spiritual life is "character." Unequivocalness, as its essential constitutive moment, distinguishes it from the daemonism of all purely sexual phenomena. (*SW* 1:335; *GS* 1:174)

Benjamin's analysis again may have been influenced by Kierkegaard's *The Concept of Anxiety*, which interpreted the demonic—or anxiety about the good—as "inclosing reserve [*det Indesluttede*] and the unfreely disclosed"[18] and as the condition of emptiness and boredom. Signaling the inauthentic temporality of satanic suddenness (*das*

Plötzliche), the demonic, Kierkegaard maintained, defied the existential instant (*Augenblick*).[19] In light of Kierkegaard's text, it appears that Ottilie's *Schein* and mythical silence were meant to denote the realm of sheer exteriority and vacant spectrality—a predicament confirmed by the fact that she was unable to demonstrate ethical resolve in decision (*Entschluß*), to attain linguistic expression, or to accomplish the process of interiorizing memory. For the entries in her diary were no more than mere epitaphs to an interiority she never achieved in the first place, Benjamin suggested, and her uncanny liveliness simply recalled the spectral beauty that also marked Goethe's Helena and Eurydice. This spectral logic, Benjamin believed, reappeared in Goethe's very writing style, his pen resembling Odysseus' sword: "Thus the aura of Hades in what the author lends to the action is confirmed: he stands before the deep ground of his poetic gift like Odysseus with his naked sword before the ditch full of blood, and like him fends off the thirsty shades, in order to suffer only those whose sparse speech [*karge Rede*] he seeks" (*SW* 1:339; *GS* 1:179).

Inasmuch as the novel bore the signs of an inauthentic liveliness and the temporality of sheer repetition, it thus lacked the diacritical force of form and the authentic temporality of the Kierkegaardian instant (*Augenblick*).[20] Only if it retained the temporal structure of the *Augenblick* could the work of art, as Benjamin envisioned it, achieve the coincidence of life and death, where temporality and eternity met. The work's endurance, or its "immortality," could be achieved only when the appearance of an organic vivacity of beauty (*das wogende Leben*) was constrained through the force of the caesura, the law of the ineffable (*das Ausdruckslose*), or the divine moral word. For while the moral word could not separate essence from mere appearance, it could nonetheless stall their inmixing. As in the preparatory fragments, the figure of the caesura thus came to signal the plastic force of the ineffable logos. When seen in light of the constraining force of the divine Logos, all attempts to bestow life onto inorganic matter—be it in the myth of the Golem or of Galatea—appeared to amount to nothing more than the bestowing of so many veils or masks. As such, the logos pointed to the condition of finality and human finitude, and it established the grounds for possible redemption. Benjamin discerned this hope of redemption in Kierkegaard's notion of the instant (*Augenblick*). For, as Kierkegaard observed in *The Concept of Anxiety*, not only did the word *Augenwurf* in Paul's prophecy portend the end of the world, which would transpire in the mere blinking of the eye (*Auge*); at the same time, this imminent catastrophe also offered a possible opening to

eternity: "By this [Paul] also expresses that the *Augenblick* is suscep-
tible (commensurable) to eternity, precisely because the *Augenblick* of
[the world's] destruction expresses eternity at the same moment [*im
gleichen Augenblick*]."[21]

Borrowing liberally from this Kierkegaardian framework, Benjamin
charged the novella with salvific power; in the resolute leap of the
"marvelous children," through which they attained reconciliation with
God, he saw realized the existential decision or instant (*Augenblick*). In
stark contrast to this, the novel appeared dominated by base passions,
mesmerized, as its characters were, by the optical, specular charms
of Ottilie. Yet for all its adherence to the power of mythical nature,
the novel in the final analysis, Benjamin suggested, also revealed a
moment of redemption. At the height of *Schein* and the rule of the
passions, the lethal forces of the daimon Eros overturned to initiate
the transition from deceptive appearances back to the realm of essence:
"In affection," Benjamin wrote, "the human being is detached from
passion. It is the law of essence that determines this, just as it determines
every detachment from the sphere of semblance and every passage to
the realm of essence; it determines that gradually, indeed even under
a final and most extreme intensification of the semblance, the change
comes about" (*SW* 1:344; *GS* 1:186).[22]

This moment of transition, through which mere affection revealed
a spiritual element that exceeded its sexual, sensual nature, was located
in the realm of the passions or, more precisely, in the state of being
moved to tears. The reference is crucial, for the motif of tears[23] recalls
Kierkegaard's discussion of the lachrymose eye in *Entweder/Oder*, which
he qualified as "the negative-infinite reflection of aesthetic man," whose
reign was to be disrupted by the intervention of ethical decisions.[24]
Benjamin, however, referred to Goethe's poem "Elegy," to the lines
"The eye grows moist, feels in loftier longing / The divine value of
[musical] sounds as of tears" (Das Auge netzt sich, fühlt im höhern
Sehnen / Den Götterwert der Töne wie der Tränen), which falsely
promised the withdrawal of the phenomenal world behind a veil of tears.
As long as these tears were shed in honor of living beauty and petty
emotions rather than in response to thorough devastation, they were
symptomatic of the shallow veil of beauty or the delusive appearance of
reconciliation (*Schein der Versöhnung*) that occluded the light of truth:

> For it is not the little emotion, which delights in itself, but only the great
> emotion of devastation [*Erschütterung*] in which the semblance of recon-
> ciliation overcomes the beautiful semblance and with it, finally, itself. The

lament full of tears: that is emotion. And to it as well as to the tearless cry of woe, the space of Dionysian shock lends resonance. "The mourning and pain of the Dionysian, as the tears that are shed for the continual decline of all life, form gentle ecstasy; it is the 'life of the cicada, which, without food or drink, sings until it dies.'" Thus Bernouilli on the one hundred forty-first chapter of *Mother Right*, in which Bachofen discusses the cicada, the creature which, originally indigenous to the dark earth, was elevated by the mythic profundity of the Greeks into the association of Uranic symbols. What else was the meaning of Goethe's meditations on Ottilie's departure from life? (*SW* 1:349; *GS* 1:192)

Benjamin added the lines about Bachofen to the Goethe manuscript around 1926, shortly after he had completed the *Trauerspiel* study (see *GS* 1:841). These lines, interestingly, located the moment of transition from the beautiful to the sublime in the tears that are shed in ecstatic mourning. Ottilie's death is compared to the soft, musical lamentation that the cicada, according to Greek mythology, was said to emit in the moment of its death. The passage thus gives proof of Benjamin's ambivalent fascination with Bachofen, whose monumental history on the roots of an originary matriarchy, as Erich Fromm noted, enticed socialists and fascists alike.[25] Scholem took great exception to Benjamin's interest in Bachofen, whose interest in gynocratics and chthonism were indicative of the same irrationalism that also characterized the thought of Ludwig Klages.[26] While in France, Benjamin wrote an essay that was meant to introduce Bachofen to the French public. Bachofen's oeuvre, he maintained, had vividly revealed the "tableau de la préhistoire" (tableau of prehistory), in which the archaic, mnemonic remainders of the ancient necropolis attested to the silent force of the prelinguistic image (*eidos*). Dating from well before the written records of history, these thanatological symbols and rites were to be seen as the remnants of an archaic, ecstatic world, "die unbeweinte Schöpfung" (*GS* 2:222).[27] In this prehistorical world, life was ruled by the promiscuous force of matter (*Stoff*), as well as by a feminine, Dionysian principle. How profound and long-lasting Benjamin's preoccupation with Bachofen would be is apparent in his Kafka essay, in which, as we shall see, the figures of Odradek and other hybrids are allocated to an intermediate world (*Zwischenwelt*), to a subterranean, telluric, prehistoric realm.

The figure of the cicada thus proved inspired by Bachofen's *Das Mutterrecht* (Mother Right), which traced how this mythological figure had moved from being an aphrodisiac, Dionysian symbol of earth and matter—evident in Plato's *Symposium* and still present even in Goethe's

Faust, I—to becoming a spiritual figure,[28] as was apparent in the ancient mysteries, where the cicada sealed the oath of silence. In Pindar's work and in Plato's *Phaedrus*, the cicada symbolized wisdom (*sophos*), and in death it attained unity with the muses Calliope and Urania. For Plato, the cicada therefore represented the figure of the philosopher who, in ascetic abstinence, attained divine intuition.[29] Benjamin clearly followed Bachofen's interpretive model when he associated Ottilie's death with the tears of the dying cicada, suggesting that in death telluric matter and materiality were turned into uranic spirit and spirituality. As he was quick to point out, however, these tears of soft ecstasy did not signal the mere flux of pathos. In accordance with a passage from the habilitation in which the act of writing figured as an instrument of sobriety that blocked the outpouring of pathos in mourning, Ottilie's death did not bring about catharsis—a point Benjamin saw substantiated by Goethe's "Nachlese zu Aristoteles's Poetik" (On Interpreting Aristotle's Poetics). Rather than being an end in itself, this state of utter devastation initiated a transition from the category of the beautiful to that of the sublime. Ultimately, Benjamin added, this moment of transition transpired as the passage to the beyond, insofar as in death the veil of the body was shed. Invoking the ancient topos of the body as veil, Benjamin thus ingeniously tied together the thematics of the veil with his discussion of phenomenal beauty.

Having returned full circle to the philosophical question of appearance that informed the essay's opening pages, Benjamin now raised the discussion to another level, promising to answer the ancient metaphysical question of whether beauty was nothing more than mere appearance (*GS* 1:193). Thus, he relegated beauty to the side of life while maintaining that it remained informed by death. Here, in a second moment of his analysis, then, the veil of beauty was no longer interpreted only as the transparent veil of phenomenalized truth. Instead it appeared as the cryptic, enigmatic cover of what could never be uncovered, except at the price of death—a truth he saw exemplified by Novalis's fable about the veiled image of Sais (*GS* 1:216; see also *O* 36). Finding its ground in the divine Logos, the veil of beauty essentially proved that human history was dependent on a necessary covering that would be repealed only at the end of time (*Unzeit*), in apocalyptic revelation (*GS* 1:195). Until then, phenomenal or aesthetic beauty remained marked by what Benjamin qualified as the deceptive play between cover and covered. Only in the biblical state of original, creatural nakedness, before the cover of shame came into existence, could the sublimity of divine creation fully express itself. It is this nakedness that was reenacted in the transition to death. For, as Benjamin's theological analysis further stressed, salvation could never be achieved through the aestheticization of the human body—a fallacy all too well symbolized by Goethe's figure of Helena, who left behind her empty garment as her body was enveloped by clouds:

The human being appears to us as a corpse and his life as love, when they are in the presence of God. Thus, death has the power to lay bare [*entblößen*] like love. Only nature cannot be unveiled, for it preserves a mystery so long as God lets it exist. Truth is discovered in the essence of language. The human body lays itself bare, a sign that the human being itself stands before God. Beauty that does not surrender itself in love must fall prey to death. (*SW* 1:353; *GS* 1:197–98)

Here it becomes obvious to what extent Benjamin drew the consequences from the Kierkegaardian existential model he had introduced earlier. What Benjamin called for in this highly charged, even pious passage could perhaps best be described as an ethico-theological freedom *unto* death. Rejecting the illusionary freedom harbored by philosophies that believed in autonomous reason (*Vernunftfreiheit*; *GS* 1:188) no less than an illusionary decisionism that promoted an absolute freedom of choice (*Wahl*), he instead defended an existential form of freedom that rested on the acceptance of one's finitude in mortality.

As such, the passage from the Goethe essay invites a comparative reading with a section in the *Trauerspiel* study that likewise advocated the absolute singularity of death. In a chapter from "*Trauerspiel* and Tragedy" Benjamin discussed the ethical dimension of death, whose moral force, he noted, radically shattered the romantic aesthetics of infinity and organicity. Insofar as it eluded all representation (*Darstellung*) and representability (delegation), death could appear only *ex negativo* in the artifact. Not by coincidence, these remarks followed a passage in which Benjamin firmly repudiated what he called Nietzsche's "abyss of aestheticism" for transforming humans into mere aesthetic phenomena or appearances (*Erscheinungen*) whose degree of self-consciousness— that is, their ability to tear the veil of Maja once and forever and to escape the doubling of Apollonian *Schein*—did not surpass the consciousness "which the soldiers painted on canvas have of the battle represented on it" (*O* 103; *GS* 1:281). Using the notions of mimesis and representation, Benjamin thus set up a rigid demarcation between the realm of the aesthetic and the fictional, on the one hand, and the domain of ethics, on the other. Clearly, the concept of mimesis here was deployed in its more negative traditional sense and thus not yet charged with the anthropological significance the term was to acquire in his later "Doctrine of the Similar," which established a magical, mimetic, and nonsensuous trait at the heart of language. Instead, in the *Trauerspiel* study Benjamin introduced a negative notion of mimesis that was linked to the Platonic *eidolon*, as well as to the Jewish interdiction against graven images (*Bilderverbot*). Strongly contesting that works of art could be copies (*eidola*) of moral phenomena, he emphasized that

fictional characters exist only in literature. They are woven as tightly into the totality of the literary work as the subjects of Gobelins into their canvas, so that they cannot be removed from it as individuals. In this respect the human figure in literature, indeed in art as such, differs from the human figure in reality, where physical isolation, which in so many ways is only apparent isolation, has its true meaning as a perceptible expression of moral seclusion with God. "Thou shalt not make unto thee any graven image"—this is not only a warning against idolatry. With incomparable emphasis the prohibition of the representation of the human body obviates any suggestion that the sphere in which the moral essence of man is perceptible can be reproduced. Everything moral is bound to life in its extreme sense, that is to say where it fulfills itself in death, the abode of danger as such. And from the point of view of any kind of artistic practice this life, which concerns us morally, that is in our unique individuality, appears as something negative, or at least should appear so. (*O* 105; *GS* 1:283–84)

Qualifying death as a singular condition, in which the individual entered into a personal confrontation with God, Benjamin thus took aim at all mythical notions of sacrifice or death in effigy.

 This passage from the *Trauerspiel* book and the Goethe essay are similar in that they adhere to an economy of salvation. Much as in the so-called theologico-political fragment, natural history is to be conceived of not only as the realm of decomposition and dissolution but also as the site of possible resurrection. Ultimately, the death of Ottilie symbolized how death overcame nature's repetitive temporality and thus pointed to the hope of redemption, which could be glimpsed in the image of the shooting star with which the Goethe essay ended. As the disappearing one (*die Schwindende*), Ottilie eventually became like the marvelous children who, in their near-fatal leap into the water—a moment that Benjamin read symbolically and typologically as a passage to the beyond—disappeared into an infinitely distant perspective. In arguing that Ottilie's distancing was similar to that of Goethe's *Neue Melusine*, he again returned to one of his favorite romantic tropes, showing how transience and finitude in the final instant opened up onto infinity.

In many ways, Ottilie's transition from dissimulating beauty to her ultimate salvation functions as a figure for the overarching redemptive movement that holds the Goethe essay together. Starting out with the realm of mythical, telluric nature, Benjamin eventually turned to the Orphic figure of hope (*elpis*), to its doctrine of immortality, and, finally, to the image of the shooting star—possibly a reference to Rosenzweig's *Star of Redemption*. Not unimportant in this context is the fact that in an earlier writing phase Benjamin had given the title "hope" to the essay's final section. And in a letter to his friend Rang, he in fact went into greater detail about the movement of ascent that the essay traced. Likening this movement to that of the "uranic symbols" of ancient Greek mythology, he described the essay's final phase as that of "the salvaged night" (*GS* 1:889). In the essay's final section, the figure of demonic nature, previously cast out, returned but this time in a salvific guise, in the image of the star. As Benjamin wrote, "that most paradoxical, most fleeting hope finally emerges from the semblance of reconciliation, just as, at twilight, as the sun is extinguished, rises the evening star which outlasts the night. Its glimmer, of course, is imparted by Venus" (*SW* 1:355; *GS* 1:200). Ending by casting the image of an enigmatic, fleeting star, the Goethe essay held up the prospect of a transcendent beyond. Promising redemption, resurrection, and hope at the moment of utter despair, this image cast the arch of a history of salvation, or "the arch of a salvational [*heilsgeschichtliche*] question" (*GS* 1:257–58), as Benjamin phrased it in the *Trauerspielbuch*. As we shall see, the star thus invoked the very economy of salvation that lay at the center of the *Trauerspiel* study and was figured by allegory.

The Allegory of Resurrection

Benjamin's figure of allegory has conventionally been read as the exemplary trope of modernity, one that radically exploded older idealistic philosophical systems, with their conceptions of totality and teleology. But the final chapter of the *Trauerspiel* study considerably complicates this interpretation. For one, in earlier sections of the study, Benjamin had introduced allegory as the tool of a Machiavellian schemer, the master of meaning (*Herr der Bedeutungen*) who, in an act of arbitrary will, bequeathed meaning to things. In other words, allegory there revealed itself to be the trope of a cryptic schemer who, celebrating the "unique ambiguity [*Zweideutigkeit*] of his spiritual sovereignty," represented pure will, as well as the very instance of irony, "esprit," and spirituality. Promising to resolve the paradox of aesthetics through a turn to theology, the final chapter first showed how an old matter–spirit dualism resurfaced in allegory. As a consequence of the loss of transcendence, Benjamin observed, the mourning play became the scene of a "satanic" inversion, opening up an abyss between, on the one hand, telluric, satanic matter and, on the other, the demonic laughter of spirit and spirituality. If the Goethe essay appealed to Greek philosophical tradition to argue that a demonic duplicity made its appearance in the realm of mythical nature and mere sensuality, now Benjamin resorted to the insights of theology to suggest that evil sprang forth from a fatal drive to knowledge and meaning:

Knowledge, not action, is the most characteristic mode of existence of evil. Accordingly, physical temptation conceived in sensual terms, as lechery, gluttony, and sloth, is far from being the sole base of its existence; indeed, strictly speaking, it is ultimately and precisely not basic to it at all. Rather is the basis of its existence revealed in the *fata morgana* of a realm of absolute, that is to say godless, spirituality, bound to the material as its counterpart, such as can be only concretely experienced through evil. Its dominant mood is that of mourning, which is at once the mother of the allegories and their content. And from it three original satanic promises are born. They are spiritual in kind. The *Trauerspiel* continually shows them at work, now in the figure of the tyrant, now in that of the intriguer. What tempts is the illusion of freedom—in the exploration of what is forbidden; the illusion of independence—in the secession from the community of the pious; the illusion of infinity—in the empty abyss of evil. For it is characteristic of all virtue to have an end before it; namely its model, in God; just as all infamy opens up an infinite progression into the depths. The theology of evil can therefore be derived much more readily from the fall of Satan, in which the above-mentioned motifs are confirmed, than from the warnings in which ecclesiastical doctrine tends to represent the snarer of souls. The absolute spirituality, which is what Satan means, destroys itself in its emancipation from what is sacred. Materiality—but here soulless materiality—becomes its home. The purely material and this absolute spiritual are the poles of the satanic realm; and the consciousness is their illusory synthesis, in which the genuine synthesis, that of life, is imitated. However, the speculation of the consciousness, which clings to the object-world of emblems, ultimately, in its remoteness from life, discovers the knowledge of the demons. According to Augustine's *The City of God,* "The word *daimones* is Greek; and demons are so called because of their knowledge." (*O* 230; *GS* 1:403–4)

Satanic, absolute spirituality arose at the moment when the spirit emancipated itself from the holy ground of the logos, illustrating how the *pneuma* of the Gospels had severed itself from the *gramma* to become profane spirit. On this reading, absolute autonomy, individuality, and empty infinitude[30] were the phantasms of a secularized spirit, which thus sought to negate human finitude and deny divine power. Doubling the fall of the angels, absolute spirit, spirituality, or pure speculation impressed its stamp on lifeless matter—an activity iconized in the baroque emblem, with its manifold, often duplicitous meanings—only to fall victim to the self-produced depths of groundless meditation. The root of evil thus surfaced in the claim of the secularized subject to absolute autonomy—an illusion that was to reach its most revealing formulation in Kant's principle of the autonomy of the will.

At the center of the *Trauerspiel* study, then, stood a postlapsarian narrative. For the trope of allegory figured the ascendance of a self-positing subjectivity that established itself in knowledge, reflection, contemplation, and abstraction.[31] In allegory, Benjamin discerned the fall from a language of names into the sphere of *Urteil*—a word that in German has analytical, ethical, and legal connotations insofar as it can mean logical proposition and legal judgment.[32] Thus the fall meant not only that a new logic replaced the loss of the divine Name but also that it brought forth an inauthentic mythical legal system at a far remove from divine judgment. As the fall from a prelapsarian concrete language of the name and naming, allegory betokened the inauguration of diacritical judgment epitomized in law and the logical proposition:

By its allegorical form evil as such reveals itself to be a subjective phenomenon. The enormous antiartistic subjectivity of the baroque converges here with the theological essence of the subjective. The Bible introduces evil in the concept of knowledge. The serpent's promise to the first men was to make them "knowing both good and evil." But it is said of God after the creation: "And God saw everything that he had made, and, behold it was very good." Knowledge of evil therefore has no object. There is no evil in the world. It arises in man himself, with the desire for knowledge, or rather for judgment. Knowledge of good, as knowledge, is secondary. It ensues from practice. Knowledge of evil—as knowledge, this is primary. It ensues from contemplation. Knowledge of good and evil is, then, the opposite of all factual knowledge. Related as it is to the depths of the subjective, it is basically only knowledge of evil. It is "chatter" [*Geschwätz*] in the profound sense in which Kierkegaard conceived the word. This knowledge, the triumph of subjectivity and the onset of an arbitrary rule over things, is the origin of all allegorical contemplation. In the very fall of man the unity of guilt and signifying emerges as an abstraction. The allegorical has its existence in abstractions; as an abstraction, as a faculty of the spirit of language itself, it is at home in the Fall. For good and evil are unnameable, they are nameless entities, outside the language of names, in which man, in paradise, named things, and which he forsakes in the abyss of that problem. For languages, the name is only a base in which the concrete elements have their roots. The abstract elements of language, however, have their roots in the evaluative word, the judgment [*Urteil*]. (*O* 233–34; *GS* 1:406–7)

Clearly, while this passage returned to the motif of the fall and to the philosophy of language of the 1916 essay "On Language as Such and the Language of Man," there remained at least one seminal difference. For the early essay relied heavily on the romantic trope of potentiation pointing to a medium of languages. By contrast, in the later text allegory became the figure of a fated subjectivity, which originated as the transcendent ground eroded. In fact, Benjamin also harked back to the epistemo-critical prologue, which defined the philosopher's task as the *anamnesis* or remembrance of Adam's act of naming. The philosopher was to reactivate a more originary hearing (*Urvernehmen*), which preceded epistemological questioning and the analytic logic of philosophy. Tellingly, in the study's final chapter Benjamin again introduced Kierkegaard, when he called these inauthentic forms of language chatter (*Geschwätz*). By doing so, he seemed to target the game of idealistic reflection and dialectical tricks that formed the target of Kierkegaard's *Kritik der Gegenwart* (Critique of the Present).[33] Here, Kierkegaard argued that the dire task awaiting the age of reflection was its disengagement from the seductions of such speculative games, "because they are so dialectical; because one single smart idea can suddenly give a new turn to the matter; because reflection, at every moment, is able to reexplain it and to let one slip away from it; because even in the final moment of a reflective decision it is still possible to turn everything around."[34] In like manner, Benjamin charged that the operation of allegory triggered meaning in the emblem, through a dialectical trick (*Kunstgriff*), as through a spring. At the deepest point of its fall or immersion (*Versenkung*) into nothingness, allegory in fact turned into a redemptive figure of itself. A metafigure of sorts, it became, ironically, a dialectical trick that imbued lifeless matter with the spirit of resurrection:[35]

Allegory, of course, thereby loses everything that was most peculiar to it: the secret, privileged knowledge, the arbitrary rule in the realm of dead objects, the supposed infinity of a world without hope. All this vanishes with this *one* about-turn in which the immersion of allegory has to clear away the final phantasmagoria of the objective and, left entirely to its own devices, rediscovers itself, not playfully in the earthly world of things but seriously under the eyes of heaven. And this is the essence of melancholy immersion: that its ultimate objects, in which it believes it can most fully secure for itself that which is vile, turn into allegories and that these allegories fill out and deny the void in which they are represented, just as, ultimately, the intention does not faithfully rest in the contemplation of bones but faithlessly leaps forward to the idea of resurrection. (*O* 232; *GS* 1:406)

In a moment of reversal (*Umschwung*), then, allegory, Benjamin concluded, turned from the realm of earthly things to the loftier spheres of the heavens. No longer faithful to the mere contemplation of a lifeless skeleton, allegory thus faithlessly leapt to the idea of resurrection.[36] Once again the movement of ascent, from the telluric to the uranic and from play to seriousness, already encountered in the Goethe essay, made its reappearance, but with one crucial difference. The moment of resurrection now appeared to be nothing more than a dialectical trick. For under the subjective gaze of melancholia, lifeless matter was reinvested with meaning.

Clearly, the antics of allegory that Benjamin described in the study's final chapter cast some doubt on the dialectical tricks that informed the Goethe essay and, indeed, the eschatological language that pervades parts of the *Trauerspiel* study. Seeming to defy the dialectical trickery he just uncovered, in the study's last lines Benjamin, curiously enough, once again called upon the resurrectional apparatus, this time to sum up the fate that awaited the *Trauerspiel*. Because the German mourning play remained trapped in the demonic game of reflexivity, in the thralls, that is, of an inauthentic time, it was unable to conjure up a single image that could transcend this base level of inauthenticity. However, on the last Day of Judgment, Benjamin predicted, would the ruinous mourning play project the true image of beauty, finally to realize to the full its potential, which it already contained in blueprint form: "[Other theatrical forms] may shine resplendently as on the first day; this theatrical form holds on to the image of beauty on the Last Day" (*O* 235; *GS* 1:409).

If it is true, then, as Adorno convincingly argued in "The Idea of Natural History," that Benjamin's theory of allegory formulated a new philosophy of natural history, it is equally true that his analysis retained the salvific model such a new conception of history was to explode. To no small degree, the final chapter thus bore witness to the self-same ironic ambiguity with which Benjamin earlier had invested allegory. With hindsight, however, it appears that the surreptitious operations of irony that form the core of allegory to a certain degree already manifested themselves in the final part of the Goethe essay. For it is doubtful that the word *Schein* was entirely free of irony when in the Goethe essay Benjamin argued that the *Schein* of reconciliation (*Versöhnung*) fleetingly appeared in the image of the shooting star. In German this phrase, it must be stressed, can mean either "the illumination" or "the illusion of reconciliation," so that in fact it becomes the object of sublime irony. Reintroducing all the ambiguities that had marked the word *Schein* when it was associated with Ottilie, the term testified to a radical discrepancy. For, seen within a German philosophical context, the image of the star cannot help but evoke Kant's *Second Critique* and, more specifically, the oft-cited phrase "The starry sky above me and the moral law within me" (Der bestirnte Himmel über mir, und das moralische Gesetz in mir). Indeed, the philosopher Karl Löwith has suggested that the phrase expressed the radical contingency and incommensurability that existed between, on the one hand, the Kantian inner realm of freedom and, on the other hand, the outer realm of natural necessity.[37] It is, incidentally, this very chasm that Lukács invoked in the opening chapter of his *Theory of the Novel*, in which he started off lamenting those happy ages "when the starry sky is the map of all possible paths—ages whose paths are illuminated by the light of the stars," noting later that "Kant's starry firmament now shines only in the dark night of pure cognition."[38] Moreover, Adorno's own early "Idea of Natural History" also allows one to shed further light on the deceptive dynamics of the term *Schein*. In the lecture, Adorno ended up establishing *Schein* as the very appearance of "second nature" and as the illusion of dialectical meaning (*Sinn*). The appearance of reconciliation, Adorno gnomically remarked, is all the more vivid the more illusionary such reconciliation really is: "the promise of reconciliation which is given in the most perfect form, where the world simultaneously appears most densely walled up by meaning [*Sinn*]."[39] It is ultimately in this sense, I believe, that one must read Benjamin's treatment of allegory in the *Trauerspiel* study. For, through allegory, Benjamin essentially meditated on the possibility of reconciliation no less than on its illusionary nature. Only from this perspective does it become understandable why allegory at once could figure the transience of natural history yet retain the fleeting promise of imminent reconciliation.

Of Stones, Animals, Human Beings, and Angels

In calling for a theory of history that would no longer be founded on the premises of historicism or hermeneutics, the *Trauerspiel* book sought to dismantle the metaphysical premises that upheld the philosophy of consciousness and reflexivity. The second part of this study will continue the analysis of what earlier had been called Benjamin's de-limitation of the subject, but it will do so by placing the issue primarily in the context of the questions of ethics and justice that his work raises. Carried on well beyond the *Trauerspiel* study, Benjamin's ethico-theological project proved to be foundational to more than a few essays he wrote while in exile. In the great literary essays from the 1930s—those on Kraus, Kafka, and Leskov—the figures of the human subject and humanity are, at times openly, at times surreptitiously, called into question by images of stones, animals, and angels. As such, these essays bear witness to Benjamin's continued engagement with the limits of the human—a line of questioning already evident in the passages the *Trauerspiel* book dedicated to the theological concept of *Kreatur*.

Like the term "natural history," the word *Kreatur* appears to be quite complex, taking on various connotations from different philosophical and theological frameworks as it traverses Benjamin's work. Originally adopted as the German translation for the Latin *creatura,* the word was commonly used in the late Middle Ages as a synonym for the German word *Geschöpf,* meaning "the totality of the world, insofar as it is related to the activity of a creator." Its usage can be traced from Luther's sermons and German mysticism (Meister Eckhart, Nicholas of Cusa, and Jakob Böhme) to the eighteenth century, when, following the rise of natural history, the word became defunct, only to be replaced by the term "nature." In present-day German, if used at all, it is used almost exclusively in its "secular" sense, as a derogatory phrase.[1] But the term has also played a major, if largely unnoticed, role in twentieth-century poetry and poetics, from Rilke's *Duino Elegies* and Heidegger's Rilke interpretations to Celan's 1960 speech "The Meridian," where it not only appears as part of his reflections on Büchner's naturalism but directly refers back to Benjamin's 1934 Kafka essay.

In the course of Benjamin's work, the term *Kreatur* underwent some significant changes in meaning. In the *Trauerspiel* study, it functioned as an overarching term for a host of divergent, often conflicting tendencies in an age marked by the rise of anthropology, the return to natural law, and the mourning play, which tended to stage humankind in the state of creation. Thus the section "Sovereign as Creature" underscored that the monarch commonly was regarded as the summit of the great chain of being, or "the lord of creatures." Playwrights and poets as varied as Opitz, Tscherning, Buchner, and Gryphius quite commonly used the term "animal" (*Thier*) to refer to the human subject. At the same time, the inherent duplicity or ambiguity of the term *Kreatur* made itself felt, for it could also signal the lowliest form of animality as well as human depravity. Glimpses of this animality appeared in the king's madness, showing that "in the ruler, the supreme creature, the beast can re-emerge with unsuspected power" (*O* 86; *GS* 1:265). Swayed by uncontrollable affects—epitomized by the crazed Herodes or by Hunold's depiction of Nebuchadnezzar as a chained animal—the tyrant was a "mad autocrat" whose erratic behavior symbolized "disordered creation" (*O* 70; *GS* 1:250). The creaturely thus not only referred to the predominance of the affects, eminently manifested in the sovereign's melancholia, but also encompassed the depravity, animality, and monstrosity that lingered in the autocratic monarch.

Already in the *Trauerspiel* study, however, this conception of the creaturely as the realm of the passions, mythical guilt, wanton melancholia, and animality—in short, a fallen nature on *this* side of transcendence and revelation—co-existed with a more positive, benign conception. Evident in the 1916 language essay, the section of the *Trauerspiel* book dedicated to natural language, and subsequent work, this positive meaning gradually became more pronounced and expressive of an ethical call for an all-inclusive turn toward nature. The signs of such an ethics, Benjamin posited, were to be detected in Kafka's attentiveness (*Aufmerksamkeit*) to the creaturely, a concern he extended even to the most abject forms of animality. But this attentiveness emerged even more vividly in the short stories of the Russian writer Leskov. In the figures of Leskov's mother and the Jewish mystic Wenzel, Benjamin welcomed the Judaic figure of the just man (*der Gerechte*), who, as the advocate of the creatural (*Fürsprech der Kreatur*), was also its highest embodiment.

To the degree that Benjamin's concern with the *Kreatur* accompanied his call to respond to what traditionally falls outside the boundaries of the human subject, it merits a brief contrastive reading with other, more recent philosophical attempts to problematize the humanistic legacy that has dominated Western philosophy. Benjamin's alternative use of the term shows affinities to the status that the theme of animality gained, for example, in Derrida's writings of the 1980s. Within the context of contemporary French philosophy the theme of animality has served to question the notion of *Dasein*—in other words, the limits of the very concept that, in much of twentieth-century philosophy, from the early Levinas to Sartre's mature work, originally was hailed as the most radical critique of the metaphysical subject. For even though Heidegger's exclusionary gestures toward "the living" were part of his encompassing project to overcome the fallacies of the philosophy of life, they nonetheless remained informed by metaphysical distinctions that regulated what traditionally counted as a subject and what counts as less than human, hence "infra-human."[2]

By reading Benjamin's writings in light of the thematization that the living has received in Derrida's, Levinas's, but also Adorno's thought, one does not simply superimpose a foreign conceptual model onto his thought. Like the work of the pre-Marxist Lukács and that of other contemporary intellectuals, Benjamin's thought came into its own in an intellectual climate that was still dominated largely by an influential vitalism (*Lebensphilosophie*).[3] After his early infatuation with the Youth Movement, several of his subsequent projects showed a sometimes subdued but often ardent interrogation of vitalism, activism, biologism, and Darwinism, falling short only of the systematic study the later Lukács was to devote to the topic.[4] If this was already evident in "Fate and Character," "Critique of Violence," or the Goethe essay, his criticism would become even more pronounced in the writings he produced in the 1930s—for example, in his "Theories of German Fascism," which indicted Ernst Jünger's *Der Krieg und die Krieger*

(War and the Warriors), as well as renouncing Kurt Hiller's activism and metaphysics of spirit.

Granted that Benjamin's attacks on vitalism share common ground with Heidegger's critique of vitalism, irreconcilable ideological and political differences remain. In view of these seeming similarities, it becomes all the more important to underscore the fundamental distinctions—a caution not least warranted by Benjamin's well-documented attempts to distinguish his own work from Heidegger's. The latter's rejection of vitalism first of all formed part of his larger project of fundamental ontology (*Fundamentalontologie*) that structured *Being and Time*. Later, this rejection returned in the *Nietzsche* study in the form of a critique of a "biologistic metaphysics"[5] and of a metaphysics of the will as technology. By contrast, Benjamin's interrogation of vitalism was motivated by a pronounced Judaic conception of justice founded in a cabalistic philosophy of language, which in the 1931 Kraus essay would be called the "Mater der Gerechtigkeit" (The Matrix of Justice). Furthermore, this criticism of vitalism seemed to draw on a utopian conception of a destructive, violent, yet redemptive technology whose alleged "purifying" force subverted organicist human creativity. Both views were explicitly linked together in the Kraus essay, as I hope to show.

But there exists yet another profound difference between these thinkers, one that might best be framed by Levinas's Celan essay in *Noms propres* (Proper Names). Thus Levinas interpreted Celan's 1959 "Conversation in the Mountains" as a critique of the philosophy of being and of the return to a Greek *phusis* that one finds in Heidegger's later work.[6] Commenting on Celan's phrase, "the Jew and nature are strangers to each other, have always been and still are, even today, even here,"[7] which seemingly confirmed Judaism's ban on nature, Levinas instead saw in it the "rupturing of [Heidegger's] naivete of the herald, messenger or shepherd of being."[8]

Several of Benjamin's texts likewise rethink the relation between nature and Judaic conceptions of law and ethics, seeking to dispel the reign of mythical nature and mere life by means of just existence. Already in the prologue to the *Trauerspiel* study, as we saw, Benjamin steered clear of the philosophy of eternal return and the concept of "nature" typical of the natural sciences, drawing instead on a Judaic tradition of revelation and history. While Benjamin thus seemingly accepted Judaism's ban on mythical nature, his work, I would submit, testified to the same ethical openness to the natural that Levinas perceived in Celan.

To address the relation between nature and justice in Benjamin's work means, however, that one must also heed the history of prejudices and stereotypes to which Judaism's alleged ban on the natural has been subjected. Thus in the history of philosophy, and specifically in German idealism, biblical and postbiblical, Talmudic Judaism often has been associated with a lethal petrification of nature and the natural. The Levinas scholar Catherine Chalier has sought to break with this interpretive tradition, proposing an alternative, innovative reading of the original covenant, which, rather than being seen as an unconditional surrender to the letter of the law, is now read to express an unlimited respect for nature and the cosmos.

If Benjamin's writings interrogate the status and predominance of the human subject, calling for a renewed attention to what traditionally was considered to be less than human, they also show the other, less benign side of this question: that of the inhuman or monstrous. Particularly in the Kraus essay, which advocated a disturbing new "humanism of the *Unmensch,*" he gestured toward the violent, monstrous limits of the human. When read in conjunction with the epistolary collection *Deutsche Menschen* (German People), which Benjamin published during the Nazi regime while in exile, the call for renewal through violence that Benjamin formulated in the Kraus essay must, to say the least, seem strangely out of place. Indeed, it remains one of the unresolved contradictions of Benjamin's work that he commonly embraced dangerously conservative figures of thought, all the while also exhibiting a marked vigilance toward the forces of fascism. Nowhere is this contradiction more apparent than in the gulf that separates texts such as "The Destructive Character" from a collection such as *Deutsche Menschen*. For with this compendium Benjamin hoped to stem the diluvian force of national socialism, seeking to rekindle the image of a lost Enlightenment humanism while at the same time pointing to the inherently inhuman aspects of the German Enlightenment. That this text sketched the ineluctable movement of the dialectic of Enlightenment, well before Adorno's and Horkheimer's joint endeavor, was recognized by Adorno in the afterword that accompanied his 1962 republication of *Deutsche Menschen*.

The following chapter, "Limits of Humanity," first of all examines some of the divergent positions on the issue of humanism that emerged in Benjamin's writings of the 1930s. Only after one has taken stock of the extent to which Benjamin's writings take issue with the stronghold of the humanistic subject can one consider his reinterpretation of the constellation nature and the law (*phusis* and *thesis*) and, finally, the de-limiting force Benjamin lodged in the concept *Kreatur*.

CHAPTER 6

Limits of Humanity

Under the title *Deutsche Menschen* (German People),
Benjamin brought together some of the letters and comments that
he published in the feuilleton of the *Frankfurter Zeitung* between
April 1931 and May 1932. The collection was comprised of twenty-five
letters, most of them by prominent German intellectuals, spanning
a period from 1783 until 1883. Later in 1936 he published the letters
in Switzerland, using the pseudonym Detlef Holz. In an apologetic
letter to Scholem, written in October 1936, Benjamin explained that
the choice of the book's somewhat questionable title was "due to the
desire to camouflage [*tarnen*] the collection, from which some may be
able to profit in Germany."[1]

How exactly Benjamin conceived the political goal of this singular
compendium can be gleaned from the undated first version of the
introduction, which, in order to escape censorship, was never included
in the 1936 edition:

The purpose of this series is to show the countenance of a "secret Germany,"
which today one all too often tries to find behind grim clouds. For a secret
Germany really exists. Only its secrecy is not only the expression of its in-
tensity and depth but—albeit in a different sense—the work of forces that
noisily and brutally denied it public effectiveness, condemning it to a secret
effectiveness. (*GS* 4:945)

The collection included such famous letters as Goethe's condolence
letter to Moritz Seebeck, Hölderlin's report following his return from
France "daß mich Apollo geschlagen," and Büchner's letter in which he

entrusted the manuscript of *Dantons Tod* to Gutzkow,[2] but it also contained little-known letters by Georg Forster, Seume, the physician Dieffenbach—in short, letters that, as Benjamin noted in one of the unpublished manuscripts, never became part of Germany's general *Bildung.*

The compendium was meant to chronicle the gradual decline of Germany's bourgeoisie, whose fall, realized by the *Gründerzeit,* truly set in with Goethe's death in 1832, as the opening letter to the collection suggested. If the tone of *Deutsche Menschen* was markedly subdued, this must first of all be ascribed to Benjamin's endeavor to circumvent German censorship. At the same time, the sobriety in tone was one of the effects Benjamin consciously strove to attain, as the motto to the collection indicates: "About honor without fame, greatness without glory, dignity without pay" (Von Ehre ohne Ruhm, von Größe ohne Glanz, von Würde ohne Sold). The preliminary drafts of the project demonstrate that Benjamin not only aimed to undo the instrumentalization of German literature, which had been put at the service of the German *Bildungsdrang;* even more so, he hoped to reclaim the "humanity" of the German classics from the canonization and eventual Nazification to which they had been subjected.

Following a gesture typical of Benjamin's historico-philosophical thought, according to which the present was to be salvaged by means of the unresolved potential of the past, Benjamin grouped together mostly little-read and often marginal letters that he considered to be exemplary of a lost German humanistic tradition. But the collection's critical potential can be deciphered only if one is attentive to its principle of montage. Only then can the reader discern the multifarious constellations formed by the letters, as well as the historical parallels and similarities the collection established between the historical past and the fascist present. In the genealogy that Benjamin traced, a covert continuity was set up between, on the one hand, national socialism, which caused him to seek exile in Paris, and, on the other hand, the ideological forces that drove Georg Forster and Hölderlin to leave the "fatherland" and Büchner to flee Darmstadt. Once one follows this strand of exegesis, the volume appears to chronicle the tension between a nationalistic construction of German identity, with its antidemocratic, exclusionary gestures, and the desire of these outcast writers to remain within German bounds, a tension Benjamin saw epitomized in Hölderlin's plea, "Deutsch will und muß ich übrigens bleiben, und wenn mich die Herzens- und Nahrungsnot nach Otaheiti triebe" (*GS* 4:213).

In the undated first version of the introduction, Benjamin defined the political goal of the letters as follows: "They represent a position that can be described as humanistic in a German sense and whose revival currently seems all the more advisable the more onesidedly those who today question German humanism—often gravely and fully conscious of their responsibility—hold on to the works of art and literature" (*GS* 4:954). As such, Benjamin's archive of a hidden Germany was meant to explode the forces of fascist nationalism. The letters were exemplary of another German people, one that questioned the boundaries of the German nation and identity from within. Thus the compendium opened onto the archive of another, silent, silenced, and secret Germany that radically called into question the hegemony and homogeneity of a nationalistic, German identity. In fact, this questioning continued a line of thinking that can be traced back to some of Benjamin's earlier writings: to the essay on the translator, who was to transgress the boundaries of a national identity, or to the 1921 "Critique of Violence," and even to the 1915 Hölderlin essay, which, in problematizing the German–Hellenistic alliance or *psyche*[3] typical of German classicism and idealism, opted for the disruptive force of the Oriental and the Judaic. As Peter Szondi and, in his footsteps, Albrecht Schöne have pointed out, the dedications in the copies of *Deutsche Menschen* that Benjamin presented to his sister Dora, Scholem, and Kracauer referred to the collection as "this ark, built according to Jewish example,"[4] which he had set out to assemble "as the fascist flood started to rise."[5] On the basis of these dedications, the critic Johannes Seiffert concluded that one ought to distinguish between the collection's ostensibly German material and its covert Judaic form, which, in line with Judaic tradition, followed the archetypical motif of the just one (*der Gerechte*), who remained hidden.[6] Seiffert proposes to read *Deutsche Menschen* as an example of the "new Midrash,"[7] a reading modeled on Ernst Simon's interpretation of the almanacs that Moritz Spitzer edited for the Schocken publishing house in Berlin from 1933 until 1938. To this reading, I would like to add that the hidden, covert reference to Noah's Ark also allows one to shed some additional light on Benjamin's own claims to identity as a German Jew and on his often complex and varied stance toward the issue of the Jewish–German symbiosis or *psyche*. Neither a simple acknowledgment of his indebtedness to the German tradition—as some critics have claimed[8]—nor an outright rejection of "the German," *Deutsche Menschen* rather sought to point to the elements of difference and alterity within "identity."

Written from a perspective that explicitly thematized what it meant to write and to philosophize after the Holocaust, Adorno's afterword to the 1962 edition of *Deutsche Menschen* couldn't but assess the collection in light of its failed utopian promises and the irretrievable loss of the image of humanity it sought to cast. The collection's confrontation with the aftermath of the Holocaust exposed the dialectics of an Enlightenment that progressively transformed its humanism into the monstrously inhuman. Seeing the collected letters as relics of a declining bourgeoisie, Adorno detected in them the last vestiges of a Kantian ethics, with its concepts of autonomy, individuality, and particularity—in short, a Kantian practical principle that sought to set boundaries or limits to the hubristic dreams of totality, universality, and collective subjectivity that typify nationalisms. The essence of these letters, Adorno suggested, could be summed up by Hölderlin's conception of "sacred sobriety" (*heilige Nüchternheit*). However, as was evident from the prologue to the central letter Johann Heinrich Kant sent to his brother Immanuel, the letters not only represented the relics of a lost, faded humanity. In their asceticism and their preoccupation with the concrete and the practical, they laid bare the conditions of possibility of humanity, as well as their very limits—limits foreshadowed by the *Gründerzeit* and fatally realized in the fascist era.

Although Adorno acknowledged Benjamin's attempt to uncover a "subterranean," "heterogeneous" German tradition—that of a failed Enlightenment—and the concomitant endeavor to undo the fascist violation of the German spirit, he questioned the effectiveness of Benjamin's project, as well as the redemptive potential of the epistolary form. The collection of letters, he suggested, was as naive as the letters it brought together—that is, marred by the illusion that it could cunningly undo the violence of the oppressive political forces:

Benjamin shared with us immigrants the erroneous belief that spirit and cunning could achieve something against a power [*Gewalt*] that no longer acknowledged the spirit [*Geist*] as something independent but only as a means to its ends and therefore did not have to fear a confrontation with it.

To the degree that these letters were the relics of an archaic, obsolete epistolary genre, they pointed to the irreparable loss of a past era: "Their irretrievability turns into a critique of a way of the world, which in wiping out the limiting forces [*das Beschränkende*] of humanity, turned itself, without realizing it, against humanity."[9]

However valid Adorno's criticism may be, one must nonetheless raise a number of questions with regard to the status of this so-called autonomous German spirit (*Geist*) to which Adorno made reference in his afterword, as well as in another short text titled "Auf die Frage: Was ist deutsch?" (On the Question: What Is German?; 1965), in which he sought to explain why he returned to Germany after his American exile.[10] In taking to task the definitions of German national identity offered by Wagner and others, the essay nonetheless retained a certain kind of specularity in the notion of an "originary" German spirit to which it seemed to subscribe. This is not to suggest that Adorno would have fallen back behind the position he first advanced, together with Horkheimer, in the 1948 "Elements of Anti-Semitism." In this chapter of the *Dialectic of Enlightenment*, Adorno and Horkheimer related anti-Semitism to what they called a "ticket mentality" and proposed to interpret Judaism as the *locus* of difference, critique (*Kritik*), and "determined negation" that undermined stabilizing notions of stereotypes, national identity, and a collective subjectivity. Even as late as 1962 Adorno reiterated this position in the lecture "Zur Bekämpfung des Antisemitismus heute" (On How to Fight Antisemitism Today), which he presented at a conference on pedagogy organized by the German Christian-Jewish alliance. As he stated in "Auf die Frage: Was ist deutsch?": "The most truthful and best in every people is that which does not adapt itself to the collective subject but, whenever possible, resists it."[11] Still, the response he himself formulated to the question of how one was to identify "the German" was rather ambiguous. On the one hand, he posited that, should one try to define what was German on historical—not essentialistic—grounds, one would have to qualify the German as "this entwinement of that which is magnificent and cannot be content with conventionally established limits, with the monstrous."[12] On the other hand, Adorno seemed to want to safeguard the stronghold of a German spirit, which he opposed to a fallen, inauthentic notion of "culture" and to the predominance of the technological. Though he was quick to point out that he did not want to fall into the trap of pitting a German notion of *Kultur* against American culture, it is hard not to read the essay in light of precisely such an opposition. As such, the essay shows some uncanny resemblances to the rather controversial essay "Scientific Experiences in America," in which Adorno, noting the absence of an English word that could adequately capture the meaning of *Geist*, took to task American empiricism for its inability to conceptualize "the spirit." Similarly, while in "Auf die Frage: Was ist deutsch?" Adorno criticized Wagner's definition of the German as "eine Sache um ihrer selbst willen tun" (to do a thing for itself),[13] he nevertheless granted the phrase some historical truth: Germany's economic and industrial backwardness during the nineteenth century allowed its spiritual productive forces to resist progressive reification, commodification, and commercialization. It was precisely this form of backwardness, still prevalent in the postwar Germany of 1962, that Adorno held to constitute the best opportunity for the German spirit.[14]

That "Auf die Frage: Was ist deutsch?" ended up, paradoxically enough, by defining the authenticity of the German as *Geist* is especially evident in its final pages, where Adorno linked his return to Germany to his love of the German idiom. More than any other language, German exhibited an "elective affinity" to philosophy, as well as a metaphysical, speculative surplus (*Überschuß*) of meaning. Most important, it was the very intranslatability of the word *Geist* that came to qualify the authenticity of the German language:

The impossibility of transposing, without doing violence, into another language, not only lengthy speculative thoughts but even some very precise concepts such as that of the spirit, the moment, and experience, while including all that resonates in the German, is indicative of a specific, objective characteristic of the German language.[15]

One must wonder, therefore, whether Adorno's text did not reintroduce some of the phantasmatic moments that typify nationalisms as it fell privy to a double gesture: the attempt to explode the German psyche coupled with the return to a covert national identity that was linked to language and (in)translatability. By contrast, Walter Benjamin's "Task of the Translator"—a text, I want to suggest, that need not be read only within a theological perspective—can be seen as a reflection on the intersections between translation, translatability, and transnationalism. Anything but a plea for a moment of intranslatability, Benjamin's text instead cherished the hope of absolute translatability and of a communicative praxis in which the translator breaks the "decayed barriers of his own language" (*I* 80; *GS* 4:19).

CHAPTER 7

Benjamin's *Unmensch:* The Politics of Real Humanism

Benjamin's attempt to retrieve the epistolary relics of a lost Enlightenment humanism invites a contrastive reading with another of his texts that was published at around the same time in the *Frankfurter Zeitung:* the essay on Karl Kraus. Unlike *Deutsche Menschen,* the Kraus essay renounced the premises of classic Enlightenment humanism that were still central to the collection of letters. Refuting not only classic humanism but also the antihumanism Nietzsche propounded with his politics of the *Übermensch,* Benjamin coined a radically new form of "humanism"—one that, paradoxically, hinged on the notion of a destructive "inhuman" (*Unmensch*). Like the 1931 essay on the destructive character, the Kraus essay ended up advocating a politics of destruction, except that now the anarchistic deployment of force was to be put at the service of divine justice.

Much as in the *Trauerspiel* book, Benjamin's projected revision of humanism called for a return to origins, notably to what he termed Kraus's humanism of the origin (*GS* 2:1,090). But the radically new humanism he envisioned defies easy classification. Indeed, the essay not only emphatically undermined the principles of liberal humanism, calling—much as the earlier "Critique of Violence" had done—for a politics of destruction. It further introduced a new type of *Unmensch,* whose task it was to bring on the dawning of a new humankind that would prove itself by destruction.[1] In trying to think such a dangerous new humanism, then, Benjamin did nothing less than announce the death of all previous conceptions of humanism.

As some of Benjamin's preparatory notes and outlines indicate, the Kraus essay was to be centered on a scathing critique of classic Enlightenment humanism or so-called *ideal* humanism (*GS* 2:1,097), which he aspired to replace with a new, *real* humanism. The subtitles for the essay's three sections—"Allmensch," "Dämon," and "Unmensch"— summed up the new images of humanity and inhumanity that Kraus's satirical work was said to depict. *Allmensch*[2] stood for the prototype of classic Weimar *Bildungshumanismus,* from Goethe's *Weltbürger* to Stifter's novellas (*GS* 2:1,097). The figure of the demon—whom Benjamin also called subhuman (*untermenschlich*)—represented abject nature, mythical guilt, and sensuality. As for the revolutionary impulse embodied by the *Unmensch,* this anarchic energy further emerged in Kraus's politics of language, in his figures of the child and the cannibal, and, finally, in Klee's *Angelus Novus.* Structured according to a tripartite model—much like the Goethe essay—the Kraus study staged a dialectical conflict between these three types, showing—as Benjamin indicated in one of the drafts—how the false justice of the *Allmensch* was to be supplanted by the anarchic justice of the *Unmensch* (*GS* 2:1,103).[3]

In the scathing criticisms of Austrian mores that appeared in *Die Fackel,* Benjamin recognized what he considered to be Kraus's moral presence of mind. When seen against Austria's cultural decadence, Kraus's sardonic moralism appeared as the last vestige of an eminently theological sense of tact or timing. Using language reminiscent of that in the *Trauerspiel* study, he noted:

Tact is the capacity to treat social relationships, though not departing from them, as natural, even as paradisiac relationships, and so not only to approach the king as if he had been born with the crown on his brow, but the lackey like an Adam in livery. Hebel possessed this *noblesse* in his priestly bearing, Kraus in armor. His concept of creation contains the theological inheritance of speculations that last possessed contemporary validity for the whole of Europe in the seventeenth century. (*R* 244; *GS* 2:339)

The yardstick Kraus used to measure social decay was creaturely naturalness, a state of moral purity that preceded and superseded all class and social oppositions. In the hands of the *Allmensch*—whose literary image was Stifter—this pristine state of creation had been corrupted. As Benjamin added:

At the theological core of this concept [i.e., creation], however, a transformation has taken place that has caused it, quite without constraint, to coincide with the cosmopolitan credo of Austrian worldliness, which made creation into a church in which nothing remained to recall the rite except an occasional whiff of incense in the mists. Stifter gave this creed its most authentic stamp, and his echo is heard wherever Kraus concerns himself with animals, plants, children. (*R* 244; *GS* 2:339–40)

Quoting from the preface to *Bunte Steine* (Stones of Many Colors), in which Stifter formulated his poetic principle of *das sanfte Gesetz* (gentle law), Benjamin concluded that Stifter's stories and novellas anthropomorphized nature. In an essay written in 1918, originally titled "About Greatness" ("Über Größe," *GS* 2:608–10), Benjamin had already strongly criticized Stifter, whom he regarded to be a conservative, essentially patriarchal writer. This early essay aptly summed up why Stifter's aesthetics of the minute or the small needed to be rejected. At stake, Benjamin emphasized, was the "sense for justice in the highest meaning of the word" (*GS* 2:608), or a divine justice beyond the smallness of earthly things, which Stifter relinquished in his myopic engagement with demonic nature.

In his glorification of the organic life of plants, animals, and children, Kraus similarly threatened to retreat from the plane of history, finding refuge in pristine creation. History, in Kraus's mind, was no more than a wilderness that forever separated human beings from creation: "As a deserter to the camp of animal creation—so he measures out this wilderness. 'And only the animal that is conquered by humanity is the hero of life': never was Adalbert Stifter's patriarchal credo given so lugubrious and heraldic a formulation" (*R* 246; *GS* 2:341). How emphatically Kraus subscribed to such an ahistorical, even essentialistic notion of nature the poem "Die Fundverheimlichung" illustrated particularly well.[4] Extolling the virtues of the dog—the "arme Kreatur"—whose faithfulness and obedience were the "creation's true mirror of virtue"[5] (*R* 246; *GS* 2:341) this poem showed all the signs, Benjamin suggested, of a questionable anthropomorphization.[6] Despite appearances, Kraus's polemical work was in the thralls of a deep-rooted, melancholic longing for a paradisiac state of nature. Against the transient, ephemeral existence of the Viennese press, Kraus held an eternally new newspaper that chronicled the history of creation, giving expression to "the eternally renewed, the uninterrupted lament" (*R* 250; *GS* 2:344–45).[7]

Structurally speaking, the essay's third part formed the antipode to the opening section, demonstrating how the *Allmensch* developed into the *Unmensch* (*GS* 2:1,102) and how classical humanism was to be supplanted by real humanism.[8] Both poles, Benjamin maintained, co-existed in Kraus's writing: the mocking, derisive invocation of Weimar classicism and humanitarian expressionism jarred with an apolitical naturalism, the result of Kraus's conversion to Catholicism. Kraus's belief in Christian original sin and his quest for moral purity were the symptoms of a lingering bourgeois state of mind. In reality, Benjamin suggested, the *Allmensch* resembled the bourgeois, "natural man," whom Marx had taken to task in his *On the Jewish Question*. But for Benjamin this Marxian term applied not only to the petty morals of the bourgeois but also to the romantics' *Naturwesen* as it found expression in Kraus's longing for cosmic nature. At the same time, this natural level apparent in Kraus's work eventually was radically shattered through the forceful intervention of a disruptive language politics, revealing the dialectical side of Kraus's writing practice. Arguing that an old and new humanism were at odds with one another in Kraus's work, Benjamin suggested that real humanism transpired through the disruptive, violent force of citation, which resolutely intervened in whatever it happened to quote.

As Benjamin's use of the term "real humanism" demonstrates, his remarks went beyond Kraus's language politics in that they also crit-ically engaged in a discussion of Marxist humanism. Sparked by the rediscovery of the early *Economic and Philosophic Manuscripts,* Marxist humanism emerged in the 1920s, counting amongst its principal dis-cussants Lukács, Korsch, and Gramsci.[9] First introduced by Marx and Engels in the jointly published *The Holy Family* (1845), real humanism targeted the concept of criticism that the Left Hegelian Bruno Bauer had proposed in his *Literatur-Zeitung* (*R* 261; *GS* 2:355).[10] It was as follows that Marx and Engels defined real humanism: "In Germany real humanism has no more dangerous enemy than spiritualism or specula-tive idealism, which replaces real individual man by 'self-consciousness' or 'spirit' and, together with the evangelist, teaches: 'The spirit is what enlivens, the flesh is of no use.'"[11] Although *The Holy Family* proved influenced by Feuerbach's anthropology, the *Theses on Feuerbach* and *The German Ideology* would take issue with Feuerbach's definition of human essence as an "abstractum that inhabits the individual."[12]

Given the centrality of the term "real humanism" in *The Holy Family,* it is interesting to note that Benjamin did not make reference to this text. Instead, he invoked another early, indeed highly controversial text of Marx's, *On the Jewish Question,* in which the term as such did not occur. However, the choice of *On the Jewish Question* may have been motivated by the fact that Kraus satirized the legacy of human rights and the classical humanitarian ideals of the French Revolution. Aphorisms such as "humanity, culture, and freedom are precious things that cannot be bought dearly enough with blood, understanding, and human dignity,"[13] collected in Kraus's *Sprüche und Widersprüche* (Dicta and Contradictions), aptly expressed the cannibalistic ferocity that marked his "antihumanistic" satire on human rights. Now it was precisely the question of human rights that formed the larger frame within which Marx placed the Jewish question. Having rejected Bauer's suggestion that the Jewish question must be resolved through a political emancipation from all forms of religion, Marx queried the political emancipation that followed the American and French Revolutions. Thus he proposed to distinguish between the *droits de l'homme,* or natural rights, established in the French constitution, which amounted to no more than the egoistic demands of the petit bourgeois, and the *droits du citoyen* or the rights of abstract political man. The real contradictions that existed in civil society "between the living individual and the citizen," he emphasized, were not to be resolved through political but through human emancipation. Only the latter could reunite individuals and abstract citizens, both in real life and in human labor.[14] In contrast to the scientific claims of the later Marx, humanist Marxism remained entrenched in the idea that human history was propelled by a creator-subject.[15]

Benjamin drastically revised Marx's real humanism when he noted that the model of progressive human creation was to be replaced by that of violent destruction. Only in this way, he suggested, could the grounds for the coming of a new humankind be laid—a humanity that, paradoxically, would realize itself through destruction. The apocalyptic figure of the *Unmensch* portended the advent of a revolutionary new human being who would arise out of the throes of self-cannibalism. What can we make, then, of the disturbing resonances that mark Benjamin's language? Why the disquieting emphasis on violence and destruction?

The topic of cannibalism resonates with the motive of eating and voracious devouring that one finds in some of Benjamin's other writings, where it is linked to the act of reading and a hermeneutics of interiorization (*Einverleibung*).[16] Its appearance in the Kraus essay, however, seems to have been motivated primarily by the tradition of satire. A choice metaphor for satirists, the image of cannibalism could be tracked, as Benjamin showed, from Swift or Nestroy's *Häuptling Abendwind* to the writings of Léon Bloy. Cannibalism best described Kraus's sardonic attack on the humanistic tradition, for satire, Benjamin noted, involved "the devouring of the adversary. The satirist is the figure in whom the cannibal was received into civilization" (*R* 260; *GS* 2:355).[17] As the privileged tool of the cannibalistic *Unmensch*, satire set an end to the subhuman powers of the demonic. Benjamin's description of Kraus's cannibalism seemed influenced by Feuerbach's anthropological materialism, which found its most compact and most playful expression in the aphorism, "Man ißt, was man ißt."[18] Cannibalism announced a new reign of sensuality, as well as the materialistic overcoming of mythical man and guilt. Only if modern humans forged a contract with the destructive forces of nature could such a materialistic overthrow come about. As he unleashed the violence and revolutionary forces locked in nature, Benjamin's *Unmensch* radically took leave of the reign of the *Allmensch*, no less than of the ahistoricity that typified mythical, demonic nature.

If earlier, under the heading *Allmensch*, Benjamin had unpacked the theological dimension of *Kreatur*, which pointed back to a paradisiac state of creation, now he introduced a new species of *Kreatur*—one that redefined itself through destruction and voracity. "While the old concept of *Kreatur* found its point of departure in love . . . the new concept of *Kreatur*, that of the *Unmensch*, starts from voracity, insofar as the cannibal at once satisfies his relation to his fellow human together with the desire for food" (*GS* 2:1,106). As traditional forms of experience waned, the *Unmensch* announced a new type of experience (*Erfahrung*), that of incorporation (*GS* 2:1,105). The figure of the cannibal thus proved related to Benjamin's theory of experience at the center of the Baudelaire essay and "Experience and Poverty" (1933).[19] Using unmistakable Krausian language, "Experience and Poverty" ascribed the entropy that typified humankind and the accompanying *Erfahrungsarmut* (poverty of experience) of modern man to the sluggishness and saturation that set in after humanity's feasting on too much culture (*GS* 2:218). Much like the Kraus study, the programmatic "Experience and Poverty" called for a relinquishing of the worn-out icons of mankind in the hope of achieving a higher, new form of humanity, one that Benjamin, in a troubling reappropriation of Nietzsche's term, described as a new barbarity. Such would be the program of the new, revolutionary modernism Benjamin envisaged and in whose vanguard he counted the likes of Loos, Brecht, Klee, Scheerbart, and Ringelnatz. Forging its new ideal of humanity by means of the artistic technique of construction, revolutionary modernism, Benjamin predicted, would destroy all metaphysical forms of artistic creativity. At the origin, then, lay originary destruction. Invoking the language of revolutionary self-generation, Benjamin argued for the drastic elimination of all metaphysical notions of origin that still believed in an original purity or fetishized a benign form of nature. In this way, the essay radically transformed the Marxist production paradigm when it suggested that technology (*techne*) was to imitate nature's destruction (*phusis*).

Benjamin's language of revolutionary destruction seemed influenced by the modernist utopianism that Adolf Loos championed in "Die moderne Siedlung" (The Modern Settlement; 1926). As Loos maintained, "if human work consists only of destruction, it is truly human, natural, noble work" (quoted in *R* 272; *GS* 2:366). The consequences Benjamin drew from this position merit considerable attention:

For far too long the accent was placed on creativity. People are only creative to the extent that they avoid tasks and supervision. Work as a supervised task—its model: political and technical work—is attended by dirt and detritus, intrudes destructively into matter, is abrasive to what is already achieved, critical toward its conditions, and is in all this opposite to that of the dilettante luxuriating in creation. His work is innocent and pure, consuming and purifying masterliness. And therefore the monster (*Unmensch*) stands among us as the messenger of a more real humanism. He is the conqueror of the empty phrase. He feels solidarity not with the slender pine but with the plane that devours it, not with the precious ore but with the blast furnace that purifies it. The average European has not succeeded in uniting his life with technology, because he has clung to the fetish of creative existence. One must have followed Loos in his struggle with the dragon "ornament," heard the stellar Esperanto of Scheerbart's creations, or seen Klee's *Angelus Novus*, who preferred to free men by taking from them, rather than make them happy by giving to them, to understand a humanity that proves itself by destruction. (*R* 272–73; *GS* 2:366–67)

Not only did the passage realign the praxis of critique to the destructive force of technology, but also it firmly tied together and brought to a close the complex relations between language and technology that Benjamin had established at the beginning of the Kraus essay. Indeed, his Kraus interpretation can be called innovative in that it sought to uncover how his destructive language politics was interwoven with an equally destructive notion of technology. The progressive technologization to which the German language had been submitted, for example, became especially apparent in the empty phrase (*Phrase*), which Kraus abhorred. The excess of ornamental phrases Kraus despised in the work of his fellow journalists documented not only to what extent German had been degraded and instrumentalized but also that it was the abortive product of technology, expressing the changed function language acquired during high capitalism. "The empty phrase of the kind so relentlessly pursued by Kraus is the label that makes a thought marketable, the way flowery language, as ornament, gives it value for the connoisseur" (*R* 242; *GS* 2:337).

In keeping, however, with Benjamin's work of the 1930s, technology proved to be dialectical in nature. If his Brecht interpretations and the artwork essay propagated the utopian dimension of a liberated technology, other texts, such as the Jünger review or the postscript to the technology essay, warned against the fascist exploitation of technology, language, and the media. Thus, even though the ornamental phrase was the label (*Wahrenzeichen*) that pointed to language's commodification and heightened rationalization, it nonetheless could become the site of possible redemption: "the liberation of language has become identical with that of the empty phrase—its transformation from reproduction to productive instrument" (ibid.). Such a redemptive kernel, Benjamin conjectured in "Experience and Poverty," lay lodged in the progressive dehumanization of language, illustrated by the pervasive changes to which Russian had been subjected after the October Revolution, or by Paul Scheerbart's "stellar Esperanto." Commenting on the characters of Scheerbart's utopian science fiction *Lesabéndio,* a novel he greatly admired, Benjamin remarked:

These creatures already speak a completely new language. For the most decisive of their characteristics is their penchant for the randomly constructive, namely in contrast to the organic. This is the unmistakable trait that marks the language of Scheerbart's human beings or better people. For they reject human likeness—this principle of humanism. They do so even in their proper names; Peka, Labu, Sofanti, and similar ones are the names of the people in this book, whose title is the name of its hero, *Lesabéndio.* The Russians too like to give their children "dehumanized" names: they call them October after the revolutionary month or Pjatiletka after the five-year plan, or Awiachim after an aircraft carrier. This is not a technical innovation of language but its mobilization in the service of the struggle or of work; in any case, it is put to the service of the alteration of reality, not its description. (*GS* 2:216–17)

The image of this new dehumanized humanity no longer conformed to the old ideal of Europe to be found in the writings of Paul Valéry, "the man at the cape of his thought, who peers, as intently as he can, for the limits of things or human sight" (*GS* 2:390). Instead of navigating the European ship of humanism, the revolutionary artists Benjamin heralded were the passengers on an allegorical ship called *Poverty*—in obvious reference to the essay "Experience and Poverty"— "which carries these emigrants from the Europe of humanism into the promised land of the cannibals" (*GS* 2:1,112) and whose blind passenger was Kraus, showing that the model for this new linguistic and technological revolution lay encapsulated in Kraus's writings.

The most important messenger (or passenger) of real humanism, however, was Klee's *Angelus Novus*. Toward the end of the Kraus essay, Benjamin drew the following profile of this creature:

Neither purity nor sacrifice mastered the demon; but where origin and de-struction come together, his rule is over. Like a creature sprung from the child and the cannibal his conqueror stands before him: not a new man; a monster, a new angel. Perhaps one of those who, according to the Tal-mud, are at each moment created anew in countless throngs, and who, once they have raised their voices before God, cease and pass into nothingness. Lamenting, chastising, or rejoicing? No matter—on this evanescent voice the ephemeral work of Kraus is modeled. Angelus—that is the messenger in the old engravings. (*R* 273; *GS* 2:367)

To be sure, the image of these ephemeral angels, who perished as they raised their voices in hymnic jubilation, had appeared earlier in Benjamin's "Ankündigung der Zeitschrift: Angelus Novus" (An-nouncement of the Journal *Angelus Novus*; 1922).[20] What warrants special consideration, however, is that the Kraus essay now accented the destructive nature of Klee's angel. This emphasis contrasts markedly with the melancholic angel of history evoked in the later theses on history. For, as the *Unmensch*'s most exalted manifestation, Klee's angel suddenly revealed its other, dark side, that of an animal-like predatory angel (*Raubengel*) equipped with claws: "New angel is the name of this painting. It is a cannibalistic angel; perhaps a predatory angel, which would rather liberate men by taking them than make them happy by giving to them" (*GS* 2:1,106, 1,112). Not only the claws but also the predatory nature of the angel point ahead to the fragment *Agesilaus Santander,* which Benjamin wrote two years after completing the Kraus study during his exile on Ibiza. Scholem observed that the title of the Ibiza fragment was in fact a near-anagram of "Der Angelus Satanas" (The Satanic Angel).[21] The violence that beset Benjamin's satanic angel far exceeded the destructiveness that distinguished the angel of the apocalypse.[22] Nor did this angel easily fit into the tradition of orthodox angelology, which, from pseudo-Dionysus to Meister Eckhart, regarded the angel to be an intermediary, a "hermeneut of the silence of the superior worlds, who restlessly passes between the visible and the invisible, witness and icon of the invisible."[23] Instead, as Scholem observed, the angel's inhumanity and his lack of human features showed a remarkable break with "the old angelogical tradition, according to which the angel of man preserves his pure, primeval [*urbildlich*] shape and thus resembles a human being."[24] By invoking this monstrous angel as the ultimate figure of the *Unmensch,* Benjamin revealed the double meaning of the term itself. No longer did it simply denote the common notion of brute, used in colloquial German, but now it evoked a creature that—no longer purely human—surpassed all humans.

Initally, it is tempting to see in Benjamin's angel a version of Nietzsche's over-man, along lines similar to Heidegger's interpretation of the angel that appears in Rilke's *Duino Elegies.* And, indeed, it rightly has been argued that Benjamin's language at times comes uncannily close to Nietzsche's.[25] Not only does the program for a new barbarism allude to *On the Genealogy of Morals,* but the predatorlike angel or *Raubengel* recalls Nietzsche's *Raubtier.*[26] At the same time, it must be noted that Benjamin carefully distinguished the *Unmensch* from the hedonism of Nietzsche's *Übermensch,* who was to overcome the "Krankheit Mensch" (the illness of being human). In a discussion of how Kraus's notion of happiness celebrated sensuality while being tempered by resignation, Benjamin noted, "one must visualize [this form of happiness] if one is to understand the urgency with which he opposed the importance the dance had for Nietzsche—not to mention the wrath with which the inhuman was bound to greet the over-man" (*R* 266; *GS* 2:361). Instead of celebrating Nietzsche, Benjamin saw his own theory of the *Unmensch,* which he claimed to have taken from Salomo Friedländer, as a corrective to the over-man.[27] Benjamin's desire to expel the specter of Nietzschean politics can also be gleaned from one of the notes to a draft version of the Kraus essay, which stated, "deepest opposition to Nietzsche: the relation of the inhuman to the over-man" (*GS* 2:1,103). Perhaps Benjamin aspired to hold the disturbing shadow of Nietzsche's over-man at bay by means of the category of sobriety, which was to dispel the irrationalism of Nietzschean intoxication. This sobriety, he thought, was most eloquently expressed in one of Kraus's self-critical aphorisms that summed up the gist of his satirical work: "All my errors stay behind to lead me" (*R* 273; *GS* 2:367).

Like Bloch, Benjamin sought to unite a Feuerbachian materialism with Jewish theology.[28] The closing paragraph to the Kraus essay suggests that the kind of revolutionary destruction Benjamin envisioned was to take the form of a divine, Judaic justice whose force was lodged in language. Divine justice alone, Benjamin believed, could bring to a halt the duplicities (*Zweideutigkeiten*) of profane law, as these formed the subject of Kraus's *Sittlichkeit und Kriminalität* (Morality and Criminal Justice). In an earlier fragment on Kraus, used as an addendum to *One-Way Street*, Benjamin likewise tried to delineate what he called Kraus's "Jewish physiognomy" (*GS* 2:1,433). As he observed: "In Kraus takes place the grand breakthrough of the exegesis of the Halacha through the German language. One doesn't understand anything about this great man as long as one does not recognize that everything, of necessity and without exception—language and fact—transpires in the sphere of right. . . . His entire fire-eating, sword-swallowing philology in his newspapers at bottom does not pursue language but right" (*GS* 2:624–25).[29] While this early text distinguished language from law, that distinction was no longer upheld in the 1931 essay. If, as that essay maintained, Kraus's work attested to a Jewish *salto mortale*, it was because it founded justice and language in one another: "To worship the image of divine justice in language—even in the German language—that is the genuinely Jewish somersault by which he tries to break the spell of the demon" (*R* 254; *GS* 2:349).

At issue was the relation between profane law or right and a divine Judaic form of justice. This more authentic principle of justice manifested itself in Kraus's citational politics, insofar as language revealed its force as the "Mater der Gerechtigkeit" (Matrix of Justice):

In the quotation that both saves and chastises, language proves the matrix of justice. It summons the word by its name, wrenches it destructively from its context, but precisely thereby calls it back to its origin. It appears, now with rhyme and reason, sonorously, congruously, in the structure of a new text. As rhyme it gathers the similar into its aura; as name it stands alone and expressionless. In quotation the two realms—of origin and destruction—justify themselves before language. And conversely, only where they interpenetrate—in quotation—is language consummated. In it is mirrored the angelic tongue in which all words, startled from the idyllic context of meaning, have become mottoes in the book of Creation. (*R* 269; *GS* 2:363)

Interestingly, the passage reads like a synopsis of Benjamin's own theory of language. Not only was the technique of citation foundational to his own writing project, as is evident in the *Trauerspiel* book or the Arcades Project, but, by associating the politics of citation with rhyme and the theory of the name, the passage also explicitly referred back to the early language essay and to Benjamin's discussion of the baroque's theory of language. In a passage that resonated with his earlier theory of origin, Benjamin cited Kraus's aphorism, "The origin is the goal," which he now—on one level at least— interpreted as Kraus's return to creatural language through the euphony of rhyme: "This ['origin']—the phenomenon's seal of authenticity—is the subject of a discovery that has a curious element of rediscovery. The theater of this philosophical recognition scene in Kraus's work is poetry, and its language rhyme" (*R* 266; *GS* 2:360).[30] The technique of rhyming remained the prerogative of the child, which "recognizes by rhyme that it has reached the summit of language, from which it can hear at the origin the rushing of all sources" (*R* 266; *GS* 2:361). Discussing Kraus's lectures on Offenbach, Benjamin suggested that Kraus's prose often lowered the word to the level of humming or the "mere creaturely voice" (*GS* 2:358)—in other words, to the level of the originary *Lautsprache* that was at the heart of baroque conceptions of language. Thus the Nürnberger school, Benjamin declared in the *Trauerspiel* study, regarded all phonetic phenomena as the manifestation of original, creatural language, which was marked by an "onomatopoeic structure" (*O* 204; *GS* 1:379). Citing from Böhme's *De signatura rerum,* according to which original language amounted to a "natural language [*Natursprache*] in which everything speaks according to its capacity and always reveals itself," Benjamin added, "spoken language is thus the domain of the free, spontaneous utterance of the creature, whereas the written language of allegory enslaves objects in the eccentric embrace of meaning" (*O* 202; *GS* 1:377–78). This adulation of primeval sound at the heart of baroque drama was reinvigorated in opera, a musical genre that directly developed out of the mourning play. Precisely this celebration of pure sound, typical of the operatic tradition, was revived in Kraus's work, whenever he pushed the word to its phonic limits, until "it finally enfeebles itself, dissolving into a merely creatural voice: a humming that is to the word what his smile is to the joke, is the holy of holies of this performer's art" (*R* 264; *GS* 2:358).[31]

Just as the *Trauerspiel* study held a language of names against the postlapsarian leveling of language to mere semantics and the logic of the proposition, so the Kraus essay argued that pure phonicity and rhyme were to be counterbalanced by the force of the name. As the lyric poets of the George circle had demonstrated, the adulation of sound could easily turn into an ecstatic, irrationalistic reverence for the *Wortleib*. Kraus's work escaped this fate only through the presence of a "Jewish certainty": "the sanctification of the name" (*R* 265; *GS* 2:359). "As rhyme, language rises up from the creaturely world; as name, it draws all creation up to it" (*R* 268; *GS* 2:362). And, "from the linguistic realm of the name, and only from within it, can we discern Kraus's basic polemical procedure: quotation. To quote a word is to call it by its name" (*R* 268; *GS* 2:362). Thus, a redemptive force lay embedded in Kraus's politics of citation—a force that, paradoxically, united both origin (rhyme) and the violence of divine destruction (name). In citation, which Benjamin called the "Mater der Gerechtigkeit," profane judicial language or the level of mere judgment (*Urteil*)—a word that again telescoped both fallen language and the fallen law of the profane, legal verdict—were radically shattered.

Only when placed, then, within the frame of this theory of language does Benjamin's disturbing call for violence appear somewhat tempered, if, to be sure, not fully abetted. This ardent belief in the redemptive power of language in fact remained a constant in his thought. Indeed, Benjamin never entirely abandoned the belief that the impetuous blow dealt by language in reality paid witness to the redemptive intervention of "an other" kind of justice or right—a divine manifestation of justice that could dispel the inadequacies of secular law.

CHAPTER 8

The Mythical Origins
of the Law

From the earliest period on through to the writings of
the 1930s, Benjamin's work probed questions of law and justice. Many
of his early texts called to account the predominance of "mere life"
(*das bloße Leben*),[1] nature, and naturality, which was often associated
with fate or the demonic. If Benjamin took to task the relics of these
mythical forces as they subsisted in the secular judicial system, he did so
mostly in the name of a divine justice and law. While, as we saw earlier,
Benjamin's critique of mere life was part of his sustained interrogation of
contemporary forms of animism, vitalism, biologism, and Darwinism,
the issue also merits a reexamination from yet another vantage point.
For inasmuch as these writings privileged a "just existence" over mere
life, they also invite a rethinking of the relation between nature and
Judaic forms of law and ethics. At the same time, one must ask to
what extent a distinction needs to be made between the early work
and the later literary essays on Leskov, Kraus, and Kafka. However,
before the intersections between nature and Judaic law in Benjamin's
work can be addressed, these terms must be set off from the negative
evaluation Judaism's alleged relation to nature has received in the
course of German idealism.

The historical and philosophical constructions to which biblical and
postbiblical Talmudic Judaism have been subjected in German idealism have been well documented.[2] In his *Jews and German Philosophy*,
Nathan Rotenstreich showed how Kant's philosophical and political de-
valuation of Judaism was based on its so-called statutory, heteronomous
character, which deprived it of the moral value he reserved for

the autonomous law and subject of his moral philosophy.[3] The shift that took place with objective idealism, evident in that Kant now could be called "the Moses of our nation,"[4] was most significant in Hegel's system. Hegel regarded the concept of *Sittlichkeit* that he developed in his *Philosophy of Right* to announce the overcoming of so-called Jewish abstraction, which he thought still afflicted Kant's formalistic morality (*Moralität*). In the fact that the Kantian subject remained separated from community, judicial law, and state, Hegel perceived a structural similarity to the abstractness he posited as constitutive of Judaism. His juvenile theological writings, *The Spirit of Christianity*, laid the foundations for the dialectical relation between abstract Judaism and organic Christianity—a relation that would still inform the dialectic of spirit of the *Phenomenology* and also underpin the *Philosophy of Right*.[5] Calling Judaism a religion of "separation" in which the Jewish people remained divided from their God, Hegel established Judaism as an earlier, more "natural" stage within the development of humankind, a stage that had been overcome and sublated by Christianity. How influential this Hegelian construction of Judaism would become was noted by Julius Carlebach, who further traced its repercussions in Feuerbach's anthropology and Marx's materialism.[6]

In his monumental *Glas*, Jacques Derrida analyzed in great detail the operations to which Hegel subjected the figure of Judaism in his *Spirit of Christianity*. Reading Hegel against the grain, Derrida pitted the Judaic—which now figured as the materialistic remnant or relic (*reste*) that obstructed the movement of sublation—against Hegel's image of Christianity and Christian love, which attested to the dialectical unification of the general and the concrete. In so doing, Derrida addressed Judaism's supposed hostile relationship to nature and the natural. As he showed, in idealism the privileged figure for this scission with nature was Abraham's departure from Chaldea, which received its most telling commentary in Hegel's *Jugendschriften*. For Hegel, Abraham's nomadic journey through the desert and his covenant with God, sealed through circumcision—a nonsublatable cut—was symptomatic of a fundamental rupture, symbolizing the Jews' alienation from earth, family, love, and beauty.[7] In contrast to the loving relation Greek culture entertained with organic nature, Judaism petrified nature, Hegel maintained, using mythical language that recalled the petrifying gaze of the Medusa.[8]

In her "Torah, cosmos et nature" and *L'Alliance avec la nature* (The Alliance with Nature), Catherine Chalier likewise refuted the received notion that Judaic law—as laid down in the Torah—was premised on the destructive domination of nature. Opposing traditional and more recent theories that speak of a rift between nature and history or that accept the alleged abstract nature of Judaism, she held that, while Judaic law was indeed "super-natural" in character, Judaism did not advocate a radical caesura from nature. As she demonstrated in *L'Alliance avec la nature*, Noah's covenant (*alliance*) with God, recorded in Genesis 9:10, did not condone anthropocentrism to the exclusion of nature. The two currents that interlaced in Judaism could not be explained by the co-presence of a Jewish cosmic mysticism, on the one hand, and a strict ethico-historical interpretation of the Torah, on the other. Instead, Chalier maintained, the observance of the law presupposed a respect for nature. Thus she granted that the Torah prescribed the observance of a "supernatural" transcendent law—"this intrusion of the supernatural in nature which is called revelation"[9]—that found its bodily inscription in circumcision. And, she added, Judaism indeed assumed a notion of the good that was separated from the human and natural realms—a conception that was historically different from either stoicism's cosmic worldview or Aristotle's ethics, which was anchored in human *phronēsis*. Nonetheless, in such diverse phenomena as the orthodox observance of the Talmudic *mitsvot*, which followed a liturgical, cosmic temporality,[10] or Levinas's "humanism of the other man," one recognized manifestations of a profoundly ethical relation to nature. Similarly, Abraham's departure from Chaldea had to be interpreted as a rejection of *mythical* nature, as the refusal, that is, to be determined by one's place of birth. Instead of a restrictive hermeneutics of the book, Chalier argued, was to come a hermeneutics of nature, "the only [hermeneutics] able to open the field of thinking and human sensibility to the generosity of welcoming the Other in the self."[11]

The complexities that shape these critical perspectives must be taken into account if one is to gauge fully Benjamin's thoughts on law, justice, and the natural order. If references to the fallen nature of profane law abound in his work, it is in his 1921 essay "Critique of Violence" [Zur Kritik der Gewalt] that Benjamin provided his most systematic analysis of the judicial system in its distinctions from divine justice. The title of the essay must be taken in at least a double sense, as the term *Gewalt* indicates. For the essay not only critically differentiated mythical, judicial, and divine manifestations of violence but also furnished a critique of "legitimate powers"[12]—that is, of institutional forms of authority, including the legal system, and the reign (*walten*) of divine violence.

Hoping to provide a general historico-philosophical analysis of violence, "Critique of Violence" charted the genealogy of a profane form of violence, which it traced from earliest mythical times, ruled by the "guilt of mere natural life" (R 297; GS 2:200), through its institutionalization in jus naturale and statutory right, to nineteenth- and twentieth-century forms of vitalism, specifically Darwinism and activism.

At first in his analysis, Benjamin took natural law to task. Based on the principle that the cause justified the means, jusnaturalism saw violence as a natural product (*Rohstoff*), much as Darwin's biology had done. However, positive, statutory right likewise did not escape the demonic, fatelike duplicity (*Zweideutigkeit*) of mythical thinking. Not even Kant's moral philosophy, Benjamin added, fully avoided being entrapped in mythical forces and demonic fate. Critical of Kant's moral system, the essay nonetheless appropriated his conceptual framework, as signaled by the fact that it found its methodological point of departure in transcendental critique (*Kritik*).[13] Furthermore, Benjamin's essay hoped to bring about a decisive rupture in the circular (Kantian) relation between means and end, upon which both natural law and statutory, or positive, right were based. As Günter Figal has observed, Kant's moral philosophy, with its notion of "just ends," subscribed to a means–end relationship that Benjamin aimed to undermine by way of a "politics of pure means" and a justice as "pure ends."[14] Kant's second formulation of the categorical imperative in the *Foundations of the Metaphysics of Morals*[15] did not, Benjamin held, safeguard against the usage of the other as means. In seeking to recognize the interests of humanity in every individual citizen, positive right merely preserved an "order imposed by fate" (R 285; GS 2:187). The degree to which law-preserving violence remained faithful to its mythical, violent origin was evident in the penal system and capital punishment.

In an earlier text, "Fate and Character" (1919), Benjamin likewise identified the judicial system with mythical violence, charging that it remained entangled in life, fate, and guilt (*Schuld, Verschuldung*). Starting with a discussion of the stoic tradition, which established fate and character as causally connected, Benjamin showed how its philosophy of eternal return culminated in Nietzsche's conception of character, evident when the latter observed that "if a man has character, he has an experience that constantly recurs" (R 306; GS 2:173). Seeking to disengage character and fate from one another, Benjamin nonetheless saw a common denominator for both. Apart from the fact that character and fate traditionally had been determined on the basis of physiognomical or other natural signs (*Zeichen der Natur*), they were related to natural man and mere life (*R* 308–9; *GS* 2:176). Benjamin thus sought to set aright yet another philosophical tradition, the one that, in relegating fate or destiny to the realm of religion, regarded the concept of character—as in Kant's notion of "intelligible character"—as the guarantor of moral freedom. In the same way that the "pseudo-moral" conception of character needed to be dislodged from ethics, so fate had to be disconnected from a theological framework and to find its proper place in the judicial system.

In several other writings, as noted, Benjamin likewise mounted a critique against what he considered to be the vestiges of mythical guilt—be it the classical form of guilt typical of the Attic-Ionic tragedies or the Christian originary guilt of the sort displayed in Calderón's drama of fate. Guilt for Benjamin to no small degree remained a metaphysical concept, unfit to be the grounding principle of an ethics of action. Further, natural law also was to be sworn off in that it allowed punitive judgment and conviction to precede action: "Fate shows itself, therefore, in the view of life, as condemned, as having, at bottom, first been condemned and then become guilty" (*R* 307–8; *GS* 2:175). The law did not instate just punishment but condemned its subjects to guilt and, in the final analysis, to expiation or atonement. Guilt could be atoned only through mythical sacrifice, showing that the law was a relic of humanity's primitive, demonic prehistory—"a residue of the demonic stage of human existence" (*R* 307; *GS* 2:174).

As Benjamin acknowledged in "Critique of Violence," Hermann Cohen had been the first to condemn what he had called the "natural law" of fate when he argued that the mythical realm itself gave rise to the emergence of evil.[16] In a section of his *Ethics* titled "Fate and Guilt," Cohen had established the rigid connections among fate, guilt, and blood that would become so central to Benjamin's own understanding of law's mythic foundations. In the mythical frame of mind, Cohen contended, fate could take its course over an entire generation only because kinship or blood relations were considered to be natural.[17] Benjamin closely followed Cohen's argument when in "Fate and Character" he established that morality was to be located in the realm of action. Thus he hoped radically to demarcate morality from the immorality of fate. As early as 1916, Benjamin had posited in "*Trauerspiel* and Tragedy" that the demonic realm of right was overcome only by the arrival of the tragic hero, who presented the earliest manifestation of the moral individual.[18] Yet, despite Benjamin's indebtedness to Cohen, there remained seminal differences between their views of the mythical. Cohen's transcendental project, which underpinned his attempt to establish an ethics of the pure will, sought to propose the science of law as a pure "theoretical factum"—that is, as the "mathematics" of the human sciences, analogous to the role mathematics had fulfilled for the natural sciences.[19] Thus he hoped to overcome what he considered to be Kant's fallacy, namely his separation of the "Rechtslehre" (doctrine of right) from the "Sittenlehre" (doctrine of ethics).[20] In consequence, Cohen carefully distinguished the notion of guilt from the realm of law, which could be defined only by the Roman judicial concepts of *dolus* or *culpa*. That is to say, while guilt in the sense of *Schuld* was relegated to the domains of religion, myth, and tragedy, the realm of law was ruled by self-determination and self-responsibility—an "action based on the regulations of causal thinking."[21] It is evident, however, that within Benjamin's conceptual framework no such transcendental position could be granted to the discipline of right, unable as it was to escape the mythical reign of fate altogether.

Benjamin's analysis of the law in "Critique of Violence" did not only aim at the primitive law of restitution (*Fehderecht*) that manifested itself in the trial by ordeal, the blood feud, or the practice of the Greek *pharmakos*.[22] It was as much directed at profane law, which failed to break with the restitutive economy of ritualistic, sacrificial practices. If in ancient Greek mythology the gods violently demarcated right from wrong, then law, he argued, did the same, as evidenced by the calamitous expiation or retribution that befell those who, in primitive times, infringed upon unwritten laws. To make this point, Benjamin invoked the Greek myth of Niobe—a reference perhaps motivated by Hölderlin's reference to Niobe in his annotations to *Antigone*. The mythical force of profane law was like the immediate, nonmediated violence exemplified in the story of Niobe, for her punishment at the hands of the gods served to establish their pure presence and power—in other words, the pure instating of right. Not until the rise of Prometheus, whose saga announced the birth of the modern tragic hero, would the ancient rights of the gods be contested. The crux of Benjamin's argument thus was directed at the distinction that needed to be made between the primitive violence of Greek mythology, on the one hand, and the divine, pure violence of biblical Judaism, on the other. The biblical account of the company of Korah demonstrated that divine, just violence was bloodless and expiatory as distinct from inauthentic justice, which had been incorporated into profane law.

Whereas "mythical violence is bloody power over mere life for its own sake, divine violence [is] pure power over all life for the sake of the living [*um des Lebendigen willen*]" (*R* 297; *GS* 2:200).

It was this mythical violence that not only returned in the modern judicial system but also found philosophical validation in contemporary forms of vitalism. Invoking the divine commandment "Thou shalt not kill," Benjamin concluded that the only sanctioned exception to this law in Judaism, namely, the right to self-defense, offered an implicit critique of those who sought to found the divine commandment on the "doctrine of the sanctity of life" (*R* 298; *GS* 2:201). At issue in this critique was Kurt Hiller, whose activism Benjamin earlier had criticized in a now lost polemical text, "Es gibt keine geistigen Arbeiter" (There Are No Intellectual Workers; *C* 160; *B* 235).[23] In *Anti-Kain*, Hiller had opposed "intellectual terrorism," which sanctioned certain forms of death, holding instead that "'we, however, profess that higher even than the happiness and justice of existence [*Dasein*] stands existence itself'" (*R* 298; *GS* 2:201). Benjamin saw in Hiller's assertion a reversal of the relationship between "mere life" and justice. In a passage that at first sight seemed to announce a form of Judaic humanism, Benjamin granted Hiller's statements a certain validity, if and only if the word *Dasein* was interpreted as "the irreducible, total condition that is 'man'" (*R* 299; *GS* 2:201)—not as mere life:

Man cannot, at any price, be said to coincide with the mere life in him, no more than with any other of his conditions and qualities, not even with the uniqueness of his bodily person. However sacred man is (or that life in him that is identically present in earthly life, death, and afterlife), there is no sacredness in his condition, in his bodily life vulnerable to injury by his fellow men. What, then, distinguishes it essentially from the life of animals and plants? And even if these were sacred, they could not be so by virtue only of being alive, of being in life. It might be well worth while to track down the origin of the dogma of the sacredness of life. Perhaps, indeed probably, it is relatively recent, the last mistaken attempt of the weakened Western tradition to seek the saint it has lost in cosmological impenetrability. (*R* 299; *GS* 2:201–2)

In Hiller's vitalism, Benjamin merely saw a nostalgia for the irrecuperable, irrevocable loss of the sacred, which needed to be radically distinguished from the ancient laws of Deuteronomy. What he above all challenged was the "ontology of life" that founded vitalism. For despite the apparent modernity of Hiller's belief in the sanctity of all life, vitalism conferred sacredness on that which, "according to ancient mythical thought [was] the marked bearer of guilt: life itself" (*R* 299; *GS* 2:202). Hiller's vitalism was a modern version of mythical violence, on this side of divine justice.

Derrida rightly has underscored that Benjamin's emphasis on the primacy of "the yet-to-come [*avenir*] of justice"[24] didn't only take the form of an interrogation of vitalism and biologism of the sort one finds in Heidegger's philosophical project. More important, it "[proceeds] like the awakening of Judaic tradition."[25] To this it could be added that Benjamin's insistence on divine justice further seems akin to Levinas's rejection of vitalism in the interview "The Paradox of Morality." Asked to comment on the theme of animality in Derrida's thought, Levinas responded that the animal could only be said to have a "face" on the basis of an analogy with the human face. Thus, he noted, "it is clear that, without considering animals as human beings, the ethical extends to all living beings. We do not want to make an animal suffer needlessly and so on. But the prototype of this is human ethics. Vegetarianism, for example, arises from the transference to animals of the idea of suffering."[26] Proposing an unorthodox reading of *Being and Time,* Levinas posited that Heidegger's conception of *Dasein* proved mired in Darwinian vitalism, evidenced by the category of *Sorge* or "care for one's being." In Levinas's ethics, to the contrary, vitalism had been radically ruptured by the advent of ethical man, who fundamentally separated himself from being and "the struggle for life." As Levinas observed:

You ask at what moment one becomes a face. I do not know at what moment the human appears, but what I want to emphasize is that the human *breaks with* pure being, which is always a persistence in being. This is my principal thesis. A being is something that is attached to being, to its own being. That is Darwin's idea. The being of animals is a struggle for life. A struggle for life without ethics. It is a question of might. Heidegger says at the beginning of *Being and Time* that *Dasein* is a being who in his being is concerned for this being itself. That's Darwin's idea: the living being struggles for life. The aim of being is being itself. However, with the appearance of the human—and this is my entire philosophy—there is something more important than my life, and that is the life of the other.[27]

Levinas's interpretation of *Being and Time* as an existential version of Darwinism must be called a "misreading" of sorts, since Heidegger's concept of *Dasein* was explicitly directed against the "ontology of life" that upheld vitalism. At the same time, this misreading served all the better to profile Levinas's conviction that justice could only be anterior to, or more primordial than, any ontology. Although "Critique of Violence" should not simply be conflated with Levinas's humanism of the other man, one can nevertheless read his vision of a disruptive, destructive violence, which came to dissolve all legal and mythical violence—no more than the "guilt of mere natural life"—as an attempt to reinstate a more primordial justice.

What needs to be stressed is that Benjamin's attempt to distinguish human beings from plants and animals, in the passage cited earlier, was based not on a "metaphysical" moment of rupture but rather on the category of justice. That is, this distinction between humans and "the living" was not ascribed to reflection, consciousness, representation, or any of the other human faculties that, as we shall see, guided Rilke's interpretation of man's privative relation to the Open (*das Offene*) in the *Duino Elegies*. Rather, the shattering of mythical violence was placed within the horizon of divine justice and, consequently, a divine form of violence that could no longer be gauged from the perspective of a theory of law and its decrepit politics of indecisiveness (*Unentscheidbarkeit*; *R* 293; *GS* 2:196). Instead, divine violence transpired as an eruptive caesura, exploding the precinct of "raging life" (*das wogende Leben*; *GS* 1:181), as Benjamin would term it in the well-known passage from the "Wahlverwandschaften" essay.[28] Seen within the perspective of Benjamin's philosophy of history, the Darwinian notion of history as a process of selection, marked by the dogmatic view that violence was "the only original means, besides natural selection, appropriate to all the vital ends of nature" (*R* 278; *GS* 2:180), was to make way for "a new historical epoch" (*R* 300; *GS* 2:202) of the sort envisioned toward the end of "Critique of Violence." In a later book review about the crisis of Darwinism, which he wrote on the occasion of a lecture by the biologist Edgar Dacqué, Benjamin still heralded this interruptive violence, recognizing it in the intellectual achievements of Husserl, Einstein, and Dacqué. There he wrote: "Husserl replaces the idealistic systems with discontinuous phenomenology; Einstein replaces infinite, continuous space with finite discontinuous space; Dacqué replaces an infinite becoming in flux with an ever renewed restarting of life in limited and countable forms" (*GS* 4:536).

That the confrontation between these two forms of history—the history of continuity and of a divine discontinuity—should take the form of an encounter between the myth of Niobe and the parable of the company of Korah, or between the Greek and the Judaic,[29] should not be cause for surprise. The same dialectic can be found in the earlier essays on Hölderlin and Goethe, where the Greek world of form (*morphē, eidos*), representation, and the symbolon was similarly shattered by the intervention of a "disruptive violence/power" (*schlagende Gewalt*)—although in the Hölderlin essay this force was qualified as the Oriental. As such, Benjamin's work, much like that of Cohen, was the product of the Greek-Hellenistic-Germanic psyche, with which these Jewish thinkers entered into discussion.[30] Perhaps no other text of Benjamin's better illustrates the extent to which this encounter between Greek, German, and Jewish cultures permeated his thought than his celebrated Kafka essay.

CHAPTER 9

Kafka's Animals

I at once appropriated for myself the Kafkaesque
formulation of the categorical imperative: "Act in such a
way that the angels have something to do."
Benjamin to Scholem, April 14, 1938[1]

When in 1934 Scholem responded to Benjamin's first draft of the Kafka essay, he hoped to call his attention to a possible contradiction and, at least, central omission in his analysis—namely, that in spite of the conspicuous position Judaic law occupied in Kafka's work Benjamin had failed to pay heed to the "*moral world of the Halakah*"[2] only to favor a profane exegesis of the law. Carried on mostly in letters, except for a brief encounter that took place in Paris in 1938, the discussion that ensued focused on Kafka's relation to the law, Judaic tradition, and its transmissibility (*Tradierbarkeit*). Already in a letter of August 1, 1931, Scholem made it clear how Benjamin was to proceed in reviewing Kafka's posthumously published *The Great Wall of China*—namely, by placing him squarely in the tradition of Jewish literature and the question of divine justice: "I advise you to begin any inquiry into Kafka with the Book of Job, or at least with a discussion of the possibility of divine judgment, which I regard as the sole subject of Kafka's production [worthy of] being treated in a work of literature." If to Scholem Kafka remained in essence a Halakist, who aimed to achieve the "*linguistic* paraphrase of a divine judgment,"[3] to Benjamin Kafka's prose instead showed up the remnants of a Haggadah that had been severed from the Halakah.

As the 1931 letter together with a didactic poem about *The Trial* Scholem sent to Benjamin in 1934 indicate,[4] Scholem's Kafka interpretation closely followed the theological reading first suggested by Margarete Susman—a reading that also partly defined Max Brod's understanding of Kafka. In her influential essay, "Das Hiob-Problem bei Kafka" (The problem of Hiob in Kafka's Work; 1929),[5] Susman held that Kafka's prose should be situated in the context of the questions of guilt and justice that the Book of Job raised. Job's singularity and individuality, as he rose against Jahweh, reflected the plight of Kafka's isolated characters. In this regard, her reading was markedly different from Adorno's later "Notes on Kafka." While Adorno acknowledged the importance of Judaic tradition in Kafka's work, he interpreted Kafka's "individualism" as a reflex to Kierkegaard's concept of interiority, thus, ironically, giving credence to the very Protestant, existentialist exegesis that Benjamin, for one, had criticized in Max Brod's and Willy Haas's Kafka interpretations.

But if Benjamin discredited Kafka's alleged indebtedness to Kierkegaard, neither did he accept Susman's thesis. Rather, his Kafka study addressed a different contradiction, one that in a plan to the 1931 lecture "Franz Kafka: The Great Wall of China" would be called the confrontation between, on the one hand, a forgotten, natural, guilt-laden primeval world (*Vorwelt*)—akin to Bachofen's "hetaeric natural being" (*BüK* 116)—and, on the other hand, Judaic law. In exposing a world filled with boglike creatures, animals, bastard offspring, half-forms, and "nebulous female creatures," Kafka's prose, Benjamin believed, uncovered the hidden side of the "legal world of Judaism" (ibid.) that resided in law itself. Thus his work revealed the natural stratum of religious law, whose traces were retained in the apotropaic normative prescriptions and ceremonial laws of the Halakah:

It is as if Kafka experimentally wanted to prove the much greater adequacy of the Torah by means of a prehistoric layer of humanity that it might itself hide. Yet this layer is not completely hidden in the Torah. The purification laws and laws of alimentation relate to a prehistoric world [*Vorwelt*], of which nothing has been retained except for the defense mechanisms against this world. In other words, only the Halakah retains the traces of this most remote existential state of humanity. Kafka's books contain the missing Haggadah to this Halakah. (ibid.)

In referring to Kafka's books as the missing rabbinical Haggadah, Benjamin introduced a term that would dominate the Kafka interpretation to follow, although the emphasis would shift from the Haggadah to the absent Halakah. Thus, in one of his 1931 diary entries that recorded his conversations with Brecht at Le Lavandou, Benjamin corrected the latter's attempt to recuperate Kafka for the cause of bolshevism. Because Kafka's works broke with the conventions of narrative prose, they were to be likened to the parabolic form of the Talmudic Haggadah—with this distinction, he hastened to add: that Kafka's Haggadah no longer reflected the normative, prescriptive doctrine (*Lehre*) of Halakah.

One might call to mind the form of the Haggadah; this is the name the Jews use for the stories and anecdotes of the Talmud, the ones that serve to explain and confirm the doctrine, the Halakah. The doctrine [*Lehre*], to be sure, nowhere is pronounced as such in Kafka. One can only try to read it from the astounding behavior of his humans, a behavior that either originated in fear or produces fear. (*BüK* 131)

Benjamin's contention that the teaching (*Lehre*) itself was absent from Kafka's work would become even more pronounced in the 1934 Kafka essay, leading Scholem to regard his reading as thoroughly misguided. At issue in the debate that unraveled as Benjamin revised the Kafka essay for publication was above all its final section, "Sancho Panza,"[6] which interpreted Kafka's students as "pupils who have lost the Holy Writ" (*I* 139; *BüK* 37)—that is, as rabbinical students whose commentaries were glosses in the margins of a place left empty. Repeatedly, Scholem cautioned that Kafka's work did not expose the complete absence of revelation in a so-called preanimistic or Bachofean world, as Benjamin held. Rather, his work showed the nonfulfillability of revelation. To accept the loss of the Torah meant to acknowledge the extinction and disappearance of revealed law. The nonfulfillment of revelation, by contrast, originated in human fallacy, as could be gleaned from the students' inability to decipher the fullness and richness of revelation. While revelation seemingly had been reduced to nothingness (*Nichts, Nullpunkt*), to "a state in which [it] appears to be without meaning, in which it still asserts itself, in which it has *validity* but no *significance*,"[7] this state merely amounted to a religious limit case (*Grenzfall*) illustrating the shortfalls of faith rather than the complete absence of the divine. If Scholem refused to see the parables as signs of the Torah's failure, Benjamin—more like Brecht—saw Kafka as one who had failed to transpose literature into the realm of religious doctrine.[8]

What already lay at the center of this controversy but would not come to the fore until a later exchange in 1938 was the issue of tradition as it pertained to religious doctrine.[9] Indeed, Benjamin's comments on Kafka harked back to thoughts on tradition and doctrine formulated in a letter of 1917 and to the discussions he had conducted with Scholem about Franz Joseph Molitor's study on tradition.[10] If earlier in our analysis Benjamin's reflections on tradition and modernity were primarily discussed in relation to hermeneutics and secular historiography, the Kafka essay and letters now unmistakably show that tradition for Benjamin also inherently referred to religious tradition. These two meanings of the word were at stake in a long letter Benjamin sent to his friend in 1938, which Scholem intended to present to the Schocken publishing house in an effort to land Benjamin a contract for another Kafka study.[11] In the letter—partly reproduced as "Some Reflections on Kafka" in *Illuminations* (*I* 141–45)[12]—Kafka's work was likened to an ellipse, of which one focal point represented modernity, the alienated experience (*Erfahrung*) of the modern urban dweller, while the other, at a far remove, was that of mystical experience and, above all, the experience of the cabala. In his essay "Offenbarung und Tradition als religiöse Kategorien im Judentum" (Revelation and Tradition as Religious Categories in Judaism), Scholem has documented how the term "cabala" literally meant "the reception of tradition."[13] As a class name, it stood for that branch of Jewish mysticism that, opposing the rabbinical notion of the written Torah, believed in the historical transmission of the *Ur-Thora* as an oral, living voice. According to Benjamin, the experience of modernity appeared mediated through mystic, cabalistic experience, as was apparent in Kafka's *Amerika*, in which mystical angels became statues for the extras in the Natural Theater of Oklahoma. Kafka's writings, then, fundamentally depicted the decline of this mystic tradition. As such, the mechanical, theatrical gestures with which Kafka's students leafed through the scriptures were similar to the loss of living tradition Benjamin captured in the trope of allegory. Allegory, as he argued in the *Trauerspiel* study, retained the relics of a past religious era, exposing the empty shrouds of the antique gods who had fled. Similarly, Kafka's parabolic writings came to stand for the Haggadah, severed from the Halakah, thus signaling the emptying out of Judaic tradition.

In what would seem to be an ironic displacement of the Judaic theologeme of "hearing," Benjamin turned Kafka into a failed prophet, destined to eavesdrop on a tradition that was no longer a living presence. What was left to register were mere rumors, spread by a theological whispered "newspaper" of rumors, for there was "no doctrine [*Lehre*] one could absorb, no knowledge one could preserve" (*R* 143; *BüK* 86). In this respect, Kafka's work exposed the "sickness of tradition." To underscore further the ailments of this tradition, Benjamin quoted from "The Storyteller" (1936), thus revealing the affinity between both studies: "wisdom," he wrote, "has sometimes been defined as the epic side of truth. Such a definition stamps wisdom as inherent in tradition; it is truth in its haggadic consistency" (*R* 143). If the loss of tradition in modernity meant the waning of wisdom or truth's "epic side," then what was really lost was the wisdom of the Jewish storyteller or the rabbinical narrator of parables. His stories, insofar as they had been laid down in the Haggadah, could never be renewed, never transmitted anew. What distinguished Kafka from other modernists, however, was that, while he relinquished truth, he nonetheless sought to retain its transmissibility (*Tradierbarkeit*) in the form of parables (*Gleichnisse*). To cast Benjamin's observations in an image: if the Haggadic parable figured as a metonymic part to the whole, then in Kafka's work the part had outgrown the whole, much like the monstrous figure of Odradek, who *survived* the primal father (*Urvater*), and much like the lowly animal creatures of the stories, who usurped all human form. Thus the parables "do not modestly lie at the feet of the doctrine [*Lehre*], as the Haggadah lies at the feet of the Halakah. Though apparently reduced to submission, they unexpectedly heave a mighty paw against it" (*I* 144; *BüK* 87). Falling behind the apotropaic measures of the Halakah, which no longer exercised its sanitizing force, these animal-like parables—heaving a "mighty paw"[14] against the Halakah—returned to the lowliest levels of life and existence, to the murky level of amphibious creatures. Kafka's parables, then, were the products of decline. They were the remainders of an epic wisdom, as was clear also from the clan of buffoons (the assistants, animals, Don Quixote, fools)—all figures that were to be read, Benjamin suggested, as sardonic displacements of the cabalistic sage (*der Gelehrte*).[15] Similarly, the useless help proffered by Kafka's assistants (*Gehilfe*) in reality signaled the deferral (*Aufschub*) of all messianic hope. No longer of use to humans, these helpers instead merely served the celestial, ethereal sphere of angels:

Folly [*Torheit*] lies at the heart of Kafka's favorites—from Don Quixote via the assistants to the animals. (Being an animal presumably meant to him only to have given up human form and human wisdom from a kind of shame—as shame may keep a gentleman who finds himself in a disreputable tavern from wiping his glass clean.) This much Kafka was absolutely sure of: first, that someone must be a fool if he is to help; second, that only a fool's help is real help. The only uncertain thing is whether such help can still do a human being any good. It is more likely to help the angels (compare the passage [in Brod's biography] about the angels who get something to do) who could do without help. Thus, as Kafka puts it, there is an infinite amount of hope, but not for us. This statement really contains Kafka's hope; it is the source of his radiant serenity. (*I* 144; *BüK* 87–88)

Insofar as Kafka's parables were the remnants of an absent Judaic law and the commentaries to scriptures no longer in place, they recall the figure of the empty Judaic tabernacle. Foundational to Hegel's *Spirit of Christianity,* this figure also surfaced in Derrida's exegesis of Kafka's "Before the Law." As Derrida explained, the inaccessibility and atopology of the law in Kafka's allegorical story bore structural resemblances to the empty tabernacle:

There is an analogy with Judaic law here. Hegel narrates a story about Pompey, interpreting it in his own way. Curious to know what was behind the doors of the tabernacle that housed the holy of holies, the triumvir approached the innermost part of the Temple, the center (*Mittelpunkt*) of worship. There, says Hegel, he sought "a being, an essence offered to his meditation, something meaningful [*sinnvolles*] to command his respect; and when he thought he was entering into the secret [*Geheimnis*], before the ultimate spectacle, he felt mystified, disappointed, deceived [*getauscht*]. He found what he sought in 'an empty space' and concluded from this that the genuine secret was itself entirely extraneous to them, the Jews: it was unseen and unfelt (*ungesehen und ungefühlt*)."[16]

When seen in light of the atopology of the law Derrida uncovered in Kafka's work, Benjamin's analysis similarly suggests that there was no longer a place to be taken up before or by Judaic law. What remained was mere emptiness, left in place of the law. To use Benjamin's vocabulary: this place left empty, which, ironically, continued to generate infinite commentary and incomprehensible gestures, was the "cloudy spot" (*I* 122) at the center of "Before the Law."[17] Referring to this very same image of the cloud, Adorno in a letter of December 12, 1934 laconically remarked to Benjamin that one should not simply take the cloud for granted but should instead "[make] the parable rain" (*BüK* 104) by twisting out of it the dialectical operation fundamental to Kafka's parables: "There is more here than simply a 'cloud,' namely a dialectic; and to dialecticize [*durchdialektisieren*] the cloudy shape (certainly not to 'clarify' it) or, in a certain sense, to make the parable rain, must remain the central concern of any Kafka interpretation" (ibid.). For if Kafka's writings testified to any hope, then this hope, according to Adorno, resided in their dialectical potential.

If in his correspondence and drafts Benjamin underscored the absence of Judaic law, the Kafka essay seemed in the final analysis to hold on to a possible, even imminent redemption. Granted, this potential for redemption was only of the weakest sort, located as it was in the many oddly shaped subhuman figures that populated Kafka's stories. Taken together, these stories exemplified the de-limitation and inversion to which the human had been subjected. Ultimately, however, Benjamin held, the Messiah would return in order to set aright (*zurechtstellen*) the many displacements to which Kafka's world paid witness. In fact, Benjamin went one step further insofar as such a redemptive displacement underlay his own Kafka reading—namely, in the figure of inversion (*Umkehrung*) that structured his interpretation. Adding interpretive layer upon layer, the essay charted the eventual transformation of profane law into divine justice, represented by the figure of Bucephalus, with which Benjamin's exegesis closed off. To understand this interpretive reversal fully, we must retrace some of the differences that emerged in Scholem and Benjamin's debate about Kafka.

Scholem's disagreement with Benjamin, registered in their correspondence, shows that he was unable to accept the profane interpretation of jurisprudence his friend recognized in Kafka's "The Judgment," "The Penal Colony," *The Trial,* and *The Castle.* To Scholem's repeated admonitions that Kafka's treatment of the law called for a theological and, vitally, Judaic exegesis, Benjamin rejoined that the law really amounted to the "the dead point in his work."[18] Similarly, when some time later he responded to Werner Kraft's criticism accusing him of having misunderstood the question of the law, Benjamin repeated that he would try to "demonstrate why the concept of the 'laws' in Kafka—as opposed to the concept of 'doctrine' [*Lehre*]—has a predominantly illusory character and is actually a sham" (*C* 463; *BüK* 98). Much like "Critique of Violence," whose argument unmistakably formed the background of Benjamin's Kafka interpretation, the Kafka essay sought to uncover the mythical origins of the power exerted by secular law. Nowhere was this more apparent than in the essay's first section, "Potemkin," where Benjamin reintroduced verbatim excerpts from "Critique of Violence" to differentiate Kafka's depiction of a mythical primeval world (*Vorwelt*)—with its secretive laws and rule of expiation—from the revealed law of the Torah. Although Benjamin pitted Kafka's primeval world against Greek mythology, which it preceded temporally, the language he used nevertheless recalled "Critique of Violence," where, as we saw, the myth of Niobe had been counterpoised to the biblical tale of Korah:

Laws and definite norms remain unwritten in the prehistoric world. A man can transgress them without suspecting it and thus become subject to atonement. But no matter how hard it may hit the unsuspecting, the transgression in the sense of the law is not accidental but fated, a destiny which appears here in all its ambiguity. In a cursory investigation of the idea of fate in antiquity Hermann Cohen came to a "conclusion that becomes inescapable": "the very rules of fate seem to be what causes and brings about the breaking away from them, the defection." It is the same way with the legal authorities whose proceedings are directed against K. It takes us back far beyond the time of the giving of the Law on twelve tablets to a prehistoric world, written law being one of the first victories scored over this world. In Kafka the written law is contained in books, but these are secret; by basing itself on them the prehistoric world exerts its rule all the more ruthlessly. (*I* 114–15; *BüK* 12)

Like "Critique of Violence," the Kafka essay launched a foundational critique against the tradition of the philosophy of right and, more in particular, I would argue, against the teleological (tripartite) model that underpinned Hegel's discussion of *Sittlichkeit* in the *Philosophy of Right.* Targeted was Hegel's account of the inception and progressive development of the history of right, from the nuclear family, to bourgeois society, and, eventually, to the crowning stage of the constitutional state. Anything but Hegelian in outlook, the secretive judicial system that K. encountered instead remained mired in the natural realm or the "hetaeric" primeval world. If Benjamin here used a term introduced by the Swiss lawyer and archeologist Bachofen, the reference was more than crucial. As a student of Savigny and his post-Hegelian "historical school of right," Bachofen did not adhere to Hegel's view of the *Volksgeist,* which lent "une empreinte commune" (a common imprint; *GS* 2:226) to a people's arts, ethics, religion, science, as well as to its system of right. Rather, Bachofen's *Mutterrecht* redirected its attention to the subterranean realms of law or right—the word Benjamin used was "sous-sols"—to unearth its roots in ancient religious customs and, finally, in a more foundational matriarchal form of right.

Seen against the background of Bachofen's *Mutterrecht,* then, the Kafka essay staged the confrontation between patriarchal law and the subversive forces of a deeper-lying matriarchy that displaced the reign of the father. Such would seem to be the significance of a strange entry in Kafka's diary, Benjamin suggested, in which the patriarch Abraham, willing to give up his time-honored place in tradition, was cast in the role of a mundane waiter out to postpone the sacrifice of Isaac. But even the helpers in *The Castle,* likened to Indian gandharvas, "celestial beings, beings in an unfinished state" (*I* 117; *BüK* 14), were said to have sprung from the womb, more particularly, the womb of nature (*BüK* 14, 138). Significantly, in an earlier version of the essay, Benjamin suggested that Odradek's survival in "The Cares of a Family Man" should be interpreted as the subjugation of the paternal to the maternal: "'The Cares of a Family Man' is the maternal, which will survive in Odradek" (*BüK* 141). The mythical world, ruled by fate, expiation, and guilt, which K. encountered in the hidden recesses and attics of the law, and which plagued Georg Bendemann in his confrontation with his father, literally was controlled by the Law of the Father. Thus the guilt that befell Georg Bendemann at the hands of his father—at once avenger and prosecutor—amounted to an original sin (*Erbsünde*). This word no longer carried Christian overtones but, instead, was to be taken quite literally—*buchstäblich,* as Adorno would say in his notes to Kafka—insofar as Bendemann had inherited (*erben*) his guilt through procreation.[19] In accordance with Cohen's *Ethik des reinen Willens,* the Kafka essay located guilt in mythical kinship, family, and blood relations, evident in the mythical visitation of the father's sins onto the son. In trying to rid himself of this mythical family burden, Bendemann's father sought to set "cosmic ages in motion in order to turn the age-old father-son relationship into a living and consequential thing" (*I* 113; *BüK* 11). In fact, Kafka's writings as a whole attested to his powerful struggle with mythical realms, Benjamin added, as he cataloged the different clans or tribes that— taken together—composed the full spectrum of Kafka's family: the helpers, assistants, messengers, fools, students; animals and vermin; the "hybrids or imaginary creatures like the Cat Lamb or Odradek" (*I* 116; *BüK* 14) and the "hetaeric" women—Frieda in *The Castle* and Leni in *The Trial,* whose "connecting web or skin" (*Verbindungshäutchen; BüK* 29; *I* 130–31) between her fingers gave away her amphibious descent. Even bastard forms such as Odradek or the *Kreuzung* were the illicit offspring, Benjamin noted, of thwarted family relations, the "monsters in the lap of the family" (*BüK* 138). Carrying the burden of this family, Kafka became the mythical figure Sisyphus, whose futile attempts to propel "the stone of history" were emblematic of a natural world of eternal repetition.

In the absence of revelation, Kafka's world appeared pervaded by forgetting and the forces of amnesia, a predicament nowhere more obvious, Benjamin held (as Willy Haas had done before him), than in

The Trial. Thus the topos of forgetting should be read as the inversion of the Judaic theme of Jehovah's memory. While the primordial, hetaeric world of myth ostensibly had been forgotten, its forces still made themselves felt in the present, despite or maybe because of the fact that they had been suppressed:

What has been forgotten—and this insight affords us yet another avenue of access to Kafka's work—is never something purely individual. Everything forgotten mingles with what has been forgotten of the prehistoric world, forms countless, uncertain, changing compounds, yielding a constant flow of new, strange products. Oblivion is the container from which the inexhaustible intermediate world in Kafka's stories presses toward the light. . . . To Kafka, the world of his ancestors was as unfathomable as the world of realities was important for him, and we may be sure that, like the totem poles of primitive peoples, the world of ancestors took him down to the animals. Incidentally, Kafka is not the only writer for whom animals are the receptacles of the forgotten. In Tieck's profound story "Fair Eckbert," the forgotten name of a little dog, Strohmi, stands for a mysterious guilt. One can understand, then, that Kafka did not tire of picking up the forgotten from animals. They are not the goals to be sure, but one cannot do without them. (*I* 132; *BüK* 30)

The manifold subhuman shapes that populated Kafka's fiction were the bastard offspring, Benjamin contended, of both individual (phylogenetic) forgetting and the primordial (ontogenetic) world. Instead of chronicling the history of progressive recollection (*Erinnerung*) of a world spirit coming to itself, Kafka's world ironically depicted the process of an ongoing forgetting. Thus the genealogy of creatures presented in Kafka's prose offered an inverse course through Hegel's *Philosophy of Right,* showing how the realm of law remained mired in the lowliest stages of the family—and, in fact, descended even further down, to the level of natural, animal religion, that is, the very religion of guilt Hegel had set forth in his *Phenomenology.*[20] Kafka's ancestors, for that matter, could be traced back not only to antiquity, to a Judaic, Chinese, or Greek layer, but even further back to the level of animals. Like Tieck's dog Strohmi, the animals that inhabited Kafka's animal parables[21]—whether the canine narrator of "Investigations of a Dog" or the mouse in "Josephine, the Singer"—were said to be the receptacles of the forgotten.

Significantly, Benjamin omitted to explore the possible latent "self-doubt" or "self-hatred" that—as some critics recently have observed[22]—may have inflected Kafka's marked obsession with animals in, for example, "The Metamorphosis" or "Report to an Academy." Benjamin did not attempt to read Kafka's obsessive delving into the animal world against the racial stereotypes that characterized the anti-Semitic rhetoric of the *Untermensch*. While, to be sure, animality for him opened up onto a hidden realm of primeval guilt, its significance was to be understood in quite different, cultural-historical terms. That is, both Benjamin's insistence on the persistence of what had been forgotten and his reference to totem poles pointed to Freud's *Totem and Taboo*, with which he undoubtedly was familiar.[23] Indeed, in the final section of *Totem and Taboo*, titled "The Return of Totemism in Childhood," Freud traced the relics of totemism in daily life to infantile animal phobias. Reviewing the literature on totemism, Freud reached the bold conclusion that "in these children's phobias some of the features of totemism reappear, but reversed into their negative,"[24] arguing that only psychoanalysis could reveal the totem animal to be a substitute (*Ersatz*) for the child's father. Freud further linked Darwin's notion of the primeval horde (*Urhorde*),[25] which was centered on an omnipotent father who laid sole claim to the female members of the clan, to totemism or the cannibalistic revolt of the sons against their father. In the same way, Benjamin's Kafka essay retraced the presence and persistence of primeval history (*Urgeschichte*) in the historical present, a Freudian project also central to the Arcades Project. Indeed, the encounter or collision between the present and primeval beginnings (*Uranfänge*) accounted for the new form of experience Kafka's work depicted: it was that of a "seasickness on shore," which Kafka had captured in the powerful image of the swing in "Children on a Country Road."

By positing a connection between forgetting and animality, Benjamin also appeared to rethink a Nietzschean tradition. Not only did Nietzsche celebrate the animal's amnesia, chained as it was to the "stake of the moment" (*Pflock des Augenblicks*),[26] but the *Genealogy of Morals* sketched humankind's development from its beginnings as a healthy, forgetful animal to the genesis of its "memory of the will," through which humans were turned into dyspeptics "who cannot 'have done' with anything."[27] What Kafka could not have done with, then, was the animalism of the body, this "forgotten alien land." Hence his peculiar habit of calling his cough "the animal" (*I* 117; *BüK* 14). What thus returned were the entrapments of the biological, physiological body or what Heidegger in his *Letter on Humanism* dismissed as the "abyssal corporeal kinship"[28] between humans and animals. Similar thoughts may have motivated Adorno when in his notes on Kafka he observed that, to trace the configurations of the human, Kafka had to retraverse the physiological and animality.

Against the force of forgetting, emanating from a mythical, primeval world (*Vorwelt*), Kafka mobilized the clan of the students and the (theological) category of study (*das Studium*). Using a figure similar to the angel of history of the theses on history,[29] Benjamin likened the pull of forgetting to a storm and the praxis of studying to a ride going against it: "It is a tempest that blows from the land of oblivion, and learning is a cavalry attack against it" (*I* 138; *BüK* 36). Like the wind that met Kafka's bucket rider or propelled the hunter Gracchus, this primeval wind was to be countered by the force of study or inversion (*Umkehr*)—that is, "the direction of learning which transforms existence into writing" (*I* 138; *BüK* 37). Significantly, Benjamin's Kafka essay thus reappropriated Kafka's technique of inversion. The term *Umkehr* first of all signaled the many displacements (*Entstellungen*) that typified Kafka's work, whether it be Alexander's horse Bucephalus turning into a man or the episode in which the servant Sancho Panza conquered his master. Second, it also stood for the force of return, of turning around one's horse, staged in a parable from the collection *Ein Landarzt* (A Country Doctor). Finally, as Stéphane Mosès was first to note, *Umkehr* also stood for religious conversion, which could only come about through *Studium*—a term to be taken in a theological sense.[30]

That Benjamin should have recognized the force of these reversals in "Der neue Advokat" (The New Attorney) is more than crucial insofar as this fable staged the encounter between the realms of animality and the law. A typical Kafkaesque transformation story, the fable introduced the attorney Bucephalus—in a previous life Alexander the Great's horse—who had resigned himself to a peaceful life of studying and reading. In an earlier draft of 1931, Benjamin had already placed great emphasis on the fact that the fable should not be read as an allegory: "Just as humans according to popular belief transform themselves into spirits and ghosts, so with Kafka humans seem to transform themselves into court functionaries after they have turned guilty" (*BüK* 117). If in this early interpretation Bucephalus's transformation from a horse into a lawyer served to confirm the mythical origin of the law, an unusual interpretative twist was introduced in the essay's final version. In the image of Bucephalus—"in the quiet lamplight, his flanks unhampered by the thighs of a rider, free and far from the clamor of [Alexander's] battle [*Alexanderschlacht*], he reads and turns the pages of our ancient tomes"[31]—Benjamin glimpsed the act of reading in the sense of theological *Studium,* in which the "gate of justice" opened itself. For "the law which is studied and not practiced any longer is the gate to justice" (*I* 139; *Bük* 37). However, with the same stroke—and in line with Kafka's logic of inversion—this figure of redemption was suddenly undercut. As Benjamin wrote: "The gate to justice is learning. And yet Kafka does not dare attach to this learning the promises which tradition has attached to the study of the Torah. His assistants are sextons who have lost their house of prayer, his students are pupils who have lost the Holy Writ. Now there is nothing to support them on their 'untrammeled, happy journey'" (ibid.). But at least once, so Benjamin continued, did Kafka succeed in capturing the uncontrolled, "breathtaking speed" of his own journey, bringing "it in line with the slow narrative pace that he presumably sought all his life" (ibid.). The precarious balance between these opposing forces was achieved in the parable of Sancho Panza. In it, the servant Sancho Panza managed to deceive his demon and master Don Quixote, diverting him with chivalrous romances and tales of adventure. Using the trick of inversion, the servant thus eventually sent his master ahead of himself: "A free man, Sancho Panza philosophically followed Don Quixote on his crusades, perhaps out of a sense of responsibility, and thus enjoyed a great and profitable entertainment to the end of his days" (ibid.). In same way, the horse Bucephalus managed to outlive his master Alexander, taking the burden of mythical guilt off his own back. Whether this deed promised final redemption was not clear, only that the difference between humans and animals no longer carried any weight. For, in the final analysis, Benjamin concluded—as he brought the figure of inversion to a logical end—Kafka's parables pushed their characters into a world where only one kind of hope was left: "Whether it is a man or a horse is no longer so important, if only the burden is removed from the back" (*I* 140; *BüK* 38).

CHAPTER 10

The Response to the *Kreatur*

*Sir, sorrow was not ordained for beasts but men, yet if men
do exceed in it they become beasts.*

Sancho Panza to Don Quixote [1]

"The flight through man into the realm of the non-human—that is
Kafka's epic trajectory," Adorno suggested in his notes to Kafka.[2] Instead of remembering or recollecting (*Eingedenken*) the human, Kafka's
writings presented "the trial run of a process of dehumanization."[3] If
Kafka's animal parables questioned the limits of the human by demonstrating the progressive biological regression of man, even more significant was the commodification, reification, and alienation to which the
human subject was submitted: "the crucial moment, however, towards
which everything in Kafka is directed, is that in which [humans] become
aware that they are not themselves—that they are things."[4] Erasing the
boundaries between the inorganic and the organic, between things
and humans—a feat best exemplified by the monstrous, nonhuman
figure Odradek at the center of "The Cares of a Family Man"—Kafka's
prose depicted a world that had been voided of all transcendence.
This world, Adorno wrote, was ruled by a perpetual "inability to die"
(*Nichtsterbenkönnen*), where neither death nor resurrection any longer
transpired but only the figures of Klee's angel, Odradek, or the hunter
Gracchus could survive. As such, these writings testified to the only
possible consequences that followed from Kierkegaard's philosophy of
existential subjectivity and expressionism: a self-enclosed hermeticism
and progressive self-objectification.

The more the I of expressionism is thrown back upon itself, the more like the excluded world of things it becomes. By virtue of this similarity Kafka forces expressionism—the chimerical aspect of which he, more than any of his friends, must have sensed, and to which he nevertheless remained faithful—into the form of a torturous epic; pure subjectivity, being of necessity [alienated] from itself as well and having become a thing, assumes the dimensions of objectivity which expresses itself through its own [alienation]. The boundary between what is human and the world of things becomes blurred. This forms the basis of the frequently noted affinity with Klee. Kafka called his writing "scribbling." The thinglike becomes a graphic sign; his spellbound [humans] do not determine their actions, but rather behave as if each had fallen into a magnetic field. It is precisely this as it were external determination of persons existing inwardly which gives Kafka's prose the [inscrutable abyssal] semblance [*Schein*] of sober objectivity. The zone in which it is impossible to die is at once the no-man's-land between [human] and thing: within it meet Odradek, which Benjamin viewed as an angel in Klee's style, and Gracchus, the humble descendant of Nimrod.[5]

Offering the inversion of Kierkegaard's existential philosophy, Kafka's prose replaced the latter's dialectical theology with the disjunctive operations of an antinomical theology. Judging Kafka from the vantage point of Kierkegaard's subjective interiority, Adorno contended that Kafka's emphasis on man's likeness to the animal was the only possible reflex reaction to the self-positing, autonomous subject he encountered as he traversed the depths of individualistic interiority. In a passage reminiscent of the *Dialectic of Enlightenment,* Kafka—locked in a game of idealistic (self-)reflexivity—turned into the trickster Oedipus, who, in stooping to the lowest strata of the organic and the inorganic, sought reconciliation with the mythical through mimicry. Seeking to break the spell of reification, the subject in reality merely reified itself.[6]

Because Kafka's gestures of dehumanization (*Entmenschlichung*) were symptomatic of humankind's progressive reification and society's ineluctable commodification, his narratives ultimately failed to explode the confining precinct of a self-enclosed subjectivity. Here it is palpably clear how much Adorno's observations in turn differed from Benjamin's Kafka interpretation. If for Benjamin Kafka's animals emblematized a state of forgetting, still they could not simply be reduced to allegories of mythical guilt or to representations of an abject exteriority and physiology. Instead, Kafka's animals ultimately expressed an ethico-political call to de-limit the category of the creaturely and to divest it of its last humanistic overtones. As such, it is crucial not to confound Benjamin's ethical project with Nietzsche's vitalistic, or even nihilistic, agenda, whether expressed in the *Second Untimely Meditation,* which envied the animal's propensity to obliviousness, or in *Zarathustra,* which meant to overcome the sickness of being human. How widely Benjamin's project diverged from Nietzsche's is particularly apparent in the section of the Kafka essay called "The Little Hunchback," in which Benjamin saluted what he, with Malebranche, called Kafka's attentiveness (*Aufmerk-samkeit*) to the creaturely. Weighed down by ageless guilt, Kafka's disfigured creatures recalled the hunchback of an old German folksong, "at home in distorted life" but bound to "disappear with the coming of the Messiah of whom a great rabbi once said that he did not wish to change the world by force, but would only make a slight adjustment in it" (*I* 134). Rejecting those Kafka interpretations that ascribed either a "mythical divination" or a (Kierkegaardian) "existential theology" to his work, Benjamin traced Kafka's openness toward the creaturely back to a more primordial ground. In a passage telling of the way in which Benjamin sought to reinscribe the theological into a seemingly abject realm of animality, he suggested the following: "Even if Kafka did not pray—and this we do not know—he still possessed in the highest degree what Malebranche called 'the natural prayer of the soul': attentiveness. And in this attentiveness he included all living creatures [*alle Kreatur*], as saints include them in their prayers" (*I* 134; *B* 32).[7]

To profile what Benjamin might have meant by this essentially theological term, I propose to frame this passage by two other prominent twentieth-century interpretations of the concept *Kreatur:* first, Heidegger's reading of Rilke's eighth Duino elegy and, second, the poetic response to the Kafka essay that Paul Celan formulated in his celebrated poetic speech "The Meridian."

Heidegger's comments on Rilke's use of the term *Kreatur* first appeared in his 1942–43 Parmenides seminar and were later developed in "What Are Poets For?" Central to his analysis were the opening verses from Rilke's eighth elegy: "With all its eyes the creature-world [*Krea-tur*] beholds / the open [*das Offene*]. But our eyes, as though reversed, / encircle it on every side."[8] These lines described man's fundamental insufficiency, for, unlike the creature-world, or the living in general (*das Lebewesen*), which was immersed in the open, humans existed in a cordoned-off realm, privy to the open only through the mediation of animals. Only in the animal's "face" (*Antlitz*), Rilke's poem suggested, could humans—vicariously and insufficiently—glimpse the open.

Proposing a philosophical reading of the elegy, Heidegger emphasized that Rilke's interpretation of the term *Kreatur* needed to be distinguished from the Christian theological tradition:

The word "creature" means in Rilke's poetry "the creations" [*Geschöpfe*]—
a word which in the more narrow sense coincides with the word and concept
"living beings" [*Lebewesen*] to the exclusion of man. This use of the words
Kreatur and *Geschöpf* does not refer in a Christian, devout manner to the
creation by the divine creator; instead, they are names for the living, which
in contrast to the living beings that have been endowed with consciousness,
i.e., man, is characteristically "helpless" and "wretched," unable to help
itself. It should be stressed once more; *Kreatur* here is not distinguished
from the *creator* and therefore is not brought into relation to God through
this distinction; instead it is the non-rational living being in its distinction
from the rational one.[9]

Yet, despite its apparent divergence from tradition, Rilke's poetry, Heidegger did not fail to add, still firmly remained rooted in the history of
metaphysics. For rather than breaking out of the circle of metaphysics,
Rilke's notion of "the open" in fact reinscribed its premises all the more
stringently. In making use of the technique of inversion, Rilke's seemingly subversive venture proved as fated as Nietzsche's equally unsuccessful attempt to leave the logic of Western metaphysics behind.
Turning upside down the relation that humans and animals traditionally were believed to entertain to the open, Rilke in fact reintroduced an
age-old assumption that lay at the foundation of the Greek philosophical tradition, notably the distinction Aristotle already drew between
man as a being endowed with language (*zōon logon echon,* in Latin,
animal rationale) and the speechless animal (*zōon a-logon*). In Rilke's
allegiance to this Western humanistic tradition, Heidegger recognized
the latest, indeed most *modern* version of metaphysics, which had come
to characterize the nineteenth and twentieth centuries.[10] In fact, Rilke's
interest in the animal, apparent also in the *Neue Gedichte,* merely continued the legacy of Schopenhauer's and Nietzsche's irrational philosophy
of life—in other words, a "biologistic metaphysics" that expressed itself
in a humanization of the animal and the concomitant animalization of
humankind.[11] Rilke's poetry, Heidegger charged, did not escape the
metaphysics of modernity and subjectivity that started with Leibniz only
to culminate in Nietzsche's will to power and the over-man. Crucially,
Heidegger's dismissal of such a biologistic metaphysics was similar to
the 1946–47 *Letter on Humanism,* which in its search for a more primordial humanism would likewise reject "the abyssal corporeal kinship
with the animal, which can hardly be thought."[12] In the end, Rilke's
and Nietzsche's attempts to invert metaphysics—through the figures of
animals, angels, or the over-man—all the more firmly installed the kind
of metaphysical humanism that the *Letter* would seek to dispel. Only a

new, more foundational humanism, the *Letter* announced, could define the proper role of human beings in relation to the "lighting of Being." Similarly, Rilke's notion of the *Weltinnenraum*, as the Parmenides lecture went on to suggest, simply reenacted the critique that Pascal had launched against Descartes's philosophy of consciousness. Pascal's logic of the heart converted Descartes's "immanence of calculating consciousness" into the "inner space [*Innenraum*] of the heart."[13] The being responsible for transforming the visible realm into the invisible recesses of the heart was no one else than the angel that appeared in the *Duino Elegies*.[14] Commenting on the letter that Rilke sent to Witold von Hulewicz in November 1925, Heidegger implied that the angel invoked the specter of Nietzsche's over-man, so that in fact it was to be read as the figure in which the metaphysics of subjectivity culminated.[15] But, for all its criticism of Rilke's submerged humanism, Heidegger's own framework, as I argued earlier, hardly remained free of the traces of a profoundly metaphysical humanism. This is particularly obvious in Heidegger's charge that the inflated, "super-human" position of the animal in Rilke's writings derived from the poet's inability to draw a firm demarcation between the (ahistorical) "living in general" and historical man.[16] This passage and similar ones prove that Heidegger's critical remarks were inspired by the same hermeneutical point of departure that had led him to ascribe a derivative, inferior status to natural history in *Being and Time*. But while this 1927 text still adopted the more sober language of existential philosophy, the *Parmenides* lecture was awash in the protofascist language that also marked the work of the 1930s, calling for a poetry that could yield a decision (*Entscheidung*) able to found history. Regardless, then, of the possible "metaphysical" overtones that imbued Rilke's poetry, Heidegger's own interpretation at best reintroduced in disguised form the traditional limits that were said to separate the living in general from humanity's "historical world." At worst, his fundamentally antimodern tract ended up affirming a hallowed precinct of Being, which it placed over and beyond the arena of human politics.

While Heidegger read Rilke's animal in relation to Nietzsche's over-man or the *super*-human, Benjamin followed quite the opposite track in his Kafka essay when he invoked the category of *Kreatur*, under which he now grouped that which traditionally counts as *infra*-human.[17] If the reference to Kafka's attentiveness (*Aufmerksamkeit*) with which he ended the essay's final section, "The Little Hunchback," might at first seem somewhat cryptic, the poet Paul Celan must be credited for having first spelled out its ethico-political implications. Delivered on the occasion of receiving the Georg Büchner Prize in 1960, Celan's speech, "The Meridian," entered into a direct dialogue with Büchner, whom he called "the poet of the *Kreatur*."[18] Written haltingly, winding through several detours, headed toward a new poetry of the other—perhaps an "*altogether other*"—this speech centrally addressed the paradoxical relation that exists between the natural and the creaturely, on the one hand, and the uncanny artificiality of art, on the other.[19] It was this tenuous relationship between art and the creaturely that Büchner's theatrical work—often seen as the precursor of late nineteenth-century naturalism—thematized. How lethal an impact art could have on the creaturely Celan saw expressed in Büchner's notion of "medusoid" art, whose artificiality and unnaturalness were emblematized by the trained monkey that appeared in the play *Woyzeck*.[20] Aware of art's propensity for excessive artificiality, Büchner—in Celan's words—reclaimed a more fundamental artistic gift, that of an attentiveness for the creaturely. What is more, Celan established a genealogical line that led from Büchner via Kafka to Benjamin:

The attentiveness that the poem devotes to everything that it encounters; its acute sense of the detail, contour, structure, color, but also of the "tremors and hints"—all this, I believe, is not the accomplishment of the eye, which every day competes with ever more precise instruments. Rather, it is a form of concentration which commemorates all our dates. "Attentiveness"— allow me to cite a phrase by Malebranche, via Benjamin's essay on Kafka— "Attentiveness is the natural prayer of the soul."[21]

It is not unlikely that Celan had in mind Benjamin's technology essay when he downplayed the effectiveness of sight—including the artifice of the optical, mechanical, photographic eye—to turn to a different kind of concentration, represented by Büchner's attentiveness. Thus the poet was to open his soul to "stones, metals, water, and plants"—to quote from Büchner's "Lenz"—so that he could "dreamfully be receptive to every essence in nature, just as flowers take in the air with the coming and going of the moon."[22] Drawing on Osip Mandelstam's conception of poetry as an encounter with the other, Celan charted how poetry was to approach a realm of freedom and utopian openness, an *Atemwende*—or turn of breath—through which it could set itself free. Setting himself free from the self, approaching the other, the poet thus moved from the position of the I to the alterity of the you. The path Celan pursued to the open (*das Offene, das Freie*) was directed toward an ethico-theological openness on the other side of art's self-enclosure. How risky such a trajectory could be became apparent from the fact that the poem's otherness bore the marks of an unmistakable duplicity, which at times also took the form of the uncanny, appearing as the dehumanized artificiality of art. Writing poetry thus also involved the risk of "going beyond what is human, stepping into a realm which is turned toward the human, but uncanny—the realm where the monkey, the automatons and with them . . . oh, art, too, seem to be at home."[23] Writing poetry therefore required the skill to discriminate between an uncanny strangeness and an authentic otherness—in other words, the skill to distinguish between two deceptively similar forms of otherness.[24]

In the state of self-forgetfulness that distinguished the writer Lenz, Celan discerned the call to take leave of the merely human; for in forgetting about his own self Lenz prepared himself for a turn to the creaturely.[25] Such a loss of self was indispensable if one was to approach the open and to reach an *Atemwende*: "Maybe . . . poetry, like art, is under way, with a self-forgotten I, to the uncanny and the strange, and sets itself—but where? in what place? with what? as what?—free?"[26] Such a path to the open further required that poets speak "from an angle of reflection which is their own existence, their own physical nature" (unter dem Neigungswinkel seines Daseins, dem Neigungswinkel seiner Kreatürlichkeit).[27] Such a path, finally, led through a Kafkaesque and Benjaminian form of *Aufmerksamkeit,* as Celan implied toward the end of his lecture when he retraced the different routes his speech had taken: "And once, by dint of an attentiveness to things and the *Kreatur,* we came to free, open space [*das Offene*] and, finally, close to utopia."[28] No one has shown better than Levinas how one is to understand this course through otherness; for in his collection of essays entitled *Proper Names* he read Celan's attentiveness back through Benjamin and Kafka, gleaning from it an originary sense of responsibility, "older than that of the *truth of being.*"[29] Attesting to the language of proximity, their writings, Levinas suggested, ultimately led back to a position that preceded the Greek-Hellenistic tradition of philosophical questioning—a position defined by a more sentient responsibility of touching, contact, and giving to the other.[30]

This ethico-theological dimension must be retained as we resume our trajectory through the otherness of Benjamin's work. For it is indeed the attentiveness toward the *Kreatur* or infra-human that distinguishes Benjamin's image of the just man (*der Gerechte*). Benjamin encountered this figure not only in Kafka's work. An eminent storyteller, Kafka shared this sensibility with the nineteenth-century Russian writer Leskov, whose work formed the center of Benjamin's 1936 study "The Storyteller." Like Celan's "The Meridian," this essay offered a balanced meditation on the clash between technological modernity and the artisanal craft of storytelling. Reaching down into the farthest recesses of history and an age-old human experience (*Erfahrung*), the essay went back to the natural history of storytelling, descending all the way down to the silenced voice of nature. Written at around the time Benjamin had started work on his much acclaimed technology essay, "The Storyteller" did not simply embrace a quaint or even conservative antimodernism. Nor did it merely seek to retrieve the plenitude of an oral, narrative tradition that predated the instrumentality of writing or the technologization of the printing press. Rather, this mystical exercise sought to reach down to a more originary level of ethical responsibility, one that antedated the destruction of experience. Above all in Leskov's stories—themselves the hybrid, "bastard" forms of legend and fairy tale—did the figure of the just man make his reappearance. As the "advocate [*Fürsprech*] for created things [*die Kreatur*] and at the same time . . . their highest embodiment" (*I* 104; *GS* 2:459), Leskov's just man often took on maternal, even hermaphroditelike features, as Benjamin suggested, showing him to be the descendent of a primeval mother figure (*Urmutter*).[31] All of Leskov's figures of justness, Benjamin wrote, proved to be "unmistakably suffused with the *imago* of his mother," who in the story "Figura" was characterized as follows:

She was so thoroughly good that she was not capable of harming any man, nor even an animal. She ate neither meat nor fish, because she had such pity for living creatures. Sometimes my father used to reproach her with this. But she answered: "I have raised the little animals myself, they are like my children to me. I can't eat my own children, can I?" She would not eat meat at a neighbor's house either. "I have seen them alive," she would say; "they are my acquaintances. I can't eat my acquaintances, can I?" (*I* 104; *GS* 2:459)

Arising from the same Bachofean matriarchal stratum that Benjamin had uncovered in Kafka's work, this ur-mother bore testimony to an antediluvian age.[32] Refusing to engage in a carnivorous incorporation of the creaturely, she proved to be the descendant of Adam who, according to Genesis, was a vegetarian.[33]

It was in the gem engraver and cabalistic mystic Wenzel, at the center of the short story "The Alexandrite," that the true figure of the just man emerged. A highly skilled gem cutter and artisan (*Hand-werker*), his exquisite work and precise gestures were products of a delicate, mystical coordination between eye, soul, and hand. Thus his gestures symbolized the movements of the storyteller, absorbed in the process of chiseling experiences (*Erfahrung*). As the representative of the just man, Wenzel maintained an undiminished contact with the creatural, even with its petrified, inanimate, lowliest stratum, that of the stone, which was exemplified by the chrysoberyl. To Wenzel the sage, it was "granted to see in this chrysoberyl a natural prophecy of petrified, lifeless nature concerning the historical world in which he himself lives" (*I* 107; *GS* 2:463).[34] Given that Benjamin sought to retrieve a more originary ethico-theological responsibility, why this surprising mystical descent to the level of the inanimate mineral, to a natural history before all human history?

That Benjamin should have glimpsed the pinnacle of justness in Wenzel's ability to commune with the chrysoberyl is no longer cause for wonder once it is understood that this semiprecious stone represented the "deepest layer of the creaturely" and expressed the voice of the nameless narrator, nature. Lending his ear to the chrysoberyl, Wenzel descended back in time, to a more original state of nature—before it was named and overnamed (*überbenennen*) by human language. Urging his own readers to become receptive to this nameless storyteller, Benjamin wrote, "only a few have ventured into the depths of inanimate nature, and in modern narrative literature there is not much in which the voice of the anonymous storyteller, who was prior to all literature, resounds so clearly as it does in Leskov's story 'The Alexandrite'" (*I* 107; *GS* 2:462–63).

Benjamin's fascination with stones does not stand as an isolated incident. Indeed, "The Storyteller" in reality harks back to the *Trauerspiel* study, in which Benjamin's discussion of stones emerged filtered through his theory of melancholia. Unobtrusive as the reference to stones in the study's chapter on melancholy may at first seem, the image of the stone nonetheless can hardly be deemed marginal. Among the more common baroque emblems used to represent melancholia, such as the dog or the sphere, Benjamin observed, there was one whose popularity in baroque emblematics had gone all but unnoticed in the scholarly work of such eminent Renaissance experts as Aby Warburg or Erwin Panofsky. And yet the stone, Benjamin stressed, was a particularly popular emblem in Renaissance and baroque art and literature through which the darker, earthbound side of the melancholic disposition could be captured. The significance of these observations can be thrown into further relief if one turns more explicitly to Benjamin's theory of melancholy.

Influenced by Panofsky and Saxl's study of Dürer's engraving, *Melencolia I,* Benjamin's theory focused on the peculiar mixture of antique and medieval conceptions of melancholia that surfaced in sixteenth- and seventeenth-century cultural productions. Thus the baroque pathology of the humors revived the old Salerno doctrine of the temperaments, as well as the belief that melancholia was physiologically generated through the spleen. Equally important, however, were the dialectical operations that were believed to characterize its symptomatology. If in the medieval Christian tradition melancholia was associated with one of the deadly sins, namely *acedia,* that is, "dullness of the heart, or sloth" (*O* 155; *GS* 1:332), then in antiquity, notably in Aristotle's *Problemata,* a more benign version of melancholia emerged, according to which the melancholic's antics really were the reverse side of his genius. It was this dialectical nature of melancholia that received attention in the writings of Renaissance humanists such as Ficino. At the same time, astrological theories of antiquity were revived, which centered on the planet Saturn, whose influence not only produced sloth (*O* 149; *GS* 1:327) but also kindled the intelligence and contemplation. Occult Renaissance natural theories hoped to separate these two faces of melancholia so as to release its beneficent, spiritual, sublime ingredients and to suppress its saturnine, materialistic, or telluric side.

Benjamin proved fascinated by the humanists' revival of a sublime, winged melancholia, but he equally indulged in describing melancholia's telluric, earthbound side. In the baroque's speculations about the physiological genesis of melancholia, he saw proof that this ailment arose from the depths of the creaturely. That melancholia could cast the most gifted individual to the lowliest state of animality was something Cervantes's Sancho Panza already knew when he exclaimed to Don Quixote, "Sir, sorrow was not ordained for beasts but men, yet if men do exceed in it they become beasts" (*O* 146; *GS* 1:324). Not only did the dog emblematize the workings of the overproductive spleen that characterized the melancholic humor. More fundamentally, melancholia, as "the most genuinely creaturely of the contemplative impulses" (*O* 146; *GS* 1:324), recalled man's uncanny likeness, indeed relatedness, to animals, thus erasing the frail boundaries between the human and animality. Deaf to "the voice of revelation" (*O* 152; *GS* 1:330), the melancholic turned his gaze toward earth, a predilection precisely captured by the emblems of the dog, the sphere, and the stone, with which the melancholic was commonly associated. Drawing again on contemporary anthropologies, Benjamin pointed to the unmistakable link Renaissance and baroque poets discerned between the melancholic's earthbound gaze and the coldness of stone, matter, or inert mass. Subjecting himself to the laws imposed by the world of objects and things, the melancholic remained bound to abject matter, a plight figured in the *Trauerspiel* by the uncanny life stage props were prone to take on.

If the *Trauerspiel* study wavered between a benign and base version of melancholy, then a similar ambiguity already loomed large in the figure of righteous, or just, man at the center of the Leskov essay. For, although Leskov's maternal figures appeared to have sprung from the world of the fairy tale—in Benjamin's work eminently the locus of possible redemption—they nonetheless also pointed to the abyss of the mythical, whose presence often appeared threateningly close. Further, there emerged another potential ambiguity in the righteous man when Benjamin described him as "the advocate [*Fürsprech*] for created things and . . . their highest embodiment." Indeed, the Benjamin scholar Irving Wohlfarth has suggested that there lurks a submerged but all the same "imperialistic humanism" in the term *Fürsprech,* which denotes both advocacy and a speaking "in the stead of."[35] As Wohlfarth showed, Benjamin relapsed into this logocentric trap when, in a 1925 imaginative text inspired by Kafka's *The Trial* and called "Idea for a Mystery Play," he depicted history as a world tribunal in which man, as the advocate of mute nature, brought a legal suit (*Klage*) against creation, litigating against the overdue appearance of the messiah.[36]

At the heart of this dilemma really lies the question whether man's predominance over language must not inevitably lead to nature's mourning in the face of its overdetermination and oversignification. It was in fact in the 1916 language essay, "On Language as Such and on the Language of Man," that Benjamin first introduced the mystical topos of nature's mourning, a figure to which the final chapter of the *Trauerspiel* study returned (*O* 224; *GS* 1:398). Arguing that every single thing was endowed with its own language, the 1916 essay initially seemed to introduce human language as but one of many languages, to be classified next to the language of inanimate things, which was marked by the "magic of matter," and the divine language of the hallowed Word. By establishing the existence of a language of things, Benjamin seemed to react against those linguistic theories that remained mired in a humanistic logocentrism. But this critical strand in the essay alternated with observations that seemed to run counter to this explosive insight. By emphasizing that only humans had been graced with "the gift of language," Benjamin again unmistakably placed humans above animals and things: "God spoke—and there was—but this man, who is not crested from the word, is now invested with the *gift* of language and is elevated above nature" (*R* 322; *GS* 2:148). Humanity's mastery over nature rested upon its ability to recognize and, ultimately, to translate (*Über-setzen*) the spiritual essence of things in a language of names. "Man is the namer, by this we recognize that through him pure language speaks. All nature, insofar as it communicated itself, communicates itself in language, and so finally in man. Hence he is the lord of nature and can give names to things" (*R* 318–19; *GS* 1:144). Benjamin implied that humanity's divinely ordained task did not amount to mere anthropomorphism. Human language instead was to be seen as one higher step in a ceaseless linguistic movement, one that, in the final analysis, remained grounded in the divine Word: "All higher language is a translation of those lower, until in ultimate clarity the word of God engulfs, which is the unity of this movement made up of language" (*R* 332; *GS* 2:157). Ultimately, however, the two sides of the dilemma to which the essay gestured can also be rephrased in terms of the two accounts of creation that one finds in Genesis. In one version, as Catherine Chalier has observed, Adam stands above nature; in the other, he merely stands on a par with the rest of nature.[37]

Oscillating between these two accounts, the language essay tried to dispel the specter of logocentrism while simultaneously suggesting that the prison house of language could not be exploded—a predicament represented by nature's silent lament. Torn between an anthropocentric account of language and one that ran counter to it, the essay at its core pointed to the figure of a silenced, mournful nature. But by introducing the image of such a mourning nature, the essay complicated matters even more: can mute nature ever speak or does nature's lament (*Klage*) already constitute a prosopopoeia and thus a logocentric anthropomorphism? Going beyond the framework of language philosophy, Benjamin thus raised larger questions about the status of nature's alterity. In so doing, he proved himself to be the interlocutor in a debate that also engaged other members and affiliates of the Frankfurt School. Thus, in his *Theory of the Novel*, Lukács indirectly raised similar questions when, in discussing Hegel's "second nature," which he saw as the product of modernity's commodification and convention, he simultaneously cast doubt on the ontological status of "first nature," presenting it as nothing but a lyrical projection. Adorno and Horkheimer further compounded the issue when, in the *Dialectic of Enlightenment,* they—ever so fleetingly—conjured up the image of a redeemed nature that escaped the reifying grip of instrumental reason.

It cannot be doubted that the objections raised regarding Benjamin's logocentrism are valid. At the same time, they should not detract from the fact that he also unmistakably and earnestly sought to break through the limitations of just such a logocentric vantage point. Nowhere is this more noticeable than in his remarks on the gesture of attentiveness; and nowhere does this become more apparent than in the earthbound cast of his melancholic gaze. To be sure, as noted earlier, the *Trauerspiel* study wavered between the two dialectical sides of melancholy, whose positive and negative influences Benjamin—donning the pose of the alchemist—seemed to want to separate from one another. Here one already recognizes the two conflictual views of melancholia that co-exist in the later work: one that associates melancholia with a retrograde method of historical analysis—the legacy of medieval *acedia*—exemplified by historicism's technique of *Einfühlung* or by the "left-wing melancholia" that characterized the work of Erich Kästner and "new objectivity"; and another that celebrated a new method of cultural analysis, a method that, through a melancholic immersion into the matter of objects, could salvage the historic potential of things.[38] Benjamin scholarship has commonly read his theory of melancholia along these lines or discussed it mainly in relation to the theses on history. Without wanting to dispute the value of these views, I wish to add another, less common meaning to this array of interpretations, one according to which Benjamin's downward gaze also reflects an ethico-theological response to the creatural. In fact, to a certain extent, these meanings already lay chiseled in the chrysoberyl hidden at the center of the Leskov essay. To be sure, this semiprecious stone might seem to conjure up the specter of the medusoid stone or the lethal petrification of ahistorical natural history; it also recalls the barren stones of Celan's "Conversation in the Mountains" or, again, the connotations of *acedia* and inertia that the stone acquired in the *Trauerspiel* book. Yet a fundamentally different reading announces itself. If Kafka's, Leskov's, Celan's, and, finally, Benjamin's gazes are turned earthward, they now no longer represent a melancholic self-absorption, which purely served to reaffirm the confines of the human subject. Instead, their gaze attests to the same kind of self-forgetfulness that Celan celebrated in Büchner's *Lenz*. Turned toward the creaturely, a radically different, dialectical side appears in Benjamin's melancholic gaze—one that fundamentally and resolutely resists incorporating the other.

Postscript

In a short text—halfway between personal testimony, parable, fable, and Talmudic gloss—titled "The Name of a Dog, or Natural Rights," Emmanuel Levinas recounts the following:

There were seventy of us in a forestry commando unit for Jewish prisoners of war in Nazi Germany. An extraordinary coincidence was the fact that the camp bore the number 1492, the year of the expulsion of the Jews from Spain under the Catholic Ferdinand V. The French uniform still protected us from Hitlerian violence. But the other men, called free, who had dealings with us or gave us work or orders or even a smile—and the children and women who passed by and sometimes raised their eyes—stripped us of our human skin. We were subhuman, a gang of apes. A small inner murmur, the strength and wretchedness of persecuted people, reminded us of our essence as thinking creatures, but we were no longer part of the world. Our comings and goings, our sorrow and laughter, illnesses and distractions, the work of our hands and the anguish of our eyes, the letters we received from France and those accepted for our families—all that passed in parenthesis. We were beings entrapped in their species; despite all their vocabulary, beings without language. . . . How to deliver a message about one's humanity which, from behind the bars of quotation marks, will come across as anything else than the language of primates.

And then, about halfway through our long captivity, for a few short weeks, before the sentinels chased him away, a wandering dog entered our lives. One day he came to meet this rabble as we returned under guard from work. He survived in some wild patch in the region of the camp. But we called him Bobby, an exotic name, as one does with a cherished dog. He would appear at morning assembly and was waiting for us as we returned, jumping up and barking in delight. For him, there was no doubt that we were men.

Perhaps the dog that recognized Ulysses beneath his disguise on his return from the Odyssey was a forebear of our own. But no! There, it concerned Ithaca and the fatherland. Here, the place was nowhere. Last Kantian of Nazi Germany, not having the brains needed to universalize maxims out of one's drives, this dog descended from the dogs in Egypt. And his friendly growling—the faith of an animal—was born from the silence of his forefathers on the banks of the Nile.[1]

Perhaps it is not altogether misguided to invoke Levinas's account of the dog Bobby, which will serve as a final interpretive gloss on Benjamin's engagement with the limits of the human—from the alterity of animality to the specter of a terrifying inhumanity. For, in the last analysis, Benjamin's writings of the 1920s and 1930s also look ahead to the critical reflections on the place of ethics after the Holocaust that one finds not only in the work of Levinas but also in that of the later Adorno. Writing in *Negative Dialectics* about Kant's critique of practical reason, Adorno questioned the viability of a Kantian ethics in the wake of the Holocaust and the ineluctable belatedness of justice. In the end, Adorno indicated, the individual stood confronted with the figure of animality; at the end of a long humanistic tradition, Adorno suggested, the individual was "left with no more than the morality for which Kantian ethics—which accords affection, not respect to animals—can muster only disdain: to try to live so that one may believe himself to have been a good animal."[2]

Levinas's text shares this fated view of humankind with Adorno, but it also does decidedly more. For in the fortuitous appearance of the dog Bobby, outside the gates of the camp, the humanness of the prisoners—reduced to abject animality—was paradoxically salvaged. Unable to pay respect to categorical imperatives as an animal, Bobby, paradoxically, appeared as the last—and perhaps only—Kantian in Nazi Germany, a dog whose welcoming bark acknowledged the humanity of the prisoners. In the midst of the worst human destitution, Bobby's friendly growling signaled the recognition of humanity, hope amid wanton misery. In Bobby, Levinas implied, lived the memory of the dogs from the Nile, evoked in Exodus 11:7, when it was prophesied that "not a dog shall growl" in the hour of the Israelites' liberation from Egyptian slavery and bondage. Pointing to a "transcendence in the animal," these dogs provided a welcome counterimage to the more common biblical conception according to which dogs were merely nonhuman, worthy only of "flesh that is torn by beasts in the field," hence unfit for human consumption (Exodus 22:31). However despairing Levinas's situation was, he glimpsed—if only with some pain—the possibility of salvation in the figure of Bobby, thus paying tribute to the same salvific potential that Benjamin all along had recognized in the less than human. It is in this way, it seems, that Levinas's exegesis of his encounter with Bobby also reflects back on Benjamin's ethical attentiveness to the so-called infra-human. For in the appearance of this dog, as Levinas implied, not only was the animal liberated from its lowliest creaturely position, on this side of transcendence; it also seemed possible—however uncertainly at first—that humanity itself might be rescued in the image of animality.

Notes

Introduction

1. Walter Benjamin, "The Task of the Translator: An Introduction to the Translation of Baudelaire's *Tableaux parisiens*," in *Illuminations*, ed. Hannah Arendt, trans. Harry Zohn (New York: Schocken Books, 1969), 69.

2. For an authoritative account of these disputes, see Ernst Bloch, Georg Lukács, Bertolt Brecht, Walter Benjamin, and Theodor Adorno, *Aesthetics and Politics*, ed. Ronald Taylor (London: Verso, 1977).

3. On Adorno's conception of natural history, see also Fredric Jameson, *Late Marxism: Adorno, or, the Persistence of the Dialectic* (London: Verso, 1990).

4. Hannah Arendt, "Introduction—Walter Benjamin: 1892–1940" in *Illuminations*, 46.

5. Walter Benjamin, *The Correspondence of Walter Benjamin, 1910–1940*, ed. Gershom Scholem and Theodor W. Adorno, trans. Manfred R. Jacobson and Evelyn M. Jacobson (Chicago: University of Chicago Press, 1994), 571–72.

6. See his letter of April 25, 1930, addressed to Scholem, in ibid., 365.

7. On the notion of *Ursprung* as "primal leap," see George Steiner, "Introduction," in Walter Benjamin, *The Origin of German Tragic Drama* (London: Verso, 1977), 16.

8. Here and in what follows I appropriate Derrida's usage of the hyphenated term "de-limitation," which brings into play a double meaning: first, de-limitation in the sense of the drawing of borders or frontiers, be they epistemological or conceptual; second, the movement of excess that surpasses and, indeed, confounds the epistemological desire for such firm borders or limits. The prefix "de" in "de-limitation" thus acquires the negative dialectical force of the French prefix *dé-* or the German *Ent-* (as in *Entgrenzung*).

9. See Jürgen Habermas, "Walter Benjamin: Consciousness-Raising or Rescuing Critique," in Gary Smith, ed., *On Walter Benjamin: Critical Essays and Recollections* (Cambridge: MIT Press, 1988), 124 and 118.

10. Ibid., 90–128. For a later analysis of Benjamin's links to conservative thinkers, see Richard Wolin, "Introduction to the Revised Edition," *Walter Benjamin: An Aesthetic of Redemption* (Berkeley: University of California Press, 1994).

11. As Lyotard, for example, observes in his collection of essays *The Inhuman,* "in 1913, Apollinaire wrote ingenuously: 'More than anything, artists are men who want to become inhuman'" (Jean-François Lyotard, *The Inhuman: Reflections on Time,* trans. Geoffrey Bennington and Rachel Bowlby [Stanford: Stanford University Press, 1991], 2).

Part I

1. Theodor W. Adorno, *Kierkegaard: Konstruktion des Ästhetischen,* in *Gesammelte Schriften,* vol. 2 (Frankfurt: Suhrkamp, 1979), 51.

2. Adorno's dissertation, "Die Transzendenz des Dinglichen und Noematischen in Husserls Phänomenologie," is published in the first volume of his collected work. For further comments on the dissertation, see Rolf Wiggershaus's helpful and comprehensive history of the Frankfurt School, *The Frankfurt School: Its History, Theories, and Political Significance,* trans. Michael Robertson (Cambridge: MIT Press, 1994), 70ff.

3. Burkhardt Lindner first pointed to this double usage of "natural history" in an early essay, "'Natur-Geschichte'—Geschichtsphilosophie und Welterfahrung in Benjamins Schriften," *Text und Kritik* 31/32 (1979): 44–45. The term would remain prominent and acquire an increased significance in Benjamin's later writings, especially the *Passagen-Werk.* Benjamin acknowledged the methodological and epistemological affinities between the *Trauerspielbuch* and the unfinished Arcades Project when he noted that the concept of *Urphänomen,* which he took from Goethe, presented the transposition of a natural category onto history. See Susan Buck-Morss's comprehensive *The Dialects of Seeing: Walter Benjamin and the Arcades Project* (Cambridge: MIT Press, 1989).

Chapter 1

1. See Susan Buck-Morss, *The Origin of Negative Dialectics: Theodor W. Adorno, Walter Benjamin, and the Frankfurt Institute* (New York: Free Press, 1977), 52ff. See also Buck-Morss's comparative analysis of the *Trauerspiel* study and the *Passagen-Werk* in *Dialectics of Seeing,* 58–77. Other readings of the theme of natural history in Benjamin's work can be found in Rolf Tiedemann, *Studien zur Philosophie Walter Benjamins* (Frankfurt: Suhrkamp, 1973), 84–89, 159–66, and Burkhardt Lindner, "'Natur-Geschichte.'" See also Martin Jay's *Adorno* (Cambridge: Harvard University Press, 1984), 62ff., which discusses Adorno and Horkheimer's critique of the domination of nature in the *Dialectic of Enlightenment.*

2. Martin Heidegger, *Being and Time,* trans. John Macquarrie and Edward Robinson (New York: Harper and Brothers, 1962), 424ff. The translators use the

term "historicality" for Heidegger's *Geschichtlichkeit*. However, I have chosen the more commonly accepted translation "historicity" instead.

3. See the chapter "Being" in Herbert Schnädelbach, *Philosophy in Germany 1831–1933*, trans. Eric Matthews (Cambridge: Cambridge University Press, 1984), 192–218. While, as Schnädelbach points out, the "history of the new ontology in Germany is characterized by the rivalry between the phenomenological conception in Heidegger's version and its alternative in the work of Nicolai Hartmann" (p. 207), Adorno's main target is Heidegger's *Being and Time*. How crucial Adorno's early Heidegger critique already was can be gleaned from the fact that over the years his scathing indictment of Heidegger's existentialism would become more pronounced, especially in *The Jargon of Authenticity*.

4. Theodor W. Adorno, "Die Idee der Naturgeschichte," in *Gesammelte Schriften*, vol. 1 (Frankfurt: Suhrkamp, 1973), 354.

5. Ibid., 350.

6. Ibid., 353.

7. Ibid., 355.

8. Ibid., 346.

9. Ibid., 355.

10. Hermann Mörchen, *Adorno und Heidegger: Untersuchung einer philosophischen Kommunikationsverweigerung* (Stuttgart: Klett-Cotta, 1981), 616, 617.

11. Georg Lukács, *The Theory of the Novel: A Historico-Philosophical Essay on the Forms of Great Epic Literature*, trans. Anna Bostock (Cambridge: MIT Press, 1971), 64.

12. Walter Benjamin, *The Origin of German Tragic Drama*, trans. John Osborne (London: New Left Books, 1977), 166.

13. Adorno, "Idee," 359–60.

14. John Pizer has dedicated a book-length study to the question of the origin. See his *Toward a Theory of Radical Origin: Essays on Modern German Thought* (Lincoln: University of Nebraska Press, 1995). As we shall see later, Benjamin's conception of origin is of a Judaic nature and inextricably linked to his philosophy of language.

15. Adorno's insistence on a primeval duplicity is further apparent toward the end of his lecture. In his attempt to dispel the belief that such an originary duplicity, such an originary entwining of the archaic and the new, reinvoked the critique Hegel mounted against Schelling's philosophy of nature, he referred to Freud's text on the contradictory meaning of primal words, as well as to the myth of Kronos—a reference inspired by Benjamin's phenomenological analysis of melancholia in the *Trauerspiel* study.

16. Theodor W. Adorno, *Negative Dialektik*, in *Gesammelte Schriften*, vol. 6 (Frankfurt: Suhrkamp, 1973), n. p.

17. Adorno, "Idee," 358.

18. "Natural growth" is the term used by the English translator of *Negative Dialectics*, trans. E. B. Ashton (New York: Seabury Press, 1973).

19. Adorno, *Negative Dialectics*, 8.

20. Ibid., 10. In the same notice to *Negative Dialektik* cited in n. 16, Adorno added that this logic formed one of the early, cellular ideas of critical theory:

"The idea of a logic of decay is the oldest of [the author's] philosophical conceptions, dating back to his student years."

21. See, for instance, Hermann Schweppenhäuser's essay "Mythisches und historisches Katastrophenbewußtsein," in *Tractanda: Beiträge zur kritischen Theorie der Kultur und Gesellschaft* (Frankfurt: Suhrkamp, 1972), 118–30, which argues for the centrality of the category of catastrophe to negative dialectics.

22. See, for example, Adorno, *Negative Dialectics*, 359.

23. Ibid., 130–31.

24. Ibid., 333.

25. Heidegger makes this point in *Being and Time*, 475.

26. Adorno, *Negative Dialectics*, 53.

27. Ibid., 52, modified translation.

28. Ibid.

29. Ibid., 331.

30. Ibid.

31. Ibid., 361, modified translation.

32. Karl Marx, *Die deutsche Ideologie*, in *MEGA*, part 1, vol. 5 (Berlin: Dietz, 1964), 567; cited by Adorno in *Negative Dialectics*, 358.

33. Adorno, *Negative Dialectics*, 360.

34. Heidegger, *Being and Time*, 432.

35. Ibid., 433.

36. Ibid., 440.

37. Ibid., 498.

38. For a related reading of Heidegger's critique of "natural history," see G. Böhme's article "Geschichte der Natur" in *Historisches Wörterbuch der Philosophie*, vol. 3 (Darmstadt: Wissenschaftliche Buchgesellschaft, 1971).

39. This, incidentally, may also explain why Heidegger tended to downplay the importance of Dilthey's endeavor to advance a theory of science (*Wissenschaftstheorie*) and to come to a "logic of the human sciences"—in marked contradistinction to the work of more recent interpreters such as Manfred Riedel, who have underscored Dilthey's lifelong, persistent attempt to found an epistemology for the human sciences. Heidegger, *Being and Time*, 450. See also O. Pöggeler, *Der Denkweg Martin Heideggers* (Pfullingen: Günther Neske, 1963), 31.

40. Martin Heidegger, "Der Zeitbegriff in der Geschichtswissenschaft," in *Frühe Schriften* (Frankfurt: Klostermann, 1972), 368.

41. Michel Haar, *Le Chant de la terre: Heidegger et les assises de l'histoire de l'être* (Paris: Éditions de l'Herne, 1985), 33ff.

42. Ibid. For a more recent discussion of Heidegger's philosophy, see Hans Sluga, *Heidegger's Crisis: Philosophy and Politics in Nazi Germany* (Cambridge: Harvard University Press, 1993).

43. In Derrida's writings of the 1980s, this critique of Heidegger's humanism is intimately linked to the project of formulating the ethico-political question of responsibility with regard to a more originary "yes" that is anterior to philosophical questioning.

44. Gianni Vattimo, *The End of Modernity* (Baltimore: Johns Hopkins University Press, 1988), esp. 113ff.

45. In *Of Spirit* and, centrally, the interview "'Il faut bien manger'" (Eating Well), Derrida takes issue with the metaphysical legacy that inhabited Heidegger's conception of "world," insofar as it remained linked to a metaphysics of spirit and to the spiritual. Analyzing the concept of world in Heidegger's Freiburg conferences of 1929–30 and his *Introduction to Metaphysics*, Derrida deconstructs Heidegger's hermeneutical "as" to show how the animal's alleged privation of world, its inability to gain access to beings as such (*comme tel*), inadvertently reflected back on the "point of departure" of fundamental ontology, that is, *Dasein*. See Jacques Derrida, "'Il faut bien manger' ou le calcul du sujet," *Cahiers confrontation* 20 (1989): 91–114; and *Of Spirit: Heidegger and the Question*, trans. Geoff Bennington and Rachel Bowlby (Chicago: University of Chicago Press, 1989), a translation of *De l'esprit: Heidegger et la question* (Paris: Galilée, 1987). I discuss these issues in more detail in "'The Correct/Just Point of Departure': Deconstruction, Humanism, and the Call to Responsibility," in Hent de Vries and Harry Kunneman, eds., *Enlightenments: Encounters between Critical Theory and Contemporary French Thought* (Kampen, The Netherlands: Kok Pharos, 1993).

46. Walter Benjamin, "Re the Theory of Knowledge," in Gary Smith, ed., *Walter Benjamin: Philosophy, History, Aesthetics* (Chicago: University of Chicago Press, 1989), 50; the original passage can be found in Walter Benjamin, *Gesammelte Schriften,* ed. Rolf Tiedemann and Hermann Schweppenhäuser, vol. 1 (Frankfurt: Suhrkamp, 1972–), 577. The passage is also cited in Claude Imbert's "Le Présent et l'histoire" in Heinz Wismann, ed., *Walter Benjamin et Paris* (Paris: Les Éditions du Cerf, 1986), 743–93.

Chapter 2

Note: Originally written in 1991, a shorter version of this chapter was published as "Philosophy at Its Origin: Walter Benjamin's Prologue to the *Ursprung des deutschen Trauerspiels,*" in *Modern Language Notes* 110 (1995): 809–33.

1. Benjamin, *Origin of German Tragic Drama,* 40. The original passage can be found in *GS* 1:221. Subsequent references to *The Origin of German Tragic Drama* will appear parenthetically in the main text as *O,* followed by page numbers. Future references to *Gesammelte Schriften* will be abbreviated *GS,* followed by volume and page numbers, and will appear in parentheses in the main text.

2. See the letter that the Orientalist Hans Heinz Schaeder sent to Hugo von Hofmannsthal, cited in Gershom Scholem, *Walter Benjamin: The Story of a Friendship* (New York: Schocken Books, 1981), 146–49.

3. On the importance of Benjamin's shift from philosophy's concern with *Reflexionsbestimmungen* to the question of Being, see also Rolf Tiedemann, *Studien zur Philosophie Walter Benjamins* (Frankfurt: Suhrkamp, 1973), 15ff. On Benjamin's critique of idealism's "subjective synthesis of reality," see Martin Jay, *Marxism and Totality: The Adventure of a Concept from Lukács to Habermas* (Berkeley: University of California Press, 1984), 248.

4. On Benjamin's interest in the Kantian term "infinite task," see Benjamin, *Gesammelte Schriften,* 6:*passim.*

5. For other accounts of Benjamin's Kant interpretation, see Michael Jennings, *Dialectical Images: Walter Benjamin's Theory of Literary Criticism* (Ithaca: Cornell University Press, 1987), and Gary Smith, "Thinking through Benjamin: An Introductory Essay," in Smith, ed., *Walter Benjamin.*

6. Walter Benjamin, *The Correspondence of Walter Benjamin,* trans. Manfred R. Jacobson and Evelyn M. Jacobson (Chicago: University of Chicago Press, 1994), 97. Further citations will appear in the text as *C,* followed by page numbers.

7. The original passage is in Walter Benjamin, *Briefe,* ed. Gershom Scholem and Theodor W. Adorno, vol. 1 (Frankfurt: Suhrkamp, 1978), 151. Subsequent citations to this work will appear in the text as *B,* followed by page numbers.

8. Walter Benjamin, "On the Program of the Coming Philosophy," in Smith, ed., *Walter Benjamin,* 3, 4, 6, 9–10; *GS* 2:160.

9. Adorno, *Negative Dialectics,* 389.

10. Benjamin, "On the Program," 5.

11. Ibid., 4. Modified translation.

12. Haar, *Le Chant de la terre,* 143.

13. Benjamin, "On the Program," 5. Cf. *GS* 2:162–63.

14. Benjamin, "On the Program," 10.

15. Ibid.

16. Rodolphe Gasché, "Saturnine Vision and the Question of Difference: Reflections on Walter Benjamin's Theory of Language," *Studies in Twentieth-Century Literature* 11, no. 1 (1986): 96.

17. Benjamin, "On the Program," 9. On the role of Hamann's philosophy in Benjamin's thought, see Winfried Menninghaus, *Walter Benjamins Theorie der Sprachmagie* (Frankfurt: Suhrkamp, 1980), 205ff.

18. Walter Benjamin, "The Concept of Criticism in German Romanticism," in *Selected Writings,* vol. 1, *1913–1926,* ed. Marcus Bullock and Michael W. Jennings (London: Harvard University Press, 1996), 158. Cf. *GS* 1:77.

19. Thus in the dissertation Benjamin invokes Novalis's notes on the Sistine Madonna, in which the a priori of the work of art is defined as its transcendental form: "Every work of art has an a priori ideal, an intrinsic necessity, to exist" (Benjamin, "Concept of Criticism," 158). This statement also figures prominently in Benjamin's Hölderlin essay, "Two Poems by Friedrich Hölderlin," and in the epistemo-critical prologue to the *Trauerspiel* study.

20. Benjamin, "Concept of Criticism," 164–65; *GS* 1:86.

21. In "Des tours de Babel," Jacques Derrida qualifies the contract of translation, *l'à-traduire,* as a quasi-transcendental structure and, at several instances, asks whether it does not also open up the possibility of thinking about another history, one no longer ruled by the genealogical categories of historical linguistics. See "Des tours de Babel," in *Psyché: Inventions de l'autre* (Paris: Galilée, 1987), 203–35, esp. pp. 212 and 220. With respect to the relation between "translatability" and the notion of "reproducibility" as it appears in the later essay "The Work of Art in the Age of Mechanical Reproduction," see also Samuel Weber, "Der posthume Zwischenfall: Eine

Live Sendung," in George Christoph Tholen and Michael O. Scholl, eds., *Zeit-Zeichen: Aufschübe und Interferenzen zwischen Endzeit und Echtzeit* (Weinheim: VCH, Acta Humaniora, 1990), 177–98.

22. Walter Benjamin, "The Task of the Translator," in Walter Benjamin, *Illuminations,* ed. Hannah Arendt, trans. Harry Zohn (New York: Shocken Books, 1969), 72 (modified translation); *GS* 4:11. Subsequent references to *Illuminations,* abbreviated *I,* will appear in the text and will be followed by page numbers.

23. See, for example, an early text of Benjamin's, "Schemata zum Psychophysischen Problem" (*GS* 6:78–87). On the figure of Fechner and psychophysics, cf. Herbert Schnädelbach, *Philosophy in Germany.*

24. See Benjamin's comments on Kurt Hiller's animism in "Critique of Violence," in Walter Benjamin, *Reflections: Essays, Aphorisms, Autobiographical Writings,* ed. Peter Demetz, trans. E. Jephcott (New York: Schocken Books, 1986), 298. Subsequent citations to *Reflections,* abbreviated *R,* will appear in the text, followed by page numbers.

25. Benjamin's view of philology is quite complex, particularly in its relation to Herder's conception of philology, and calls for a closer study than is possible in the present context. On the interrelations between philology and Benjamin's philosophy of history, see also Jeanne-Marie Gagnebin, *Zur Geschichtsphilosophie Walter Benjamins* (Erlangen: Palm and Enke, 1978), and Heinrich Kaulen, *Rettung und Destruktion: Untersuchungen zur Hermeneutik Walter Benjamins* (Tübingen: Max Niemeyer, 1987). On Nietzsche's view of translation in *Die fröhliche Wissenschaft,* see Hans Joachim Störig, ed., *Das Problem des Übersetzens* (Darmstadt: Wissenschaftliche Buchgesellschaft, 1969, c. 1963).

26. See Derrida, "Des tours de Babel," on the notion of an economy of indebtedness and restitution. This economy of restitution is most likely related to the Torah, which is the very instance of restitutive tradition in Judaic orthodoxy. Gershom Scholem discusses the interrelations among Judaic tradition, the Torah, and orthodoxy's tensions with utopian Messianism in "Die Krise der Tradition im jüdischen Messianismus," in *Judaica: Studien zur jüdischen Mystik,* vol. 3 (Frankfurt: Suhrkamp, 1970), 152–97.

27. Walter Benjamin, "Doctrine of the Similar," trans. Knut Tarnowski, *New German Critique* 17 (1979): 65–69. In a remarkable analysis of the "ontologico-temporal structure" of Benjaminian translation, Andrew Benjamin has argued that the interaction between pure language and languages in general can be typified as "the temporality of inhering." Rereading de Man's analysis of the fragmented vessel, according to which the Jewish motive of *tikkun* would be an empty structure—since it does not imply an original but rather an originarily displaced language—Andrew Benjamin interprets pure language, in a Heraclitean sense, as "the anoriginal presence of original difference; of original conflict; of differential plurality." Crucially, the Greek Heraclitean model of *harmonia* is said to set adrift the Platonic "privileg[ing]" of being over becoming." See Andrew Benjamin, *Translation and the Nature of Philosophy: A New Theory of Words* (London: Routledge, 1989), 100ff. Indeed, as we shall see, by the time Benjamin drafts the introduction to *The Origin of German Tragic Drama,* such a setting adrift of Platonic ontology has moved to the center of his

attention, for it is intimately related to his historical thinking and the endeavor to mediate between the timeless Platonic Ideas and historical change. At the same time, this project remains explicitly bound up with Jewish tradition.

28. See the notes by Rolf Tiedemann and Hermann Schweppenhäuser in the collected edition's *Werkapparat, GS* 1:888. For further comments on this letter to Rang, see also Jennings, *Dialectical Images,* 141–42.

29. My translation is based on the one in *C* 224. I have chosen to translate "Welt der Verschlossenheit" by a somewhat cumbersome paraphrase, however, so as to foreground the double meaning of 'silence' and 'closure' that the term implies. The underlying dualism between a fallen temporality and a timeless sphere—constitutive of early phenomenology and as such the target of Adorno's "Die Idee der Naturgeschichte"—gradually undergoes significant transformations in the course of Benjamin's intellectual trajectory. While in the letter to Rang this duality is recast as the paradox that the historicity of the artwork consists in its "timelessness," the project of the prologue to "animate" the realm of stationary essences by means of a natural history, by contrast, amounts to the very crossing of the boundaries between atemporal "nature" and "history."

30. See also Bernd Witte, *Walter Benjamin—Der Intellektuelle als Kritiker: Untersuchungen zu seinem Frühwerk* (Stuttgart: Metzlersche Verlagsbuchhandlung, 1976), 107; Jennings, *Dialectical Images,* 194ff.; and Timothy Bahti, *Allegories of History: Literary Historiography after Hegel* (Baltimore: Johns Hopkins University Press, 1992), *passim.*

31. See Tiedemann, *Studien,* 18ff.

32. For a historical account of the inversion between epistemology and truth in Benjamin's early writings, see Rodolphe Gasché, "Saturnine Vision."

33. For a detailed analysis of Benjamin's indebtedness to Hamann, see Menninghaus, *Walter Benjamins Theorie der Sprachmagie,* esp. p. 205ff.

34. On this merger, see also Benjamin's famous letter to Scholem, of February 19, 1925, in which he writes the following about the epistemo-critical prologue: "This introduction is unmitigated chutzpah—that is to say, neither more nor less than the prolegomena to epistemology, a kind of second stage of my early work on language (I do not know whether it is any better), with which you are familiar, dressed up as a theory of ideas" (*C* 261; *B* 372). The comic effect in the letter derives not only from the Yiddish "chutzpah" but also from the stark contrast between the mention of "rubbish" and a seemingly high Kantian discourse. Benjamin's confession to Scholem is at first sight puzzling insofar as it suggests that the prologue merely rethought the 1916 language essay, supplemented by the Platonic doctrine of Ideas, as if the Ideas, rather than forming the core of the prologue, were merely ornamental or decorative. On the basis of similar remarks Benjamin was to make to Max Rychner and Adorno, Scholem concluded in his Benjamin biography that the cabalistic subtext of the prologue "for all purposes left me as the only reader who was close at hand" (Scholem, *Benjamin,* 125). The question of intended readership is an interesting one, considering that in the same letter to Scholem Benjamin noted that "with Rang's death [my book on the baroque] has lost the reader for whom it is intended" (*C* 262; *B* 374). However, rather than seeing these two intellectual strands as opposites or antinomies, one must view

them as part of Benjamin's endeavor to intertwine Jewish and Greek figures of thought.

35. Franz Rosenzweig, *Der Stern der Erlösung* (Frankfurt: Suhrkamp, 1988), 23–24.

36. Martin Heidegger, *Nietzsche*, trans. David Farrell Krell, 2 vols. (San Francisco: Harper and Row, c. 1979–87), 2:198–208.

37. Ibid., 200.

38. Ibid., 201n.

39. See Guy Oakes's "Rickert's Theory of Historical Knowledge," in Heinrich Rickert, *The Limits of Concept Formation in Natural Science: A Logical Introduction to the Historical Sciences*, ed. and trans. Guy Oakes, abridged ed. (Cambridge: Cambridge University Press, 1986).

40. Cf. ibid., ix. See further Schnädelbach, *Philosophy in Germany*, 57ff.

41. Thorleif Boman, *Hebrew Thought Compared with Greek* (Philadelphia: Westminster Press, 1960), 168–83.

42. Georg Simmel, *Goethe* (Leipzig: Klinkhardt and Biermann, 1913), 50–96.

43. On the relations between the ur-phenomenon in the *Trauerspielbuch* and the *Passagen-Werk*, see Buck-Morss, *Dialectics of Seeing*, 71ff.

44. For another reading of the first version of the prologue in its relation to revelation, see also Jeanne-Marie Gagnebin, *Zur Geschichtsphilosophie Walter Benjamins* (Erlangen: Palm and Enke, 1978). The fact that the link between the origin and revelation was later more or less suppressed confirms Scholem's remark in *"Und alles ist Kabbala"* that, though the term "revelation" was to gradually disappear from Benjamin's writings, the topos itself nonetheless remained present as a tacit intertext. See Gershom Scholem, *"Und alles ist Kabbala": Gershom Scholem im Gespräch mit Jörg Drews* (Munich: Edition Text und Kritik GmbH, 1980), 18–19.

45. For a related reading of this passage, see also Bahti's *Allegories of History*, 259ff.

46. For a discussion of these dynamics of *feststellen*, see also Tiedemann, *Studien*, and Bahti, *Allegories of History*, 260ff. Following Samuel Weber, I have translated *Vor-und Nachgeschichte* (or the work's natural history) by pre- and post-history.

47. See Tiedemann, *Studien*, and *Allegories of History*, 262.

48. See Tiedemann, *Studien*, 62ff.

Chapter 3

1. *GS* 5:571, 573. See also Buck-Morss, *Dialectics of Seeing, passim*.

2. The phrase Benjamin used was "die Geschichte wandert in den Schauplatz hinein" (*GS* 1:271). The English translation does not do justice to the element of *Ostentation* or *zur Schau stellen* central to Benjamin's analysis of baroque drama. On this point, see further Rainer Nägele, *Theater, Theory, Speculation: Walter Benjamin and the Scenes of Modernity* (Baltimore: Johns Hopkins University Press, 1991).

3. Wolf Lepenies, *Das Ende der Naturgeschichte: Wandel kultureller Selbstverständlichkeiten in den Wissenschaften des 18. und 19. Jahrhunderts* (Munich:

C. Hanser, 1976), 34, 41. See also Michel Foucault, *The Order of Things: An Archaeology of the Human Sciences* (New York: Vintage, 1970).

4. Wilhelm Dilthey, *Die Funktion der Anthropologie in der Kultur des 16. und 17. Jahrhunderts*, in *Weltanschauung und Analyse des Menschen seit Renaissance und Reformation: Abhandlungen zur Geschichte der Philosophie und Religion*, in *Gesammelte Schriften*, ed. Georg Misch, vol. 2 (Leipzig: B. G. Teubner, 1929), 417. See also Georg Misch's "Vorwort" in the same volume (p. v).

5. Dilthey, "Funktion der Anthropologie," 417.

6. Ibid., 441.

7. On the relations between Benjamin and Schmitt, see also my "On the Politics of Pure Means: Benjamin, Arendt, Foucault," in Hent de Vries and Samuel Weber, eds., *Violence, Identity, and Self-Determination* (Stanford: Stanford University Press, 1997).

8. Odo Marquard, *Schwierigkeiten mit der Geschichtsphilosophie: Aufsätze* (Frankfurt: Suhrkamp, 1982), 235n. 88.

9. Marquard, *Schwierigkeiten*, 125.

10. Michael Makropoulos, *Modernität als ontologischer Ausnahmezustand?: Walter Benjamins Theorie der Moderne* (Munich: Wilhelm Fink, 1989). See also Samuel Weber, "Taking Exception to Decision: Walter Benjamin and Carl Schmitt," in Harry Kunneman and Hent de Vries, eds., *Enlightenments: Encounters between Critical Theory and Contemporary French Thought* (Kampen, The Netherlands: Kok Pharos, 1993). Hans Blumenberg, *Säkularisierung und Selbstbehauptung: Erweiterte und überarbeitete Neuausgabe von "Die Legitimität der Neuzeit,"* pts. 1 and 2 (Frankfurt: Suhrkamp, 1974), 10. On the status of secularization in the *Trauerspiel* study, see also Lindner, " 'Natur-Geschichte,' " 43.

11. Exceptions are Bernd Witte's *Walter Benjamin—Der Intellektuelle als Kritiker*, and Jennings, *Dialectical Images*, 42ff.

12. Benjamin, quoted in Smith, ed., *Walter Benjamin*, 62–63; *GS* 5:590.

13. Walter Benjamin, *Passagen-Werk*, N3, 1.

14. Benjamin, quoted in Smith, ed., *Walter Benjamin*, 50.

15. Apart from the reference in the original draft of the epistemo-critical prologue, cited earlier, according to which historical time could be broached only by means of the concept of origin, the term as such does not occur in the *Trauerspielbuch*. On the question of historical time, see also Jennings, *Dialectical Images*, 42ff.

16. See Witte, *Walter Benjamin*, Jennings, *Dialectical Images*, and Bahti, *Allegories of History*.

17. Georg Simmel, "Das Problem der historischen Zeit," *Philosophische Vorträge, veröffentlicht von der Kantgesellschaft* 12 (1916): 3–31. About Heidegger's 1915 inauguration lecture, see further David Couzens Hoy, "History, Historicity, and Historiography in *Being and Time*," in M. Murray, ed., *Heidegger and Modern Philosophy: Critical Essays* (New Haven: Yale University Press, 1978). Samuel Weber's "Der posthume Zwischenfall: Eine *Live* Sendung" charts the missed encounter between Benjamin and Heidegger.

18. Simmel, "Das Problem der historischen Zeit," 30.

19. Ibid., 26.

20. See also Pöggeler, *Denkweg Martin Heideggers,* 30.

21. Heidegger, "Der Zeitbegriff in der Geschichtswissenschaft," 359.

22. Ibid.

23. Ibid., 374.

24. On the notion of "empty time," see Hans-Georg Gadamer, "Über leere und erfüllte Zeit," *Kleine Schriften III: Idee und Sprache* (Tübingen: J.C.B. Mohr, Paul Siebeck, 1972), 221–236.

25. In *Being and Time,* Heidegger would label this temporal modality *Jetztzeit,* only to reject it as a vulgar, inauthentic interpretation of time that covered up *Dasein*'s authentic temporality. While Heidegger's Freiburg lecture still stopped short at presenting physical time as endemic to the natural sciences, the last section of *Being and Time* would condemn the metaphysical tradition as a whole, from Aristotle through Hegel to Bergson, for being based on an inauthentic spatialization of temporality. As such, one would need to explore the pronounced differences between Heidegger's rejection of *Jetztzeit* and Benjamin's revalidation of the term as dialectical "now" in the Arcades Project.

26. On the distinction between these modalities of time, see also Boman, *Hebrew Thought,* 123ff.

27. See Helmut Pfotenhauer, "Benjamin und Nietzsche," in Burkhardt Lindner, ed., *"Links hatte noch alles zu enträtseln . . . ": Walter Benjamin im Kontext* (Frankfurt: Syndikat, 1978).

28. Herbert Cysarz, *Deutsche Barockdichtung: Renaissance-Barock-Rokoko* (Leipzig: Haessel, 1924), 26.

29. Ibid., 28.

30. See also "Critique of Violence," where Benjamin uses the term *Naturprodukt* (*GS* 1:180).

31. The original reads as follows: "das berechenbare Triebwerk der Kreatur" (*O* 96; *GS* 1:274).

32. Henri Bergson, *Essai sur les données immédiates de la conscience* (Paris: Félix Alcan, 1904), 173, 76.

33. Adorno, *Negative Dialectics,* 334.

34. Benjamin, *Illuminations,* 157–58; *GS* 1:609. See also section x of the Baudelaire essay (*I* 180–85; *GS* 1:637–44).

35. Bergson, *Essai,* 176.

36. On this phrase, see also Nägele, *Theater, Theory, Speculation.*

Chapter 4

1. Vattimo, *End of Modernity,* 63.

2. The image Benjamin painted of a decaying nature resembled the one evoked in the essay "On Transience," which Freud wrote at the height of World War I. The essay tried to shed some light on the interrelations between nature's transience and man's propensity to mourn, only to conclude that the mourning over transience seems small in the face of human forms of destruction inflicted during war.

3. In a letter to Scholem, dated April 17, 1920, Benjamin made reference to *The Plaint of Nature* but confessed that he hadn't read the tract. The figure of nature's mourning already appeared in "*Trauerspiel* and Tragedy" and is worked out in the *Trauerspielbuch*'s final chapter. See Irving Wohlfarth, "On Some Jewish Motifs in Benjamin," in Andrew Benjamin, ed., *The Problems of Modernity: Adorno and Benjamin* (London: Routledge, 1989), 157–215. See also chapter 10, below.

4. Theodor W. Adorno, *Ästhetische Theorie*, in *Gesammelte Schriften*, vol. 7 (Frankfurt: Suhrkamp, 1970), 192.

5. See also Philippe Lacoue-Labarthe and Jean-Luc Nancy's *The Literary Absolute: The Theory of Literature in German Romanticism*, trans. Philip Barnard and Cheryl Lester (Albany: State University of New York Press, 1988), which discusses Benjamin's theory of the fragment.

6. This attempt to endure explained the tendency to "spatialization" that he recognized in the elaborate graphic embellishments and frames that frequently adorned editions of baroque plays. "It was not felt that these products were intended to spread by growth over a period of time, so much as to fill up their allotted place here and now" (*O* 181; *GS* 1:357).

7. See also Kaulen, *Rettung und Destruktion, passim*.

8. See also Wolin, *Walter Benjamin*.

9. Cf. Kaulen, *Rettung und Destruktion, passim*.

10. See also Benjamin's critique of idealist and fascist forms of aesthetics in "Literaturgeschichte und Literaturwissenschaft" (*GS* 3:286). Relatively early on in his writerly career, Benjamin questioned the ideological baggage of terms such as *Schöpfertum* or geniality—for example, in the Goethe essay. This was not the case with the mystical notion of secrecy, which figured centrally in both the dissertation and the Goethe interpretation. In the Trauerspiel book, Benjamin defined the mourning play as a genre devoid of such secrecy.

11. This conception of aura also sheds light on the Baudelaire studies. The 1939 Baudelaire essay demystified the philosophy of life as a movement that vowed to recapture "lived experience" in an industrial age, by means of such reified and spatialized notions of time as Bergson's *durée*. The loss of the auratic, experience and tradition resulted from the introduction of a new, modern temporality, driven by far-reaching forms of mechanization and acceleration. Revising Proust's philosophy of time, Benjamin concluded that the modern condition came about through a split in the faculty of memory, so that voluntary, individual memory was sundered from involuntary memory or the realm of collective tradition. The auratic itself had withdrawn into the buried realms of involuntary memory. In a passage similar to the theses on history, Benjamin held that these mnemonic layers could be conjoined through the collective experience of religious cults, while the collective celebration and re-collection (*Eingedenken*) of important historical calendar dates joined qualitative to quantitative time.

12. The "desire of contemporary masses to bring things 'closer' spatially and humanly" was "just as ardent as their bent toward overcoming the uniqueness of every reality by accepting its reproduction" (*I* 223; *GS* 1:479).

13. On allegory as a historico-philosophical term, see also Wolin, *Walter Benjamin*.

14. Martin Heidegger, "Der Ursprung des Kunstwerks," in *Holzwege Gesamtausgabe,* ed. Friedrich-Wilhelm von Herrmann, 1st ser., vol. 5 (Frankfurt: Klostermann, c. 1977).

15. Adorno, *Ästhetische Theorie,* 12–13.

16. Ibid., 48.

17. Ibid., 50.

18. Ibid., 12.

19. Ibid., 191.

20. Ibid., 192.

21. Adorno, *Negative Dialectics,* 359–60. Modified translation.

22. Jacques Derrida, "Ousia et Grammè," in *Marges de la philosophie* (Paris: Les Éditions de Minuit, 1972), 76.

23. Adorno, *Negative Dialectics,* 55. Modified translation.

24. See Marx, *Die deutsche Ideologie,* 17.

25. Adorno, *Negative Dialectics,* 361.

Chapter 5

Note: This chapter was first presented at the 29th Annual Meeting of the Society for Phenomenology and Existential Philosophy at Villanova University, Philadelphia in 1990.

1. Theodor W. Adorno, "Die Aktualität der Philosophie," in *Gesammelte Schriften,* vol. 1 (Frankfurt: Suhrkamp, 1973), 338. The term "negative hermeneutic" is used by Kaulen, *Rettung und Destruktion,* and by Andrew Arato and Eike Gebhardt, eds., *The Essential Frankfurt School Reader* (New York: Continuum, 1993).

2. The critic Burkhardt Lindner observes that Benjamin seemed to propose a salvational model that was typical of *Geistesgeschichte,* thus in effect undercutting the destructive potential of natural history. See Lindner, "Natur-Geschichte," 62ff.

3. See Benjamin's remarks on these different strata ("die Welt in ihren Schichtungen") in *GS* 6:97.

4. English translation in Benjamin, *Selected Writings,* 1:303. I have translated "tragische Szene" as "tragic scene." Hereafter, references to *Selected Writings* will appear in the text and be abbreviated *SW,* followed by volume and page numbers.

5. Cf. the article on "Eros" in August Friedrich von Pauly, *Paulys Real-Encyclopädie der classischen Altertumswissenschaft,* ed. G. Wissowa, 24 vols. (Stuttgart: J. B. Metzlersche Verlagsbuchhandlung, 1894–1963).

6. See also Wolin, *Walter Benjamin.*

7. Friedrich Nietzsche, *Die Geburt der Tragödie aus dem Geiste der Musik,* in *Werke,* ed. Giorgio Colli and Mazzino Montinari, Dritte Abteilung, vol. 1 (Berlin: Walter de Gruyter, 1972), 39. Friedrich Nietzsche, *The Birth of Tragedy and the Case of Wagner,* trans. Walter Kaufmann (New York: Vintage, 1967), 22.

8. Nietzsche, *Birth of Tragedy,* 22–23.

9. On this point, see also Martin Heidegger, *Nietzsche,* vol. 1 (Pfullingen: Neske, 1961).

10. Translated as "The Curious Tale of the Childhood Sweethearts"; see Benjamin, *Selected Writings*, 1:331.

11. Ernst Tugendhat, *Ti Kata Tinos: Eine Untersuchung zu Struktur und Ursprung aristotelischer Grundbegriffe* (Freiburg: Alber, 1958), 3.

12. As Benjamin observed: "Mörike's profound verse: 'Was aber schön ist, selig ist [*sic*] es in ihm selbst' combines appearance [*Schein*] with beauty, that is to say, the beauty of art" (*GS* 1:829). Benjamin's misquotation of *ist* for *scheint* may stem from Rosenzweig's *Star of Redemption*. See the latter's faulty citation of the line in his discussion of the mythico-metaphysical "Abgeschlossenheit" that marks the work of art. Franz Rosenzweig, *Der Stern der Erlösung* (Frankfurt: Suhrkamp, 1988), 41.

13. On the seals of creation, see Gershom Scholem, "Der Name Gottes und die Sprachtheorie der Kabbala," in *Judaica: Studien zur jüdischen Mystik*, vol. 3 (Frankfurt: Suhrkamp, 1970). See also Nägele, *Theory, Theater, Speculation*, 101–2.

14. Søren Kierkegaard, *Der Begriff Angst* (Cologne: Eugen Diederichs, 1983), 84n.

15. Ibid., 69. My translation is based on, but alters, the English translation; see Søren Kierkegaard, *The Concept of Anxiety: A Simple Psychologically Orienting Deliberation on the Dogmatic Issue of Hereditary Sin*, trans. Reidar Thomte and Albert B. Anderson (Princeton: Princeton University Press, 1980), 69.

16. Clearly, Benjamin's early work embraces the flawed gender politics that also mars Nietzsche's philosophical work. For excellent analyses of the representation of femininity in Benjamin's later work, see Buck-Morss's *Dialectics of Seeing* and Christine Buci-Glucksmann's *Baroque Reason: The Aesthetics of Modernity*, trans. Patrick Camiller (London: Sage Publications, 1994).

17. On the interiority of character, see also Søren Kierkegaard, *Kritik der Gegenwart*, trans. Theodor Haecker (Basel: Hess, 1914), 20. This edition, which Benjamin most likely used, is cited in *GS* 2:936.

18. Kierkegaard, *Concept of Anxiety*, 123; cf. Kierkegaard, *Der Begriff Angst*, 127.

19. Kierkegaard, *Der Begriff Angst*, 122ff.

20. The term "instant" here is used for *Augenblick* so as to set it off from Kierkegaard's *Moment* (*momentum*), which refers to a fallen, linear succession of atomic time.

21. Kierkegaard, *Der Begriff Angst*, 89n; Kierkegaard, *Concept of Anxiety*, 88n.

22. My translation is based on Walter Benjamin, *Selected Writings*, vol. 1 (Cambridge: Harvard University Press, 1996), 348.

23. See also Werner Hamacher, "History, Teary: Some Remarks on *La Jeune Parque*," *Yale French Studies* 74 (1988): 67–94.

24. Adorno, *Kierkegaard*, 179.

25. See Benjamin's reading list (*GS* 2:970) and the reference to Fromm cited in the Bachofen essay.

26. Scholem, *Walter Benjamin*, 79. See also Richard Wolin's "Introduction to the Revised Edition" of *Walter Benjamin*, which provides a comprehensive analysis of Benjamin's flirtation with conservative and protofascist thinkers.

27. The phrase "unbeweinte Schöpfung"—a citation from theological tradition—appears in German in Benjamin's French Bachofen essay. Literally, it means creation that has not been mourned or lamented.

28. Johann Jakob Bachofen, *Das Mutterrecht*, in *Gesammelte Werke*, ed. Karl Meuli, vol. 3 (Basel: Benno Schwabe, 1948), 792.

29. Ibid., 798.

30. This is corroborated by a line from one of the drafts: "The *Schein*, in which nothingness appears [*erscheint*]" (*GS* 1:831).

31. Irving Wohlfarth's essay "On Some Jewish Motifs in Benjamin" also offers a reading of this "fall into the abyss of subjectivity" (160). See further Bahti, *Allegories of History*, 281ff., and Nägele, *Theater, Theory, Speculation*, 167ff.

32. Wohlfarth, "On Some Jewish Motifs."

33. On the trickery of dialectics, see Kierkegaard, *Kritik der Gegenwart*, 35 and 19–20.

34. Kierkegaard, *Kritik der Gegenwart*, 53.

35. See also Bahti, *Allegories of History*, *passim*.

36. See also ibid.

37. Karl Löwith, "Natur und Geschichte," in *Sämtliche Schriften*, vol. 2 (Stuttgart: J.B. Metzlersche Verlagsbuchhandlung, 1983), 290. On this figure, see also Adorno, *Kierkegaard*, 130.

38. Lukács, *Theory of the Novel*, 29, 36.

39. Adorno, "Idee der Naturgeschichte," 365.

Part II

1. My discussion of the term is based on J. Wiebering, "Kreatur," in *Historisches Wörterbuch der Philosophie*, vol. 4 (Darmstadt: Wissenschaftliche Buchgesellschaft, 1971–), 1,204–11.

2. Especially Derrida's *Geschlecht* cycle and *Of Spirit* addressed the ethico-political implications of Heidegger's inability to thematize the living in general (*Lebewesen*).

3. The influence of vitalism is particularly noticeable in Georg Lukács's *Die Seele und die Formen: Essays* (Neuwied: Luchterhand, 1971). See also Rainer Nägele, "Benjamin's Ground," *Studies in Twentieth-Century Literature* 11, no. 1 (1986): 5–24.

4. Georg Lukács, *Die Zerstörung der Vernunft*, in *Werke*, vol. 9 (Neuwied: Luchterhand, 1962).

5. Martin Heidegger, *Parmenides*, in *Gesamtausgabe*, ed. Friedrich-Wilhelm von Herrmann, 2d ser., vol. 54 (Frankfurt: Klostermann, c. 1982), 226.

6. Emmanuel Levinas, "Paul Celan: De l'être à l'autre," in *Noms propres* ([Montpellier]: Fata Morgana, 1976), 49–56.

7. Paul Celan, "Conversation in the Mountains," in *Collected Prose*, trans. Rosemarie Waldrop (Riverdale-on-Hudson, N.Y.: Sheep Meadow Press, 1990), 18. The original reads, "der Jud und die Natur, das ist zweierlei, immer noch, auch heute, auch hier" (Paul Celan, "Gespräch im Gebirg," in *Gesammelte*

Werke, vol. 3 [Frankfurt: Suhrkamp, 1983], 169). Also cited by Hent de Vries, *Theologie im Pianissimo und Zwischen Rationalität und Dekonstruktion: Die Aktualität der Denkfiguren Adornos und Levinas'* (Kampen, The Netherlands: J. H. Kok, 1989), 302; Catherine Chalier, *L'Alliance avec la nature* (Paris: Cerf, 1989), 51.

8. Levinas, *Noms propres,* 54.

Chapter 6

Note: Originally presented at the 1991 Convention of the Modern Language Association.

1. Gershom Scholem, ed., *The Correspondence of Walter Benjamin and Gershom Scholem, 1932–1940,* trans. Gary Smith and Andre Lefevre (New York: Schocken Books, 1989), 186. Cf. also Albrecht Schöne, "'Diese nach jüdischem Vorbild erbaute Arche': Walter Benjamin's *Deutsche Menschen,*" in Stéphane Moses and Albrecht Schöne, eds., *Juden in der deutschen Literatur: Ein deutsch-israelisches Symposion* (Frankfurt: Suhrkamp, 1986), 350–65. See also Anson Rabinbach, "Introduction," in Scholem, ed., *Correspondence of Walter Benjamin and Gershom Scholem,* vii ff.

2. See Theodor W. Adorno, "Zu Benjamins Briefbuch *Deutsche Menschen,*" in *Noten zur Literatur,* in *Gesammelte Schriften,* vol. 11 (Frankfurt: Suhrkamp, 1974), 687.

3. I use the word "psyche" here in the sense coined by Jacques Derrida in "Interpretations at War: Kant, the Jew, the German," *New Literary History* 22, no. 1 (1991): 39–95—that is, first, as "a psychic locus of the fantasies that drive us" (93) and, second, in the French sense of "a great pivoting mirror, a device of specular reflection" (94). Part of a series of writings that addressed the question of nationalisms, "Interpretations at War" analyzed aspects of the German–Jewish symbiosis or psyche in Hermann Cohen's *Deutschtum und Judentum.* Further, the article uncovered some of the phantasmatic, specular, and metaphysical moments that have marked the attempts in German history, most obviously by Wagner and Nietzsche but also by Cohen and Adorno, to provide an answer to the question, "Was ist deutsch?"

4. Peter Szondi, "Hoffnung im Vergangenen: Über Walter Benjamin," in *Schriften,* vol. 2 (Frankfurt: Suhrkamp, 1978), 294.

5. Schöne, "'Diese nach jüdischem Vorbild erbaute Arche,'" 365.

6. Johannes Ernst Seiffert, "*Deutsche Menschen*: Vorläufiges zu Walter Benjamins Brief-Anthologie," *Jahrbuch des Instituts für deutsche Geschichte* 1 (1972): 159.

7. Ibid., 161; see also Schöne, "'Diese nach jüdischem Vorbild erbaute Arche.'"

8. See, for example, Peter von Haselberg's highly problematic article, "Der Deutsche Walter Benjamin," which tries to recuperate "the German Benjamin," and Gershom Scholem's critique in his "Peter von Haselberg über den Deutschen Walter Benjamin," in Gershom Scholem, *Walter Benjamin und sein Engel: Vierzehn Aufsätze und kleine Beiträge,* ed. Rolf Tiedemann (Frankfurt: Suhrkamp, 1983), 180–85. It is above all Gershom Scholem who,

on various occasions, has pointed to the fact that Benjamin—like Kafka and Freud—never saw himself as a "German," only as a "German writer." See particularly the essays in *Judaica: Studien zur jüdischen Mystik*, vol. 2 (Frankfurt: Suhrkamp, 1970), in which Scholem rejects the idea of a Jewish–German symbiosis, and Habermas's response in "Gershom Scholem: Die verkleidete Thora," in *Philosophisch-politische Profile* (Frankfurt: Suhrkamp, 1981).

9. Adorno, "Zu Benjamins Briefbuch *Deutsche Menschen*," 686, 692.

10. Theodor W. Adorno, "Auf die Frage: Was ist deutsch?" in *Stichworte: Kritische Modelle 2* (Frankfurt: Suhrkamp, 1969), 102–12. Cf. also Jacques Derrida, "Force of Law: The 'Mystical Foundation of Authority,'" *Cardozo Law Review* 11 (1990): 977n.

11. Adorno, "Auf die Frage: Was ist deutsch?" 102.

12. Ibid., 105.

13. Ibid., 104.

14. Ibid., 110.

15. Ibid., 111.

Chapter 7

1. Benjamin, *Reflections*, 273; *GS* 2:367.

2. Translated in *Reflections* as "cosmic man." In Benjamin's notes to the Kraus essay, however, the term is used more or less interchangeably with *Vollmensch*, a term Benjamin borrowed from Salomo Friedländer's *Schöpferische Indifferenz*.

3. The following reading will address mainly the first and third sections of the Kraus essay.

4. Karl Kraus, "Worte in Versen II," in *Schriften*, ed. Christian Wagenknecht, vol. 9 (Frankfurt: Suhrkamp, 1989), 108–15.

5. Ibid., 111.

6. The counterpart to this anthropomorphization of the dog forms an intriguing piece, which Benjamin wrote at around the same time, in 1930, for the *Berliner Rundfunk*. Called "Wahre Geschichten von Hunden" (True Stories about Dogs), published in *GS* 7:243–49, this radio lecture offered a bizarre catalogue of canine images, from Linnaeus's baroque elaboration on the characteristics of dogs, to the ferocious blood dogs Fernando Cortez and his crew encountered as they conquered Mexico, to a British newspaper report about a *Trauerhund* (mourning dog), who invariably accompanied funeral processions. For a remarkable interpretation of these canine stories, see Jeffrey Mehlman's *Walter Benjamin for Children: An Essay on His Radio Years* (Chicago: University of Chicago Press, 1993), 83ff. On the figure of the dog, see also my "'The Correct/Just Point of Departure.'" See, furthermore, chapter 10, below.

7. If these and other analogies indicate to what degree Kraus's prose for Benjamin captured the spirit of baroque mourning, then the point is made even more persuasively in one of the unpublished notes to the essay, where Kraus acquires the stature of Saint Francis. See *GS* 2:1114.

8. On the question of real humanism in Benjamin's Kraus essay, see also Wolin's "Introduction to the Revised Edition," *Walter Benjamin*, xxviii.

9. For a discussion of Marxist humanism, see Kate Soper, *Humanism and Anti-Humanism* (La Salle, Ill.: Open Court, 1986); Martin Jay, "The Frankfurt School's Critique of Marxist Humanism," in *Permanent Exiles: Essays on the Intellectual Migration from Germany to America* (New York: Columbia University Press, [1985] c. 1986).

10. This point is also made by Alfred Schmidt, "Adorno: Ein Philosoph des realen Humanismus," *Neue Rundschau* (1969): 654–72. Also cited by Martin Jay, *Permanent Exiles*, 18–19. Schmidt's article analyzed Adorno's version of real humanism, focusing on the *Minima Moralia*, and suggested that, while Adorno no longer accepted Marx's "romantically inflected identity of humanism and materialism" (669), he professed to a humanism based on a "remembrance of nature in the subject" (671). Martin Jay further develops Alfred Schmidt's position when he takes issue with the Althusserian Göran Therborn, who held that the Frankfurt School's alleged replacement of real history with the philosophical construction of the dialectic of Enlightenment presented nothing less than a falling behind Marx to reclaim the position of the Young Hegelians. See also Alfred Schmidt, *The Concept of Nature in Marx* (London: New Left Books, 1971).

11. Karl Marx and Friedrich Engels, *Die heilige Familie oder Kritik der kritischen Kritik: Gegen Bruno Bauer und Konsorten*, in *Werke*, vol. 2 (Berlin: Dietz, 1962), 7.

12. Schmidt, "Adorno," 655.

13. See also Karl Kraus, *Sprüche und Widersprüche*, in *Schriften*, ed. Christian Wagenknecht, vol. 8 (Frankfurt: Suhrkamp, 1986), 71. Translated as *Dicta and Contradictions* in *In These Great Times: A Karl Kraus Reader*, ed. Harry Zohn (Chicago: University of Chicago Press, 1990).

14. Karl Marx, "Zur Judenfrage," in *Werke*, vol. 1 (Berlin: Dietz, 1964), 355, 370.

15. This is the charge Therborn levels at Marxist humanism; cited in Jay, *Permanent Exiles*, 16.

16. See Werner Hamacher, "*Pleroma*: Zu Genesis und Struktur einer dialektischen Hermeneutik bei Hegel," in Georg Wilhelm Friedrich Hegel, *"Der Geist des Christentums": Schriften 1796–1800*, ed. Werner Hamacher (Frankfurt: Ullstein, 1978); and *GS* 4:374ff.

17. Benjamin suggested that Kraus donned the mask of the misanthrope to become Shakespeare's Timon or the man-eater Caliban, thus embodying the inhumanity of the actor. See also Edward Timms, *Karl Kraus Apocalyptic Satirist: Culture and Catastrophe in Habsburg Vienna* (New Haven: Yale University Press, 1986), especially 175ff., for a discussion of Kraus's early wish to become an actor and the traces it left on his nontheatrical writings.

18. Feuerbach's aphorism remains untranslatable. Literally it reads, "One eats what one eats," but the third person singular of *essen*, *ißt* is homophonous with *ist* (of *sein*, to be), so that the line really is a pun on "One is what one is." In other words, existential being is defined by the act of eating.

19. See also the *Werkapparat* of Benjamin's collected works, where the editors frequently point to the close similarities between these texts.

20. On the figure of these transient angels, see Scholem's "Lyrik der Kabbala?" *Der Jude 6 (1921–22): 55–69*, a book review of Meïr Wiener's *Die Lyrik der Kabbala: Eine Anthologie* in which he discussed the relationship between Jewish mysticism and the status of the hymn. Scholem, *Walter Benjamin und sein Engel*. See also Robert Alter, *Necessary Angels: Tradition and Modernity in Kafka, Benjamin, and Scholem* (Cambridge: Harvard University Press, 1991), 113ff.

21. Scholem, *Walter Benjamin und sein Engel*, 50.

22. Massimo Cacciari, *The Necessary Angel*, trans. Miguel E. Vatter (Albany: State University of New York Press, 1994), 12 and 17. Cacciari discerns the angel of the apocalypse in Rilke's angel, which was at once "wonderful" and "horrific."

23. Cacciari, *Necessary Angel*, 2. This is not to say that Benjamin would not have been aware of this tradition. On the contrary, apart from the extensive discussion he had with Scholem about Judaic and Christian angelologies, Benjamin also had important contact with Hugo Ball, the author of *Byzantinisches Christentum* (1923) and the editor of pseudo-Dionysus's *The Celestial Hierarchy*. Benjamin may have come into contact with Hugo Ball's work on pseudo-Dionysus already in 1919, when, as Scholem reported, Ball visited Benjamin and afterward in his diary noted Benjamin's possession of a "cabalistic book of spells with demonic images" (*Flucht aus der Zeit*, 243; quoted in *Walter Benjamin und sein Engel*, 69n).

24. Scholem, *Walter Benjamin und sein Engel*, 53.

25. See Irving Wohlfarth, "Der 'Destruktive Charakter': Benjamin zwischen den Fronten," in Lindner, ed., *"Links hatte noch alles sich zu enträtseln . . ."*; and Burkhardt Lindner, "Positives Barbarentum—aktualisierte Vergangenheit: Über einige Widersprüche Benjamins," *Alternative* 23 (June/August 1980): 130–39.

26. On Benjamin's links to Nietzsche, see Wohlfarth, "Der 'Destruktive Charakter,'" 75.

27. On Salomo Friedländer, cf. *GS* 2:1102. Significantly, Nietzsche used the term *Unmensch* in the sense of "brute" in *Genealogy of Morals*. In a passage rife with antisemitic invectives, Nietzsche discussed the notion of a so-called Jewish form of "ressentiment," whose interplay with the ideal of classical Roman culture he sketched throughout the ages, to end up with the figure of Napoleon, whom he heralded as the corporeal reincarnation of the antique ideal. As the synthesis of inhuman and over-man, he overcame the rule of ressentiment that resurged in the wake of the French Revolution. See Friedrich Nietzsche, *On the Genealogy of Morals and Ecce Homo*, trans. Walter Kaufmann (New York: Vintage Books, 1969), 54. Compare also Friedländer's comments in his monograph on Nietzsche, a study Benjamin much admired: *Friedrich Nietzsche: Eine intellektuale Biographie* (Leipzig: Göschen, 1911), 104.

28. See Benjamin's letter to Max Rychner (*C* 371–73; *B* 522–24).

29. Cf. *GS* 2:349 (*R* 254), where part of the passage returns.

30. I have substituted the word "origin" for the translator's "source."

31. See also *GS* 3:452–80.

Chapter 8

1. See also Lindner, "Natur-Geschichte," 42.

2. See, for example, Nathan Rotenstreich's writings, particularly *Jews and German Philosophy: The Polemics of Emancipation* (New York: Schocken Books, 1984); Julius Carlebach's analysis of the Jewish question in *Karl Marx and the Radical Critique of Judaism* (London: Routledge and Kegan Paul, 1978); Susan A. Handelman's "The Legacy of German Idealism," in *Fragments of Redemption: Jewish Thought and Literary Theory in Benjamin, Scholem, and Levinas* (Bloomington: Indiana University Press, 1991), 93–115.

3. Rotenstreich, *Jews and German Philosophy*, 3–6.

4. Cf. Hölderlin's letter to his brother of January 1, 1799: Friedrich Hölderlin, *Sämtliche Werke*, vol. 6 (Stuttgart: Cotta, 1954), 304.

5. Peter Szondi's study of tragedy charts the development of this dialectic; see "Poetik der Tragödie und Philosophie des Tragischen," in *Schriften*, vol. 1 (Frankfurt: Suhrkamp, 1978), 151–260.

6. Carlebach, *Karl Marx*, 104–10. Carlebach, for example, comments on Marx's more than problematic adoption of the tradition that links Judaism to abject matter, materiality, and exteriority in the second part of his *On the Jewish Question*.

7. Jacques Derrida, *Glas* (Paris: Denoël/Gonthier, 1981), 58a, 56a.

8. Ibid., 62a, 63a.

9. Catherine Chalier, "Torah, cosmos et nature," *Les Nouveaux cahiers* 79 (1984–85): 9.

10. In his study on Benjamin and Rosenzweig, Stéphane Mosès argued that the reference to prayer in the appendix to the historico-philosophical theses followed the "sacred time" or "phenomenology of religious time," which Rosenzweig first analyzed in *Star of Redemption* (Stéphane Mosès, "Walter Benjamin and Franz Rosenzweig," in Smith, ed., *Walter Benjamin*, 244). Chalier's study, *L'Alliance*, similarly underscored that the time of liturgical observance followed an organic, cosmic temporality.

11. Chalier, *L'Alliance*, 15.

12. Derrida, "Force of Law," 926.

13. On this transcendental project, see also Werner Hamacher, "Afformative, Strike," *Cardozo Law Review* 13 (1991): 1133–57.

14. Günter Figal, "Die Ethik Walter Benjamins als Philosophie der reinen Mittel," in Günter Figal and Horst Folkers, eds., *Zur Theorie der Gewalt und Gewaltlosigkeit bei Walter Benjamin*, ser. A, no. 10 (Heidelberg: Forschungsstätte der Evangelischen Studiengemeinschaft, 1979); see also Günter Figal, "Recht und Moral bei Kant, Cohen und Benjamin," in Hans-Ludwig Ollig, ed., *Materialien zur Neukantianismus-Diskussion* (Darmstadt: Wissenschaftliche Buchgesellschaft, 1987), 163–83.

15. See also Adorno, *Negative Dialectics*, 254.

16. Hermann Cohen, *Ethik des reinen Willens*, 3d ed. (Berlin: Bruno Cassirer, 1921), 365.

17. Ibid., 366.

18. See *GS* 1:286; see also Mosès, "Walter Benjamin and Franz Rosenzweig," on the possible relations to Rosenzweig's work.

19. Cohen, *Ethik des reinen Willens,* 78.

20. Ibid., 69.

21. Ibid., 370.

22. Cf. René Girard, *Violence and the Sacred* (Baltimore: Johns Hopkins University Press, 1977), especially 15–18. If one follows Girard's argument, it is evident that Benjamin's notion of sacrifice was essentially theological in nature in that it bore on man's relations to his deities. Thus, in line with what Norbert Bolz and Bernd Witte have revealed to be Benjamin's Weberian background, the practice of a bloody, mythical sacrifice and its disappearance signaled the transition from polytheism to a Judaic monotheism. Going against these received views of anthropology and ethnology, Girard's *Violence and the Sacred* essentially analyzed sacrifice as a means of societal equilibrium, one that served to stem or quell violence in the primitive community. Eventually, the structure of vengeance was displaced by the instating of a judicial system, founded on the intervention of a sovereign, independent body.

23. On the figure of Hiller, see Hans Puttnies and Gary Smith, eds., *Benjaminiana* (Giessen: Anabas, 1991), and Witte, *Walter Benjamin.*

24. Derrida, "Force of Law," 1029.

25. Ibid.

26. Emmanuel Levinas, "The Paradox of Morality," in Robert Bernasconi and David Wood, eds., *The Provocation of Levinas: Rethinking the Other* (London: Routledge, 1988), 172. Also cited by John Llewelyn, "Am I Obsessed by Bobby? (Humanism of the Other Animal)," in Robert Bernasconi and Simon Critchley, eds., *Re-Reading Levinas* (Bloomington: Indiana University Press, 1991).

27. Levinas, "Paradox of Morality," 172, first italics added.

28. See also Hamacher, "Afformative, Strike," 1153.

29. Derrida, "Force of Law," 980.

30. See Derrida, "Interpretations at War," *passim.*

Chapter 9

1. Benjamin made these comments in 1938 in a letter to Scholem, which included a scathing review of Max Brod's Kafka biography. He implied that he only retained Kafka's displaced Kant citation from his reading of the biography. See *C* 554. The original reads: "Handle so, daß die Engel zu tun bekommen." Cited in Walter Benjamin, *Benjamin über Kafka* (Frankfurt: Suhrkamp, 1981), 83. This Suhrkamp paperback contains all of Benjamin's completed writings on Kafka: namely, the 1934 essay "Franz Kafka: On the Tenth Anniversary of His Death" (*I* 111–40), published in the *Jüdische Rundschau*; a 1931 radio lecture entitled "Franz Kafka: Beim Bau der chinesischen Mauer" (Franz Kafka: On the Great Wall of China); and two polemical texts against Max Brod, one from 1929, called "Kavaliersmoral," first published in *Die literarische Welt,* and the other from 1938, which Benjamin wrote in response to a request of Scholem's. The latter text, a letter to Scholem of June 12, 1938, appears in translation in *C* 560–66.

2. Scholem, ed., *Correspondence of Walter Benjamin and Gershom Scholem,* 127; see also Benjamin, *Benjamin über Kafka,* 75.

3. Gershom Scholem to Walter Benjamin, August 1, 1931, reprinted in Scholem, *Walter Benjamin,* 171; see also Benjamin, *Benjamin über Kafka,* 65.

4. Scholem, ed., *Correspondence of Walter Benjamin and Gershom Scholem,* 123–25.

5. This essay was later reprinted under the title "Früheste Dichtung Franz Kafkas" in a collection of essays by Susman, *Gestalten und Kreise* (Stuttgart: Diana, 1954), 348–66. Benjamin was not familiar with the study until Werner Kraft called his attention to it; see Benjamin, *Benjamin über Kafka,* 157. Hereafter, citations to this last work, abbreviated *BüK* and followed by page numbers, will appear in the text.

6. See, for example, Benjamin's letter of August 11, 1934, which seeks to redress Scholem's criticism, in Scholem, ed., *Correspondence of Walter Benjamin and Gershom Scholem,* 134–36.

7. Ibid., 142; *BüK* 82.

8. As Benjamin noted: "He did fail in his grandiose attempt to convert poetry into doctrine, to turn it into a parable and restore to it that stability and unpretentiousness which, in the face of reason, seemed to him to be the only appropriate thing for it. No other writer has obeyed the commandment 'Thou shalt not make unto thee a graven image' so faithfully" (*I* 129; *BüK* 27–28).

9. For a similar reading, see Alter, *Necessary Angels,* 106ff.

10. *B* 45–46; Scholem, *Walter Benjamin,* 38.

11. Scholem, *Walter Benjamin,* 214.

12. Ibid.

13. Gershom Scholem, "Offenbarung und Tradition als religiöse Kategorien im Judentum," in Rolf Tiedemann, ed., *Judaica,* vol. 4 (Frankfurt: Suhrkamp, 1984), *passim.*

14. This is the term offered by Gary Smith and Andre Lefevre, the translators of the Benjamin-Scholem correspondence.

15. On the figure of *der Gelehrte* in cabalism, see Scholem's *Von der mystischen Gestalt der Gottheit: Studien zu Grundbegriffen der Kabbala* (Frankfurt: Suhrkamp, 1977), 83–134.

16. Jacques Derrida, "Before the Law," in Derek Attridge, ed., *Acts of Literature* (New York: Routledge, 1992), 208.

17. See Werner Hamacher, "The Word *Wolke*—If It Is One," *Studies in Twentieth-Century Literature* 11, no. 1 (1986): 133–62.

18. Scholem, ed., *Correspondence of Walter Benjamin and Gershom Scholem,* 135, modified translation; see *BüK* 79.

19. Irving Wohlfarth offers a similar reading in "On Some Jewish Motifs in Benjamin," 185.

20. Cf. G.W.F. Hegel, "Die Pflanze und das Tier," in *Phänomenologie des Geistes,* in *Werke,* vol. 3 (Frankfurt: Suhrkamp, 1986), 507–8.

21. See also Margot Norris, *Beasts of the Modern Imagination: Darwin, Nietzsche, Kafka, Ernst, and Lawrence* (Baltimore: Johns Hopkins University Press, 1985).

22. On the complex representation of the *Ostjude* in Kafka's "Report to an Academy," see Sander L. Gilman, *Jewish Self-Hatred: Anti-Semitism and*

the Hidden Language of the Jews (Baltimore: Johns Hopkins University Press, 1986), 282, 285.

23. It should, however, be pointed out that there were numerous anthropological studies on totemism—some of which also form the foundation of Freud's own study—that may have inspired Benjamin, such as Frazer's groundbreaking work on myth (*The Golden Bough*) or, another likely source, Wilhelm Wundt's *Elemente der Volkspsychologie,* also cited by Freud.

24. See also Sigmund Freud, *Totem and Taboo and Other Works,* in *The Standard Edition of the Complete Psychological Works of Sigmund Freud,* ed. James Strachey, vol. 13 (London: Hogarth Press, 1955), 129.

25. Ibid., 171.

26. See his *Second Untimely Meditation.* See also Margot Norris, *Beasts of the Modern Imagination.* In her analysis of Kafka's last story, "Josefine the Singer, or the Mouse Folk," Norris quotes Nietzsche's second meditation, severing it from the discussion of history and historicism: "the narration constitutes a bestial gesture that marks the trajectory from signification to obliteration, from remembering to forgetting. Becoming the beast is remembering to forget, as being the beast is forgetting to remember, a moment presented by Nietzsche in a hypothetical interlocution. 'The human may well ask the animal one day, "Why do you not talk to me of your bliss and only look at me?" The animal really wants to answer and say: "It comes of always forgetting right away what I wanted to say." But it forgot even this answer and was mute: so that the human could only wonder'" (119). Norris examines "the critique of anthropocentrism at the hands of 'beasts'" (1) or the "biocentric critique of anthropocentrism," specifically "human being as a cultural creature, as implicated in the Symbolic Order" (3). Benjamin's work, I would argue, falls outside what Norris terms the biocentric tradition. Further, insofar as his critique of biocentrism—to adopt the term—was inspired mostly by a Judaic conception of language, it cannot merely be seen as an exponent of the "Symbolic Order," which Norris pits against the biocentric tradition.

27. Nietzsche, *On the Genealogy of Morals and Ecce Homo,* 58.

28. Martin Heidegger, *Über den Humanismus* (Frankfurt: Klostermann, 1981), 17. See also chapter 10, below.

29. Cf. Stéphane Mosès, "Brecht und Benjamin als Kafka-Interpreten," in Stéphane Mosès and Albrecht Schöne, eds., *Juden in der deutschen Literatur: Ein deutsch-israelisches Symposion* (Frankfurt: Suhrkamp, 1986), 237–56.

30. Ibid., 254.

31. Franz Kafka, *"The Metamorphosis," "The Penal Colony," and Other Stories,* trans. Willa Muir and Edwin Muir (New York: Schocken, 1975), 136.

Chapter 10

1. Quoted in *O* 146; *GS* 1:324.

2. Theodor W. Adorno, "Notes on Kafka," in *Prisms,* trans. Samuel Weber and Shierry Weber (Cambridge; MIT Press, 1981), 255 (modified translation); see also Theodor W. Adorno, "Aufzeichnungen zu Kafka," *Prismen,* in *Gesammelte Schriften,* ed. Rolf Tiedemann, vol. 10 (Frankfurt: Suhrkamp, 1986), 262.

3. Adorno, "Notes on Kafka," 255; "Aufzeichnungen zu Kafka," 267.

4. Ibid.

5. Adorno, "Notes on Kafka," 262–63 (slightly modified translation); "Aufzeichnungen zu Kafka," 275–76.

6. Adorno, "Notes on Kafka," 270.

7. Rainer Nägele recently addressed the topic of *Aufmerksamkeit* in "Die Aufmerksamkeit des Lesers: Aufklärung und Moderne," in Harry Kunneman and Hent de Vries, eds., *Enlightenments: Encounters between Critical Theory and Contemporary French Thought* (Kampen, The Netherlands: Kok Pharos, 1993).

8. Rainer Maria Rilke, *Duino Elegies,* trans. J.B. Leishman and Stephen Spender (New York: Norton, 1939), 67.

9. Martin Heidegger, *Parmenides,* in *Gesamtausgabe,* ed. Friedrich-Wilhelm von Herrmann, 2d ser., vol. 54 (Frankfurt: Klostermann, 1982), 229.

10. Rilke's conception of the relation between humans and animals was the latest instance of a metaphysical current that really had started with the onset of an abject modernity. Heidegger, typically, located modernity temporally in the shift from Greek to the predominance of Roman culture, exemplified by the translation of the Greek *zōon logon echon* into the Latin *animal rationale.*

11. Heidegger, *Parmenides,* 226.

12. Heidegger, *Über den Humanismus,* 17. The translation offered in Martin Heidegger, *Basic Writings: From* Being and Time *(1927) to* The Task of Thinking *(1964),* ed. David Farrell Krell (New York: Harper Collins, 1977), 206, omits this crucial phrase.

13. Martin Heidegger, "Wozu Dichter?" in *Holzwege,* in *Gesamtausgabe,* ed. Friedrich-Wilhelm von Herrmann, 1st ser., vol. 5 (Frankfurt: Klostermann, c. 1977), 311.

14. Ibid., 312. Cf. Rainer Maria Rilke, *Briefe aus Muzot 1921 bis 1926* (Leipzig: Insel, 1935), 337.

15. "To what extent the relation to such an essence within the completion of modern metaphysics belongs to the Being of beings; to what extent the essence of Rilke's angel, despite all differences in content, is metaphysically speaking the same as the figure of Nietzsche's Zarathustra, can only be shown by a more originary development of the essence of subjectivity" (Heidegger, "Wozu Dichter?" 312–13). These comments illustrated the argument Heidegger also set forth in his "Nietzsches Wort 'Gott ist tot.'" Indeed, the will to power of technology and the over-man were thought to be part of the history of modern metaphysics, which absorbed the totality of beings (*das Seiende*) into the immanence of subjectivity: "The over-man never takes up the position of God; instead, the position the over-man aims to achieve is that of another realm that provides another foundation for beings in another Being. This other Being of beings in the meantime, signaling the beginning of modern metaphysics, is subjectivity" (Heidegger, "Nietzsches Wort 'Gott ist tot,'" in *Holzwege,* 255).

16. "Because in Rilke's poetry too the essential boundary between the secret of the living (plants, animals) and the secret of the historical (i.e., man) can be neither experienced nor maintained, this poetic word nowhere reaches the pinnacle of a decision that founds history. It almost appears as if there is in this poetry a boundless and groundless humanization of the animal at work,

through which the animal, as it relates to the original experience of being as a whole, is placed above man, and, in a certain sense, even is turned into over-man [*Übermensch*]" (Heidegger, *Parmenides,* 239).

17. On the notion of the "infra-human," see also my "'The Correct/Just Point of Departure.'"

18. Paul Celan, "The Meridian: Speech on the Occasion of Receiving the Georg Büchner Prize, Darmstadt, 22 October 1960," in *Collected Prose,* 43. Modified translation. The original German can be found in Paul Celan, "Der Meridian: Rede anläßlich der Verleihung des Georg-Büchner-Preises," *Gesammelte Werke,* vol. 3 (Frankfurt: Suhrkamp, 1983), 192.

19. Celan, "The Meridian," 48.

20. Ibid., 38.

21. Ibid., 50, modified translation. As John Felstiner observes, "Reading Benjamin in December 1959, Celan had underlined this maxim" (*Paul Celan: Poet, Survivor, Jew* [New Haven: Yale University Press, 1995], 164).

22. Georg Büchner, *Werke und Briefe* (Munich: Hanser, 1980), 75.

23. Celan, "The Meridian," 42–43.

24. Ibid., 47; in German: "zwischen Fremd und Fremd zu unterscheiden" (Celan, "Der Meridian" 196).

25. Celan, "Der Meridian," 193; "The Meridian," 44.

26. Celan, "Der Meridian," 193; "The Meridian," 44.

27. Celan, "Der Meridian," 197; "The Meridian," 49.

28. Celan, "The Meridian," 52, modified translation.

29. Levinas, *Noms propres,* 50.

30. Ibid., 52–53.

31. Cf. the *Werkapparat* to Benjamin's collected writings in *GS* 2:1315.

32. On the figure of the ur-mother, see Chalier, *L'Alliance,* 120.

33. On this point, see Emmanuel Levinas, "The Name of a Dog, or Natural Rights," in *Difficult Freedom: Essays on Judaism,* trans. Seán Hand (Baltimore: Johns Hopkins University Press, 1990), 151.

34. See also *GS* 2:460, 461, 465: "The storyteller is the figure in which the righteous man encounters himself." On the figure of *Aufmerksamkeit,* see also Nägele, "Die Aufmerksamkeit des Lesers."

35. Wohlfarth's "On Some Jewish Motifs in Benjamin" provides a compelling, thorough analysis of this constellation in Benjamin's writings. In his analysis, Wohlfarth traces the tension between an apparent Judaic logocentrism and the otherness of nature. In a transposition of Adorno's aphorism that "foreign words are the Jews of language," Wohlfarth comes to hold that "nature—which speaks no audible language, not even a foreign one—might in turn be called the (Jew)ess of the Logos. She would thus be the Jew(ess) of Judaism itself, the burnt offering or holocaust it bore within itself" (197). This remark is reintroduced in a footnote, which discusses the figure of exile in the Lurianic Cabala, for which exile stands at the center of creation: "nature's exile is ineradicably inscribed in the logic of the Word. It is, as it were, internal exile, an internal Jewish matter. Is nature, then, not merely the Jew(ess) as scapegoat but the scapegoat of the Jews? How to square such structural exclusion with the all-inclusiveness to which any self-respecting Messianism has often laid claim?" (215n. 66). Further, Wohlfarth notes that it was "one of the tasks awaiting

Benjamin's generation . . . to complete the deliverance of Judaism from the dictatorship it had been forced to impose on the mythical order" (205)—that is, nature. Indeed, precisely such a project lies at the heart of Adorno's and Benjamin's engagements with natural history. Wohlfarth places a great deal of emphasis on the underlying anthropomorphic and "imperialistic humanism" of the term *Fürsprech*. While such a reading is warranted, especially in view of the motif of "the plaint of nature," one would nevertheless have to ask whether such an observation is not similar to Levinas's observation that one can speak of animal suffering only in analogy to human suffering—a statement that is perhaps the reverse side of Rilke's lament that humans have been turned away from the open at birth. In the development of Benjamin's notion of *Kreatur*, a decisive shift seems to have occurred in the Leskov essay, for Wenzel's openness to the language of otherness is foregrounded there.

36. See *GS* 2:1153–54; see also Wohlfarth, "On Some Jewish Motifs in Benjamin," 188.

37. Chalier, *L'Alliance avec la nature*, 55.

38. For the most comprehensive account of the duplicitous nature melancholy acquired in Benjamin's work, see Susan Sontag, "Introduction," in Walter Benjamin, *"One-Way Street" and Other Writings*, trans. Edmund Jephcott and Kingsley Shorter (London: Verso, 1985), 7–28.

Postscript

1. Emmanuel Levinas, "The Name of a Dog, or Natural Rights," in *Difficult Freedom: Essays on Judaism*, trans. Seán Hand (Baltimore: Johns Hopkins University, 1990), 152–53. Modified translation. See also Llewelyn, "Am I Obsessed by Bobby?"

2. Adorno, *Negative Dialectics*, 299.

Bibliography

Adorno, Theodor W. "Die Aktualität der Philosophie." In *Gesammelte Schriften.* Ed. Rolf Tiedemann. Vol. 1. Frankfurt: Suhrkamp, 1973.
———. *Ästhetische Theorie.* Ed. Gretel Adorno and Rolf Tiedemann. Frankfurt: Suhrkamp, 1970. In *Gesammelte Schriften.* Ed. Rolf Tiedemann. Vol. 7.
———. "Aufzeichnungen zu Kafka." *Prismen.* In *Gesammelte Schriften.* Ed. Rolf Tiedemann. Vol. 10. Frankfurt: Suhrkamp, 1986.
———. "Auf die Frage: Was ist deutsch?" In *Stichworte: Kritische Modelle 2.* Frankfurt: Suhrkamp, 1969.
———. "Die Idee der Naturgeschichte." In *Gesammelte Schriften.* Ed. Rolf Tiedemann. Vol. 1. Frankfurt: Suhrkamp, 1973.
———. *The Jargon of Authenticity.* Trans. Knut Tarnowski and Frederic Will. Evanston, Ill.: Northwestern University Press, 1973.
———. *Kierkegaard: Konstruktion des Ästhetischen.* In *Gesammelte Schriften.* Ed. Rolf Tiedemann. Vol. 2. Frankfurt: Suhrkamp, 1979.
———. *Minima Moralia: Reflexionen aus dem beschädigten Leben.* Frankfurt: Suhrkamp, 1969.
———. *Negative Dialectics.* Trans. E. B. Ashton. New York: Seabury Press, 1973.
———. *Negative Dialektik.* In *Gesammelte Schriften.* Ed. Rolf Tiedemann. Vol. 6. Frankfurt: Suhrkamp, 1973.
———. "Notes on Kafka." In *Prisms.* Trans. Samuel Weber and Shierry Weber. Cambridge, Mass.: MIT Press, 1981.
———. *Über Walter Benjamin: Aufsätze, Artikel, Briefe.* Ed. Rolf Tiedemann. Frankfurt: Suhrkamp, 1990.
———. "Zu Benjamins Briefbuch *Deutsche Menschen.*" In *Gesammelte Schriften.* Ed. Rolf Tiedemann. Vol. 11. Frankfurt: Suhrkamp, 1974.
Adorno, Theodor W., and Max Horkheimer. *Dialectic of Enlightenment.* Trans. John Cumming. New York: Continuum, 1993.
Alter, Robert. *Necessary Angels: Tradition and Modernity in Kafka, Benjamin, and Scholem.* Cambridge, Mass.: Harvard University Press, 1991.

Arato, Andrew, and Eike Gebhardt, eds. *The Essential Frankfurt School Reader.* New York: Continuum, 1993.

Arendt, Hannah. "Introduction—Walter Benjamin: 1892–1940." In Walter Benjamin, *Illuminations.* Ed. Hannah Arendt, trans. Harry Zohn. New York: Schocken Books, 1969.

Bachofen, Johann Jakob. *Das Mutterrecht: Eine Untersuchung über die Ginaikokratie der alten Welt nach ihrer religiösen und rechtlichen Natur.* In *Gesammelte Werke.* Ed. Karl Meuli. Vol. 3. Basel: Benno Schwabe and Co. Verlag, 1948.

Bahti, Timothy. *Allegories of History: Literary Historiography after Hegel.* Baltimore: Johns Hopkins University Press, 1992.

Benjamin, Andrew. *The Problems of Modernity: Adorno and Benjamin.* London: Routledge, 1989.

———. *Translation and the Nature of Philosophy: A New Theory of Words.* London: Routledge, 1989.

Benjamin, Walter. *Benjamin über Kafka.* Frankfurt: Suhrkamp, 1981.

———. *Briefe.* Ed. Gershom Scholem and Theodor W. Adorno. 2 vols. Frankfurt: Suhrkamp, 1978.

———. *The Correspondence of Walter Benjamin.* Trans. Manfred R. Jacobson and Evelyn M. Jacobson. Chicago: University of Chicago Press, 1994.

———. "Doctrine of the Similar." Trans. Knut Tarnowski. *New German Critique* 17 (Spring 1979): 65–69.

———. *Gesammelte Schriften.* Ed. Rolf Tiedemann and Hermann Schweppenhäuser. 7 vols. Frankfurt: Suhrkamp, 1972–.

———. *Illuminations.* Ed. Hannah Arendt, trans. Harry Zohn. New York: Schocken Books, 1969.

———. *The Origin of German Tragic Drama.* Trans. John Osborne. London: Verso, 1985.

———. *Reflections: Essays, Aphorisms, Autobiographical Writings.* Ed. Peter Demetz, trans. Edmund Jephcott. New York: Schocken Books, 1986.

———. *Selected Writings.* Ed. Marcus Bullock and Michael W. Jennings. Cambridge, Mass.: Harvard University Press, 1996.

Bergman, Samuel Hugo. *The Philosophy of Solomon Maimon.* Trans. Noah J. Jacobs. Jerusalem: Magnes Press, The Hebrew University, 1967.

Bergson, Henri. *Essai sur les données immédiates de la conscience.* Paris: Félix Alcan, 1904.

Bloch, Ernst, Georg Lukács, Bertolt Brecht, Walter Benjamin, and Theodor Adorno. *Aesthetics and Politics.* Ed. Ronald Taylor. London: Verso, 1977.

Blumenberg, Hans. *Säkularisierung und Selbstbehauptung: Erweiterte und überarbeitete Neuausgabe von "Die Legitimität der Neuzeit," erster und zweiter Teil.* Frankfurt: Suhrkamp, 1974.

Böhme, G. "Geschichte der Natur." In *Historisches Wörterbuch der Philosophie.* Vol. 3. Darmstadt: Wissenschaftliche Buchgesellschaft, 1971.

Bolz, Norbert W. *Auszug aus der entzauberten Welt: Philosophischer Extremismus zwischen den Weltkriegen.* Munich: Fink, 1989.

Boman, Thorleif. *Hebrew Thought Compared with Greek.* Philadelphia: Westminster Press, 1960.

Büchner, Georg. *Werke und Briefe.* Munich: Hanser, 1980.

Buci-Glucksmann, Christine. *Baroque Reason: The Aesthetics of Modernity*. Trans. Patrick Camiller. London: Sage, 1994.

Buck-Morss, Susan. *The Dialectics of Seeing: Walter Benjamin and the Arcades Project*. Cambridge, Mass.: MIT Press, 1989.

———. *The Origin of Negative Dialectics: Theodor W. Adorno, Walter Benjamin, and the Frankfurt Institute*. New York: Free Press, 1977.

Cacciari, Massimo. *The Necessary Angel*. Trans. Miguel E. Vatter. Albany: State University of New York Press, 1994.

Carlebach, Julius. *Karl Marx and the Radical Critique of Judaism*. London: Routledge and Kegan Paul, 1978.

Celan, Paul. "Conversation in the Mountains." In *Collected Prose*. Trans. Rosemarie Waldrop. Riverdale-on-Hudson, N.Y.: Sheep Meadow Press, 1990.

———. "Gespräch im Gebirg." In *Gesammelte Werke*. Vol. 3. Frankfurt: Suhrkamp, 1983.

———. "Der Meridian: Rede anläßlich der Verleihung des Georg-Büchner-Preises." In *Gesammelte Werke*. Vol. 3. Frankfurt: Suhrkamp, 1983.

———. "The Meridian: Speech on the Occasion of Receiving the Georg Büchner Prize, Darmstadt, 22 October 1960." In *Collected Prose*. Trans. Rosemarie Waldrop. Riverdale-on-Hudson, N.Y.: Sheep Meadow Press, 1990.

Chalier, Catherine. *L'Alliance avec la nature*. Paris: Éditions du Cerf, 1989.

———. "Torah, cosmos et nature." *Les Nouveaux cahiers* 79 (Winter 1984–85): 3–13.

Cohen, Hermann. *Ethik des reinen Willens*. 3d ed. Berlin: Bruno Cassirer, 1921.

Cysarz, Herbert. *Deutsche Barockdichtung: Renaissance-Barock-Rokoko*. Leipzig: H. Haessel Verlag, 1924.

Derrida, Jacques. "Before the Law." In Derek Attridge, ed., *Acts of Literature*. New York: Routledge, 1992.

———. "Eating Well." In Eduardo Cadava, Peter Connor, and Jean-Luc Nancy, eds., *Who Comes after the Subject?* New York: Routledge, 1991.

———. "Force of Law: The 'Mystical Foundation of Authority.'" *Cardozo Law Review* 11 (1990): 920–1,045.

———. *Glas*. Paris: Denoël/Gonthier, 1981.

———. "'Il faut bien manger' ou le calcul du sujet." *Cahiers Confrontation* 20 (Hiver 1989): 91–114.

———. "Interpretations at War: Kant, the Jew, the German." *New Literary History* 22, no. 1 (Winter 1991): 39–95.

———. *Marges de la philosophie*. Paris: Éditions de Minuit, 1972.

———. *Of Spirit: Heidegger and the Question*. Trans. Geoff Bennington and Rachel Bowlby. Chicago: University of Chicago Press, 1989.

———. "Des Tours de Babel." In *Psyché: Inventions de l'autre*. Paris: Galilée, 1987.

De Vries, Hent. *"Theologie im Pianissimo" und "Zwischen Rationalität und Dekonstruktion": Die Aktualität der Denkfiguren Adornos und Levinas'*. Kampen: J. H. Kok, 1989.

Dilthey, Wilhelm. *Weltanschauung und Analyse des Menschen seit Renaissance und Reformation: Abhandlungen zur Geschichte der Philosophie und Religion*. In *Gesammelte Schriften*. Ed. Georg Misch. Vol. 2. Leipzig: B. G. Teubner, 1929.

Felstiner, John. *Paul Celan: Poet, Survivor, Jew*. New Haven: Yale University Press, 1995.

Figal, Günter. "Die Ethik Walter Benjamins als Philosophie der reinen Mittel." In Günter Figal and Horst Folkers, eds., *Zur Theorie der Gewalt und Gewaltlosigkeit bei Benjamin*. Ser. A, no. 10. Heidelberg: Forschungsstätte der Evangelischen Studiengemeinschaft. 1979.

———. "Recht und Moral bei Kant, Cohen und Benjamin." In Hans-Ludwig Ollig, ed., *Materialien zur Neukantianismus-Diskussion*. Darmstadt: Wissenschaftliche Buchgesellschaft, 1987.

Foucault, Michel. "Nietzsche, Genealogy, History." *Semiotexte* 3 (1987): 78–94.

———. *The Order of Things: An Archaeology of the Human Sciences*. New York: Vintage, 1970.

Franck, Didier. "Being and the Living." In Eduardo Cadava, Peter Connor, and Jean-Luc Nancy, eds., *Who Comes after the Subject?* New York: Routledge, 1991.

Freud, Sigmund. *Totem and Taboo and Other Works*. In *The Standard Edition of the Complete Psychological Works of Sigmund Freud*. Ed. James Strachey. Vol. 13. London: Hogarth Press, 1955.

Friedländer, Salomo. *Friedrich Nietzsche: Eine intellektuale Biographie*. Leipzig: Göschen, 1911.

Fürnkäs, Josef. "Zitat und Zerstörung: Karl Kraus und Walter Benjamin." In J. Le Rider and G. Raulet, eds., *Verabschiedung der (Post-) Moderne*. Tübingen, 1987.

Gadamer, Hans-Georg. "Über leere und erfüllte Zeit." In *Kleine Schriften III: Idee und Sprache*. Tübingen: J. C. B. Mohr, Paul Siebeck, 1972.

Gagnebin, Jeanne-Marie. *Zur Geschichtsphilosophie Walter Benjamins*. Erlangen: Verlag Palm and Enke, 1978.

Gasché, Rodolphe. "Saturnine Vision and the Question of Difference: Reflections on Walter Benjamin's Theory of Language." *Studies in Twentieth-Century Literature* 11, no. 1 (1986): 83–104.

Gilman, Sander L. *Jewish Self-Hatred: Anti-Semitism and the Hidden Language of the Jews*. Baltimore: Johns Hopkins University Press, 1986.

Girard, René. *Violence and the Sacred*. Baltimore: Johns Hopkins University Press, 1977.

Haar, Michel. *Le Chant de la terre: Heidegger et les assises de l'histoire de l'être*. Paris: Éditions de l'Herne, 1985.

Habermas, Jürgen. "Gershom Scholem: Die verkleidete Thora." In Jürgen Habermas, *Philosophisch-politische Profile*. Frankfurt: Suhrkamp, 1981.

———. "Walter Benjamin: Consciousness-Raising or Rescuing Critique." In Gary Smith, ed., *On Walter Benjamin: Critical Essays and Recollections*. Cambridge, Mass.: MIT Press, 1988.

Hamacher, Werner. "Afformative, Strike." *Cardozo Law Review* 13 (1991): 1,133–57.

———. "History, Teary: Some Remarks on *La Jeune Parque*." *Yale French Studies* 74 (1988): 67–94.

———. "*Pleroma*: Zu Genesis und Struktur einer dialektischen Hermeneutik bei Hegel." In Georg Wilhelm Friedrich Hegel, *"Der Geist des Christentums": Schriften 1796–1800*. Ed. Werner Hamacher. Frankfurt: Ullstein, 1978.

——. "The Word *Wolke*—If It Is One." *Studies in Twentieth-Century Literature* 11 (1986): 133–62.

Handelman, Susan A. *Fragments of Redemption: Jewish Thought and Literary Theory in Benjamin, Scholem, and Levinas*. Bloomington: Indiana University Press, 1991.

Hanssen, Beatrice. "'The Correct/Just Point of Departure': Deconstruction, Humanism, and the Call to Responsibility." In Harry Kunneman and Hent de Vries, eds., *Enlightenments: Encounters between Critical Theory and Contemporary French Thought*. Kampen, The Netherlands: Kok Pharos, 1993.

——. "Elfriede Jelinek's Language of Violence." *New German Critique* 68 (1996): 79–112.

——. "On the Politics of Pure Means: Benjamin, Arendt, Foucault." In *Violence, Identity, and Self-Determination*. Stanford: Stanford University Press, 1997.

Hegel, Georg Wilhelm Friedrich. *"Der Geist des Christentums": Schriften 1796–1800*. Ed. Werner Hamacher. Frankfurt: Ullstein, 1978.

——. *Phänomenologie des Geistes*. In *Werke*. Vol. 3. Frankfurt: Suhrkamp, 1986.

——. *Vorlesungen über die Philosophie der Geschichte*. In *Werke*. Vol. 12. Frankfurt: Suhrkamp, 1986.

Heidegger, Martin. *Being and Time*. Trans. John Macquarrie and Edward Robinson. New York: Harper and Brothers, 1962.

——. *Die Grundbegriffe der Metaphysik*. In *Gesamtausgabe*. Ed. Freidrich-Wilhelm von Herrmann. 2d ser., vol. 29/30. Frankfurt: Klostermann, 1983.

——. *Holzwege*. In *Gesamtausgabe*. Ed. Friedrich-Wilhelm von Herrmann. 1st ser., vol. 5. Frankfurt: Klostermann, c. 1977.

——. *Nietzsche*. Trans. David Farrell Krell. 2 vols. San Francisco: Harper and Row, c. 1979–87.

——. *Nietzsche*. 2 vols. Pfullingen: Neske, 1989.

——. *Parmenides*. In *Gesamtausgabe*. Ed. Friedrich-Wilhelm von Herrmann. 2d ser., vol. 54. Frankfurt: Klostermann, c. 1982.

——. *Sein und Zeit*. In *Gesamtausgabe*. Ed. Friedrich-Wilhelm von Herrmann. Vol. 2. Frankfurt: Klostermann, 1977.

——. *Über den Humanismus*. Frankfurt: Klostermann, 1981.

——. "Der Ursprung des Kunstwerks." In *Holzwege*, in *Gesamtausgabe*. 1st ser., vol. 5. Frankfurt: Klostermann, 1982.

——. "Wozu Dichter?" In *Holzwege*. In *Gesamtausgabe*. Ed. Friedrich-Wilhelm von Herrmann. 1st ser., vol. 5. Frankfurt: Klostermann. c. 1977.

——. "Der Zeitbegriff in der Geschichtswissenschaft." In *Frühe Schriften*. Frankfurt: Klostermann, 1972.

Hölderlin, Friedrich. *Sämtliche Werke*. Vol. 6. Stuttgart: COTTA, 1954.

Hoy, David Couzens. "History, Historicity, and Historiography in *Being and Time*." In M. Murray, ed., *Heidegger and Modern Philosophy: Critical Essays*. New Haven: Yale University Press, 1978.

Imbert, Claude. "Le Présent et l'histoire." In Heinz Wismann, ed., *Walter Benjamin et Paris*. Paris: Éditions du Cerf, 1986.

Jameson, Fredric. *Late Marxism: Adorno, or, the Persistence of the Dialectic*. London: Verso, 1990.

Jay, Martin. *Adorno*. Cambridge, Mass.: Harvard University Press, 1984.

———. *Marxism and Totality: The Adventure of a Concept from Lukács to Habermas.* Berkeley: University of California Press, 1984.

———. *Permanent Exiles: Essays on the Intellectual Migration from Germany to America.* New York: Columbia University Press, [1985], c. 1986.

Jennings, Michael. *Dialectical Images: Walter Benjamin's Theory of Literary Criticism.* Ithaca: Cornell University Press, 1987.

Kafka, Franz. *"The Metamorphosis," "The Penal Colony," and Other Stories.* Trans. Willa Muir and Edwin Muir. New York: Schocken, 1975.

Kaulen, Heinrich. *Rettung und Destruktion: Untersuchungen zur Hermeneutik Walter Benjamins.* Tübingen: Max Niemeyer Verlag, 1987.

Kierkegaard, Søren. *Der Begriff Angst.* Cologne: Eugen Diederichs Verlag, 1983.

———. *The Concept of Anxiety: A Simple Psychologically Orienting Deliberation on the Dogmatic Issue of Hereditary Sin.* Trans. Reidar Thomte and Albert B. Anderson. Princeton: Princeton University Press, 1980.

———. *Kritik der Gegenwart.* Trans. Theodor Haecker. Basel: Hess, 1914.

Kraus, Karl. *Dicta and Contradictions.* In Harry Zohn, ed., *In These Great Times: A Karl Kraus Reader.* Chicago: University of Chicago Press, 1990.

———. *Schriften.* Ed. Christian Wagenknecht. 12 vols. Frankfurt: Suhrkamp, 1989.

Kunneman, Harry, and Hent de Vries, eds. *Enlightenments: Encounters between Critical Theory and Contemporary French Thought.* Kampen: Kok Pharos Publishing, 1993.

Lacoue-Labarthe, Philippe, and Jean-Luc Nancy. *The Literary Absolute: The Theory of Literature in German Romanticism.* Trans. Philip Barnard and Cheryl Lester. Albany: State University of New York Press, 1988.

Lepenies, Wolf. *Das Ende der Naturgeschichte: Wandel kultureller Selbstverständlichkeiten in den Wissenschaften des 18. und 19. Jahrhunderts.* Munich: C. Hanser, 1976.

Levinas, Emmanuel. *Humanisme de l'autre homme.* Paris: Fata Morgana, 1972.

———. "The Name of a Dog, or Natural Rights." In *Difficult Freedom: Essays on Judaism.* Trans. Seán Hand. Baltimore: Johns Hopkins University Press, 1990.

———. "The Paradox of Morality." In Robert Bernasconi and David Wood, eds., *The Provocation of Levinas: Rethinking the Other.* London: Routledge, 1988.

———. "Paul Celan: De l'être à l'autre." In *Noms propres.* Paris: Fata Morgana, 1976.

Lindner, Burkhardt. " 'Natur-Geschichte'—Geschichtsphilosophie und Welterfahrung in Benjamins Schriften." *Text und Kritik* 31/32 (1979): 41–58.

———. "Positives Barbarentum—aktualisierte Vergangenheit: Über einige Widersprüche Benjamins." *Alternative* 23 (June/August 1980): 130–39.

Llewelyn, John. "Am I Obsessed by Bobby? (Humanism of the Other Animal)." In Robert Bernasconi and Simon Critchley, eds., *Re-Reading Levinas.* Bloomington: Indiana University Press, 1991.

Löwith, Karl. "Natur und Geschichte." In *Sämtliche Schriften.* Vol. 2. Stuttgart: J. B. Metzlersche Verlagsbuchhandlung, 1983.

———. *Nietzsches Philosophie der ewigen Wiederkehr des Gleichen.* In *Sämtliche Schriften.* Vol. 6. Stuttgart: J. B. Metzlersche Verlagsbuchhandlung, 1987.

Lukács, Georg. *Die Seele und die Formen: Essays*. Neuwied am Rhein: Luchter-hand, 1971.

———. *The Theory of the Novel: A Historico-Philosophical Essay on the Forms of Great Epic Literature*. Cambridge, Mass.: MIT Press, 1971.

———. *Die Zerstörung der Vernunft*. In *Werke*. Vol. 9. Neuwied am Rhein: Luchterhand, 1962.

Lyotard, François. *The Inhuman: Reflections on Time*. Trans. Geoffrey Benning-ton and Rachel Bowlby. Stanford: Stanford University Press, 1991.

Makropoulos, Michael. *Modernität als ontologischer Ausnahmezustand?: Walter Benjamins Theorie der Moderne*. Munich: Wilhelm Fink, 1989.

Marquard, Odo. *Schwierigkeiten mit der Geschichtsphilosophie: Aufsätze*. Frank-furt: Suhrkamp, 1982.

Marx, Karl, and Friedrich Engels. *Die deutsche Ideologie*. In *Werke*. Part 1, Vol. 5. Berlin: Dietz, 1964.

———. *Die heilige Familie oder Kritik der kritischen Kritik: Gegen Bruno Bauer und Konsorten*. In *Werke*. Vol. 2. Berlin: Dietz, 1962.

———. "Zur Judenfrage." In *Werke*. Vol. 1. Berlin: Dietz, 1964.

Mehlman, Jeffrey. *Walter Benjamin for Children: An Essay on His Radio Years*. Chicago: University of Chicago Press, 1993.

Menninghaus, Winfried. *Walter Benjamins Theorie der Sprachmagie*. Frankfurt: Suhrkamp, 1980.

Mörchen, Hermann. *Adorno und Heidegger: Untersuchung einer philosophischen Kommunikationsverweigerung*. Stuttgart: Klett-Cotta, 1981.

Mosès, Stéphane. "Brecht und Benjamin als Kafka-Interpreten." In Stéphane Mosès and Albrecht Schöne, eds., *Juden in der deutschen Literatur: Ein deutsch-israelisches Symposium*. Frankfurt: Suhrkamp, 1986.

———. "Walter Benjamin and Franz Rosenzweig." In Gary Smith, ed., *Walter Benjamin: Philosophy, History, Aesthetics*. Chicago: University of Chicago Press, 1989.

Nägele, Rainer. "Benjamin's Ground." *Studies in Twentieth-Century Literature* 11, no. 1 (1986): 5–24.

———. *Theater, Theory, Speculation: Walter Benjamin and the Scenes of Moder-nity*. Baltimore: Johns Hopkins University Press, 1991.

Nietzsche, Friedrich. *The Birth of Tragedy and The Case of Wagner*. Trans. Walter Kaufmann. New York: Vintage, 1967.

———. *Die Geburt der Tragödie aus dem Geiste der Musik*. In *Werke*. Ed. Giorgio Colli and Mazzino Montinari. Berlin: Walter de Gruyter, 1972.

———. *On the Genealogy of Morals and Ecce Homo*. Trans. Walter Kaufmann. New York: Vintage Books, 1969.

Norris, Margot. *Beasts of the Modern Imagination: Darwin, Nietzsche, Kafka, Ernst, and Lawrence*. Baltimore: Johns Hopkins University Press, 1985.

Oakes, Guy. "Rickert's Theory of Historical Knowledge." In *Heinrich Rickert: The Limits of Concept Formation in Natural Science: A Logical Introduction to the Historical Sciences*. Ed. and trans. Guy Oakes. Abridged ed. Cambridge: Cambridge University Press, 1986.

Ollig, Hans-Ludwig, ed. *Materialien zur Neukantianismus-Diskussion*. Darm-stadt: Wissenschaftliche Buchgesellschaft, 1987.

Pfotenhauer, Helmut. "Benjamin und Nietzsche." In Burkhardt Lindner, ed., *"Links hatte noch alles zu enträtseln . . . ": Walter Benjamin im Kontext.* Frankfurt: Syndikat, 1978.

Pizer, John. *Toward a Theory of Radical Origin: Essays on Modern German Thought.* Lincoln: University of Nebraska Press, 1995.

Pöggeler, Otto. *Der Denkweg Martin Heideggers.* Pfullingen: Günther Neske, 1963.

———. *Spur des Worts: Zur Lyrik Paul Celans.* Freiburg: Verlag Karl Alber, 1986.

Puttnies, Hans, and Gary Smith, eds. *Benjaminiana: Eine biografische Recherche.* Giessen: Anabas Verlag, 1991.

Rabinbach, Anson. "Introduction." In Gershom Scholem, ed., *The Correspondence of Walter Benjamin and Gershom Scholem, 1932–1940.* New York: Schocken, 1989.

Ramnoux, Clémence. *La Nuit et les enfants de la nuit dans la tradition grecque.* Paris: Flammarion, 1959.

Riedel, Manfred. "Einleitung." In Wilhelm Dilthey, ed., *Der Aufbau in der geschichtlichen Welt in den Geisteswissenschaften.* Frankfurt: Suhrkamp, 1981.

Rilke, Rainer Maria. *Briefe aus Muzot 1921 bis 1926.* Leipzig: Insel, 1935.

———. *Duino Elegies.* Trans. J. B. Leishman and Stephen Spender. New York: Norton, 1939.

Rosenzweig, Franz. *Der Stern der Erlösung.* Frankfurt: Suhrkamp, 1988.

Rotenstreich, Nathan. *Jews and German Philosophy: The Polemics of Emancipation.* New York: Schocken Books, 1984.

Schmidt, Alfred. "Adorno: Ein Philosoph des realen Humanismus." *Neue Rundschau* (1969): 654–72.

———. *The Concept of Nature in Marx.* London: New Left Books, 1971.

Schnädelbach, Herbert. *Philosophy in Germany, 1831–1933.* Trans. Eric Matthews. Cambridge: Cambridge University Press, 1984.

Scholem, Gershom, ed. *The Correspondence of Walter Benjamin and Gershom Scholem, 1932–1940.* Trans. Gary Smith and Andre Lefevre. New York: Schocken Books, 1989.

———. "Die Krise der Tradition im jüdischen Messianismus." In *Judaica: Studien zur jüdischen Mystik.* Vol. 3. Frankfurt: Suhrkamp, 1970.

———. "Lyrik der Kabbala?" *Der Jude* 6 (1921–22): 55–69.

———. "Der Name Gottes und die Sprachtheorie der Kabbala." In *Judaica: Studien zur jüdischen Mystik.* Vol. 3. Frankfurt: Suhrkamp, 1970.

———. "Offenbarung und Tradition als religiöse Kategorien im Judentum." In *Judaica: Studien zur jüdischen Mystik.* Vol. 4. Frankfurt: Suhrkamp, 1984.

———. *"Und alles ist Kabbala": Gershom Scholem im Gespräch mit Jörg Drews.* Munich: Edition Text und Kritik GmbH, 1980.

———. *Von der mystischen Gestalt der Gottheit: Studien zu Grundbegriffen der Kabbala.* Frankfurt: Suhrkamp, 1977.

———. *Walter Benjamin: The Story of a Friendship.* New York: Schocken Books, 1981.

———. *Walter Benjamin und sein Engel: Vierzehn Aufsätze und kleine Beiträge.* Ed. Rolf Tiedemann. Frankfurt: Suhrkamp, 1983.

———. *Zur Kabbala und ihrer Symbolik.* Zürich: Rhein, 1960.

Schöne, Albrecht. " 'Diese nach jüdischem Vorbild erbaute Arche': Walter Ben-
    jamins *Deutsche Menschen.*" In Stéphane Mosès and Albrecht Schöne, eds.,
    Juden in der deutschen Literatur: Ein deutsch-israelisches Symposion. Frank-
    furt: Suhrkamp, 1986.
Schweppenhäuser, Hermann. *Tractanda: Beiträge zur kritischen Theorie der
    Kultur und Gesellschaft.* Frankfurt: Suhrkamp, 1972.
Seiffert, Johannes Ernst. "*Deutsche Menschen*: Vorläufiges zu Walter Benjamins
    Brief-Anthologie." *Jahrbuch des Instituts für deutsche Geschichte* 1 (1972): 159–
    70.
Simmel, Georg. *Goethe.* Leipzig: Klinkhardt and Biermann, 1913.
———. "Das Problem der historischen Zeit." *Philosophische Vorträge,
    veröffentlicht von der Kantgesellschaft* 12 (1916): 3–31.
Sluga, Hans. *Heidegger's Crisis: Philosophy and Politics in Nazi Germany.* Cam-
    bridge, Mass.: Harvard University Press, 1993.
Smith, Gary. "Thinking through Benjamin: An Introductory Essay." In Gary
    Smith, ed., *Benjamin: Philosophy, History, Aesthetics.* Chicago: University of
    Chicago Press, 1989.
Sontag, Susan. "Introduction." In Walter Benjamin, *"One-Way Street" and
    Other Writings.* Trans. Edmund Jephcott and Kingsley Shorter. London:
    Verso, 1985.
Soper, Kate. *Humanism and Anti-Humanism.* La Salle, Ill.: Open Court,
    1986.
Steiner, George. "Introduction." In Walter Benjamin, *The Origin of German
    Tragic Drama.* London: Verso, 1977.
Störig, Hans Joachim, ed. *Das Problem des Übersetzens.* Darmstadt: Wis-
    senschaftliche Buchgesellschaft, 1969, c. 1963.
Susman, Margarete. "Früheste Dichtung Franz Kafkas." In *Gestalten und Kreise.*
    Stuttgart: Diana Verlag, 1954.
Szondi, Peter. "Hoffnung im Vergangenen: Über Walter Benjamin." In
    Schriften. Vol. 2. Frankfurt: Suhrkamp, 1978.
———. "Poetik der Tragödie und Philosophie des Tragischen." In *Schriften.* Vol.
    1. Frankfurt: Suhrkamp, 1978.
Tiedemann, Rolf. *Studien zur Philosophie Walter Benjamins.* Frankfurt:
    Suhrkamp, 1973.
Timms, Edward. *Karl Kraus Apocalyptic Satirist: Culture and Catastrophe in
    Habsburg Vienna.* New Haven: Yale University Press, 1986.
Tugendhat, Ernst. *Ti Kata Tinos: Eine Untersuchung zu Struktur und Ursprung
    aristotelischer Grundbegriffe.* Freiburg: Alber, 1958.
Vattimo, Gianni. *The End of Modernity.* Baltimore: Johns Hopkins University
    Press, 1988.
Voigts, Manfred. " 'Die Mater der Gerechtigkeit'—Zur Kritik des Zitat-Begriffs
    bei Walter Benjamin." In Norbert W. Bolz and Richard Faber, eds., *Antike
    und Moderne: Zu Walter Benjamins "Passagen."* Würzburg: Königshausen
    and Neumann, 1986.
Weber, Samuel. "Der posthume Zwischenfall: Eine *Live* Sendung." In Georg
    Christoph Tholen and Michael O. Scholl, eds., *Zeit-Zeichen: Aufschübe und
    Interferenzen zwischen Endzeit und Echtzeit.* Weinheim: VCH, Acta Human-
    iora, 1990.

———. "Taking Exception to Decision: Walter Benjamin and Carl Schmitt." In Harry Kunneman and Hent de Vries, eds., *Enlightenments: Encounters between Critical Theory and Contemporary French Thought*. Kampen: Kok Pharos, 1993.

Wiebering, J. "Kreatur." *Historisches Wörterbuch der Philosophie*. Vol. 4. Darmstadt: Wissenschaftliche Buchgesellschaft, 1971–.

Wiggershaus, Rolf. *The Frankfurt School: Its History, Theories, and Political Significance*. Trans. Michael Robertson. Cambridge, Mass.: MIT Press, 1994.

Witte, Bernd. *Walter Benjamin—Der Intellektual als Kritiker: Untersuchungen zu seinem Frühwerk*. Stuttgart: J. B. Metzlersche Verlagsbuchhandlung, 1976.

Wohlfarth, Irving. "Der 'Destruktive Charakter': Benjamin zwischen den Fronten." In Burkhardt Lindner, ed., *"Links hatte noch alles sich zu enträtseln . . . ": Walter Benjamin im Kontext*. Frankfurt: Syndikat, 1978.

———. "On Some Jewish Motifs in Benjamin." In Andrew Benjamin, ed., *The Problems of Modernity: Adorno and Benjamin*. London: Routledge, 1989.

Wolin, Richard. *Walter Benjamin: An Aesthetic of Redemption*. Berkeley: University of California Press, 1994.

Index

Designer: Barbara Jellow
Compositor: Publication Services, Inc.
Text: Galliard
Display: Galliard
Printer: BookCrafters
Binder: BookCrafters